THE CALL
FROM HOME

THE CALL FROM HOME

An autobiographical self-help memoir written as an ascension manual to help people emerging from hell, on the journey back home

By Anthony Torres

New Aeon Solutions Publishing

NEW AEON SOLUTIONS
—— PUBLISHING ——

THE CALL FROM HOME

Produced by Anthony Torres
Published by New Aeon Solutions

NEW AEON SOLUTIONS
—— PUBLISHING ——

3151 Airway Ave., Suite L1, Costa Mesa, CA, 92626
© 2022 New Aeon Solutions. All rights reserved.
For permissions contact: info@gold-encompass.com

Cover Design: Rob Williams
Editor: Hill Hughes & Harriet Beauchemin

For information about sales promotions, fundraising, educational needs, and special discounts available for bulk purchases, please contact New Aeon Solutions Publishing at:

info@gold-encompass.com

DISCLAIMER:

This is a nonfiction book written through recall of memory. It is an attempt to recreate events, locales, and experiences from recollection of experiences over time. Although the author has made every effort to ensure that the information in the book was correct, many names and identifying details of individuals have been changed for privacy protection purposes. Some events have been compressed or altered, and some locations have been changed. The author does not assume, and hereby disclaims, any liability to any party for any loss, damage, or disruption caused by errors, omissions, or changes in the details of this book, whether the errors, omissions, or changes were caused by negligence, accident, or any other cause. This book is not intended as a substitute for the medical advice of physicians.

DEDICATED TO:

*My Guardian Angels and
my Grandma Diane*

I would like to deeply thank all my family and friends who shared their love and helped me

Special Acknowledgments to my teachers & mentors:

Josiah Osuagwu

Peter & Anne Selby

Kathleen Milner

Jeanne Johnson

John Kappas

Thank you!

CONTENTS

PREFACE

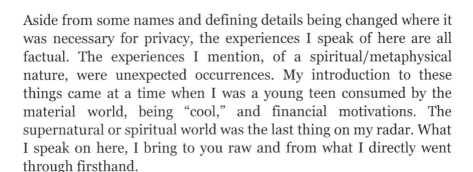

Aside from some names and defining details being changed where it was necessary for privacy, the experiences I speak of here are all factual. The experiences I mention, of a spiritual/metaphysical nature, were unexpected occurrences. My introduction to these things came at a time when I was a young teen consumed by the material world, being "cool," and financial motivations. The supernatural or spiritual world was the last thing on my radar. What I speak on here, I bring to you raw and from what I directly went through firsthand.

This was written for anyone battling through life's adversities while consciously on the path of spiritual awakening.

This is for those who found the escape route from hell and the path to the open door of Heaven.

This is also for the underdogs in life: for anyone overcoming the limiting beliefs others have placed on them, whether it be your parents, family, friends, colleagues, or foes.

My message is one of overcoming what was once a monster of myself. It is a story of gnarly triumph and unforeseeable transformation. For the people who have created a nightmare, we all have within us the seed of transformation.

I hope to inspire young men/women born without fathers and those with single, drug-addicted mothers to love themselves and know that their circumstances do not define them. Sometimes, when a soul chooses a dark, steep path it opens the door to tremendous achievement and God's workings. For such people, I pray that my story helps you to stay strong, push forward, and believe in yourself through hell and high water.

INTRODUCTION

What you're about to read is a true story detailing the fierce game of tug-of-war the inertia of my darkened past played versus my healing, my soul's awakening, and my destiny.

Born of a drug-addicted mother on the streets of Venice Beach, Los Angeles, I barely escaped childhood, wandering through my early years in shell shock and confusion.

Eventually adopted by family members, I felt like a dispensable, abandoned outcast. I ran away at sixteen and morphed from an innocent skateboarder into a drug trafficker whose entire self-identity was bound to. I lived in self-perpetuating darkness seduced by a nasty methamphetamine addiction, and for a while it seemed the only road for me was one of a life-long drug dealer. Statistics predicted I would be dead or in prison, and my life choices supported both options.

However, as it turned out, my experience of the underground drug world was a cosmically-crafted vehicle for spiritual initiation. I faced multiple supernatural experiences with entities, both Angels and astral demons, which opened my eyes to the things at play within existence. These experiences, some of which quite traumatizing to the soul at that time, were intense and blatant. I faced the darkest of temptations from literal evil at my lowest, most vulnerable drug-addicted point, where my soul was able to persevere by a thread of remembrance of the love of God within.

From the depths of death, my eventual ascent came through wholehearted surrender and asking The Creator to show me the way forward. I cleared my head of the demons and overcame the monstrosity I had become. This opened the door for wisdom and guidance from mentors which allowed me to develop and discover inner gifts that were beyond me. Eventually I was able to discover true peace and realize Self spiritually. This prepared me for something indescribable: the love that is our Home, the love our Creator has for us all equally and eternally.

Now I want to share my journey from darkness to healing with you, showing that it's possible to die to lesser past versions of ourselves and resurrect into the genuine expression of who we really are within our soul. No matter where your life has taken you or where you are now, through belief in yourself and focused effort, you can create an abundant life for yourself.

Enjoy!

My mom and I as a baby

CHAPTER 1

✸ CALIFORNIA SON ✸

⚙ Into the Physical

I entered this world on June 25th, 11:03 p.m., in the year 1977, in Santa Monica Hospital, Los Angeles. I was born of a rebellious-spirited, drug-addicted mother. I was a premature baby, weighing only 3.5 pounds. I was born so small that I couldn't be circumcised. My great-grandmother used to jokingly say that when I was brought home from the hospital, I was so small that I looked like a pot roast. Because of my size at birth, I spent the first three or so weeks of my life in an incubator-like device at the hospital.

Once I was taken home from the hospital, and the dust settled from the turbulence of my birth, I would be faced with the most adversity a young child could be met with — the adversity of being raised by a single mother on a lunatic mission.

I inherited my mother's stubborn determination and extremely addictive personality. Because of this, it would require inhuman strength and fortitude of spirit to overcome various addictions at times throughout my life.

My father, Martine, was a good man whose life took an unexpected turn into a homicidal nightmare. I never got to know him, and I only remember seeing him briefly on two occasions. He was never able to be a part of my life.

My father and mother were never married. They got together while he was out on bond, awaiting a court sentencing. Their night of passion produced my opportunity to be on this earth. At the time, he was in his early fifties, thirty-some-odd years older than my mother, who was around 20 years old when she had me.

Martine, or Marty as he was called, was a quiet type, a loner in nature. He was a mild-mannered, laid-back Chicano, Mexican American. Being a California native raised in Los Angeles, his favorite place was Venice Beach; he was a local there. He was the type of guy you would find at Venice Beach playing an acoustic guitar, smoking a joint, and drinking a beer near the boardwalk.

Before I was born, my father was charged with murdering two men who raped his then-fiancé. He was awaiting trial when I was born. His reaction to what happened to his fiancé was an act of blind rage and revenge. An act which led to him living out the rest of his days in San Quentin State Prison while serving two life-sentences.

My father was not affiliated with any gangs, and contrary to his fate, he was not a violent type of person. Considering he was older than fifty at the time of his sentencing, it was presumed he died in prison. I was kept away from his family and never knew my grandmothers, grandfathers, aunts, or uncles from his side.

Although my will is of nonviolence, I can understand, and I respect my father's decision.

My mother was a truly troubled soul. She was raised by a very loving mother, my grandmother, and an absentee father who was absent physically and emotionally neglectful. Her feelings surrounding her father would become the fuel for an unstoppable inferno of self-destruction.

Venice Beach was my mother's stomping ground as a young runaway. She was a hellion on a warpath and someone who was as contrary to reason as could be. She was addicted to crack cocaine and heroin. Her addictions (as do most everyone's) served to mask the pain and fill the void of a father's love missing from her heart.

She had the best of intentions for being a mother, but she was in the most destructive of places within herself. I was caught in her romantic notion of having a child, while her actual ability to raise me was consumed by drug abuse.

There was no hope of getting through to her. Going to jail couldn't stop her; having a child didn't stop her; being homeless wouldn't stop her, and the love of her own mother could never reach her. She was like a runaway locomotive in her pursuits to quench her thirst for drugs, and her approach to obtaining those drugs was truly psycho.

While excitement is certainly an important aspect of a child's life growing up, my mother took that to a dangerously unhealthy level in the worst of ways. It goes without saying that the drug world isn't a place for a young child to be exposed to on a daily basis – or any time at all for that matter.

I remember we lived in apartments right on the Venice Beach Boardwalk. We would walk up and down that boardwalk constantly while my mom jived and chopped it up with everyone on the block. They would all be hanging out drinking beers and doing drugs at the pagodas. My mom was an expert at impulsively doing whatever she wanted.

In the late '70s and early '80s (and still now), Venice Beach was a mecca for chilling and having fun. My mom's irresponsibility was not the best example for my sponge-like child mind. This period of my life programmed my subconscious in a way that wasn't the healthiest for my future self. Throughout life there seemed to be an unconscious force working against my ability to be disciplined. That part of my early childhood programming became something I would have to dig deep to transmute. It took sincere effort to overcome this and successfully arrive at who I am now.

Apartment where we lived on Venice Beach Boardwalk

All throughout my childhood, my mom and I were without a car or money to get a new one. To get around, we would walk and hitchhike through Los Angeles. I remember many days of us walking down the 405 Freeway hitchhiking. One of those occasions was in summer being barefooted. I remember us thumbing for a ride on the Highway during the middle of the day, the concrete scorching hot on my feet, the sun blazing overhead. Most of our outings were so she could obtain more drugs.

When my mom would finally be coming down from her multi-day tirade on drugs, she would knock out, cold asleep, for what seemed like days. On one such occasion, I remember waking up one morning and making myself a bowl of cereal — except there was no milk for my cereal. I remember feeling helpless and having to eat the bowl of cereal with tap water. Sitting there, the feeling was a mix between broken and frustrated, looking at my mom passed out in a coma-like sleep, coming down off drugs. I remember walking down to the convenience store below our apartment, right there on Venice Boardwalk, to get a jug of milk. I grabbed the jug, walked up to the counter, and set it down. I looked up at the store owner at the register and asked if I could have the milk. He told me the cost. I said, "I don't have any money." His reply was, "Then, no, you can't have the milk."

I remember just turning around and walking away, feeling even more frustrated and helpless.

The memory of that moment would remain deep in my subconscious throughout my life. It created a scarcity mindset. My poverty consciousness and survival fears took decades to fully overcome.

My mom, only half in her head, would space out on the normal day-to-day human needs. She would also spend our food and bill money on drugs. Because of this, we often went without food. The scarcity and poverty consciousness I developed due to this was something that lived with me until I grew up and learned subconscious reprogramming techniques. My grandmother would do everything she could to help us, but with a daughter who could spend a week's worth of grocery money in one day on drugs, it was impossible for her to always keep us afloat.

I was always by my mother's side in the most precarious of settings and situations. One time, I remember her getting in a fight over drugs with a big, bald white man who stood at about 6 foot, 4 inches, who weighed about 300 pounds. They both started throwing empty glass beer bottles at each other, which led to smashing them onto each other's heads. I still have a small scar on my right leg from the altercation that night. It was the first time I remember freaking out of my head. I was four years old.

During the fight, I desperately tried to help my mom. I had no clue what to do. At one point, I remember running into the hallway and screaming for my father, to no avail. I remember then jumping from the top of the couch onto this mountainous man's back, trying to choke him to get him off my mother. He swatted me off his back like a fly. I remember in the aftermath of it all walking with her to the emergency room with her head bleeding, so she could get stitches for the wounds on her head from the glass bottles.

The stories are too many to document here. It was a rare form of insanity.

Between my mother's conflicted soul and the formative cultural tone of the '80s crack cocaine epidemic in the streets of Los Angeles, the odds of her becoming a responsible mother were majorly stacked against her. She had the best of intentions. Good intentions are easily swallowed whole by extreme adversity.

Regardless of all of this, as contrary as it may sound, my mother loved me with all her heart and soul. She'd make it known to me in every way she was capable — aside from being a responsible parent. As a very gifted singer-songwriter and guitar player, she would sing songs to me about my *big brown eyes* and how much she loved me. She did the best she could despite her addictions.

The market where I asked for a gallon of milk

There were times when my mother would get arrested and be in jail for months. My grandmother would have to find arrangements and places for me to live, which ranged from an array of different people, including family members and friends of the family. At one point, I lived with friends of the family on a ranch, who spoke only Spanish. There as a little boy, waiting for my mom to get out of jail, for close to nine straight months, I spoke only Spanish as a requisite of my environment and survival.

As a kid I was reserved and introverted. I had a quiet, distant demeanor. I was traumatized and in a state of dissociative shell shock. For my first twenty years, even while living with my aunt and uncle, I felt like I was sleepwalking through life. I would discover during my training to become a hypnotherapist that there was a name for this sleepwalking-like state of consciousness caused by trauma: somnambulism. It wasn't until twenty years later when I grew into my healing arts career that I was able to heal and reintegrate into myself.

⊛ God-Like Grandmotherly Intervention

A little before I was born, my grandmother had remarried a big pharma businessman, who was an alumnus of the University of Southern California. He didn't want to have anything to do with my mom and her problematic scenarios. All my grandmother's assistance, which was seemingly always, she had to keep veiled and discreet.

Although her husband didn't want my mom anywhere around, I could still visit and spend time with my grandmother in the safety of her comfortable world. The time I spent with my grandmother was the healthiest thing I had going for me in my life.

My grandmother was very classy, kind, and responsible. She was like the prototypical fairy godmother who would spoil me and offer me a much-needed escape from the ever-present dangers of my clan-destined mother's world and decision-making.

I remember the time when my grandmother had rescued my mother and I from a horrible situation. While in the car they got in a huge fight. Once my mom got out of the car I remember being in the middle of a tug-o-war, each of them holding and pulling one of my hands, fighting over if I was going to go with my mom or stay in the car and go with my grandma.

The polarity of their two uniquely-different worlds was a mind-bender. One moment I would be hand in hand with my mother storming through the alleyways and criminal streets of Venice. The next day I would be with my grandmother at her plush three-story condominium in Marina Del Rey, safely watching cartoons.

My grandma, my mom, and me

A short while after I turned five years old, things were about to change. A painful change, but for my best. When my mom was unable to get me to school properly, my grandmother began to try and convince her to surrender her rights to raise me. The pressures of the day-to-day responsibilities became too much for my mom in her condition. She was faced with having to make one of the most difficult unselfish (yet selfish) decisions of her entire life-the decision to give up her only child.

Ultimately, addiction and drug use would be her choice. A choice made over her health and over her ability to raise me. This would be a choice that she'd never recover from emotionally. The guilt from this decision would drive her further into a perpetual apocalypse of oblivion. Having to give up her firstborn son, a little boy she loved more than her own life itself, would crumble her to even smaller pieces.

The dilemma she was forced with was a process that my grandmother and the rest of the family had seen coming for a while, and they had been preparing for it.

As children, we believe we are the center of the universe and a core cause of virtually everything that is happening to and around us, good or bad. Not having a psychologically-developed and mature ability to reason at that age, I felt like I was the reason I'd been taken from her. This feeling would morph into various self-worth issues.

Her decision to surrender me created sinking feelings of abandonment, guilt, and personal failure within me. All those feelings would follow me through my childhood, adolescence, and young adult life.

I would go on to create a view of myself that I was a bad kid, unworthy of love. My guilt would lead me to be more reserved and avoidant than was natural. I always felt like I had to walk on eggshells to avoid getting in more trouble or messing up. It was quite a confusing ride emotionally — a ride that I never spoke to anyone about. I remember there being a point in my twenties where I noticed this recurring tendency and decided to do something about it. With love, I sternly told myself: *No! You've done nothing wrong! You don't have to try and avoid confrontation. I'll always come from a good place towards others, and if ever needed, I'll make changes to improve!*

CHAPTER 2

✸ EASTERN NORTH CAROLINA ✸

⊛ Crushed into Silence

When my grandmother brought me to North Carolina from Los Angeles, she brought me under the pretense that we were *just* going for a visit to see my uncle and aunt and their newborn baby.

My Uncle Steve, my mom's big brother, and his wife, my Aunt Barbara, would be the ones to step in and raise me — thankfully!

Steve had recently married Barbara, whom he met in Santa Barbara while she was on vacation from eastern North Carolina. Shortly after meeting, Steve and Barbara married, and they had a child, my cousin/sister Carrie. After having Carrie, they decided to move back to North Carolina, where Barbara grew up. Relocating to eastern North Carolina allowed them to have the support and assistance of Barbara's family.

Barbara's family was a large, healthy family. They were considered pillars in the community of Atlantic and the surrounding areas of eastern coastal North Carolina. They were all very welcoming and loving toward me. I'm grateful to this day for their kindness and openness to take me in and raise me. It was a healing to witness and be a part of a healthy, vast, loving family structure growing up.

As I was on my way to North Carolina with my grandmother, it felt like just another magical journey with grandma. She was associated with care and nurturing which my soul so deeply needed. Going places and doing anything with her always brought me great happiness, and that was all the same while we were on the way to North Carolina. However, this excursion with her would not end with great happiness. What I thought was a short visit would end up being an unbeknownst ten-plus-year stay for me.

She and I arrived in North Carolina and visited. Everything was as normal. The day we were supposed to be flying back to California, I thought it was time for me to go with her. My grandmother had all her things packed and was headed to the airport to go back to California. That's when I discovered I wouldn't be going with her. The next thing I knew, my visit was becoming permanent, and I was beginning life with three people I didn't know. This was while carrying a head-full of unresolvable emotional conflicts and despair. It would be an understatement to say I was crushed. I was utterly confused. It was something I just could not wrap my head around, nor did I want to.

What made the situation worse was that my grandmother's plane kept getting delayed and rescheduled. She kept returning from the airport, then turning around and leaving again! This happened twice. It drove the knife in my heart even deeper every time I had to watch her go again.

My little heart was in pieces. I cried every tear I could shed. Then... I became quiet and distant. My life had already been traumatically confusing. Now the one ray of light in my life, my grandmother, was leaving me behind. My emotions faded to black and things went dark within.

I was a mix of confused, heartbroken, abandoned, ashamed, and guilty. The shame was because I felt like she wasn't bringing me back to California with her because I was a bad kid and unwanted. In my child mind I felt like I was the central reason both my mom and grandma didn't want me.

I was left there to figure it all out, without my grandmother, my mother, or a father, whom I never even got a chance to know.

Although I was left in caring, responsible hands, I went mute. I didn't speak a word to anyone for around seven months straight. I wasn't emotionally open to anyone. I didn't trust. I shut down completely. Introversion is one thing, but introversion induced by a shattered heart is a whole other thing. My seven months of not speaking was a silence motivated by the deepest of frustration, confusion, and heartbreak.

Ten months or so went by, and I gradually came around and became more comfortable as time progressed. Nevertheless, due to my past, I was always a bit removed and felt like an outsider. I would spend much of my time by myself drawing. Any trust I was able to muster up in my heart for anyone was still protective. I remained socially withdrawn.

My uncle was a Berkeley graduate and part of the counterculture, anti-Vietnam war movement of the younger, progressive generation, but he wasn't a full-blown hippie. He was more like a down-to-earth, responsible Southern California surfer, who was facing the reality of unexpectedly raising a child — and with me added, two children. He was an even-keeled, easygoing, passive type of personality. He showed his care by being soft-spoken and by consistently providing. He led by example. He never rocked the boat and was a man of few words. In hindsight, he may have been carrying some of the same unresolved issues associated with his father as my mom had been carrying within her. However, unlike my mom, Steve was a calm presence. He was the chef of the house, he worked eight hours a day, and he enjoyed a beer with his nightly meal. He was like an older brother that kindly kept to himself.

Uncle Steve

My Aunt Barbara was a social worker for the state of North Carolina. Her vocation was foretelling, considering she was fostering and raising me. She was, by far, the more dominant of my two caretakers. She naturally had an intense presence and seemed to have a quiet, almost intimidating energy about her.

Although Barbara was not my paternal mother, we were very much alike. We even looked similar. Both of our personalities were extremely strong, while my sister/cousin, Carrie, and Uncle Steve were more passive and easygoing.

Barbara was always very present with us kids. She had a watchful eye. She put sincere effort into the things in my life, which my drug-addicted mom was dysfunctional at providing.

They had to re-raise me and fill in a lot of the gaps left by my mother's irresponsibleness. Although they got me when I was already five going on 6 years old, Barbara had to teach me the correct hygiene practices. She covered all the bases and was very present in her role as a mom. They made sure birthdays and Christmas were always special occasions.

She and my uncle did everything needed to give me a stable, consistent life. They had me participating in all three school sports when I was growing up. Football was my favorite. They always supported my hobbies. They both set healthy examples of what it meant to be a human. They did an excellent job of raising me.

Although Barbara accepted me with open arms and did everything required to provide me with a healthy upbringing, I had a tough time opening my heart to her — or anyone for that matter. In hindsight, I realize it must've been hard for her to raise this shut-down little boy with a removed disposition, who was almost unreachable emotionally.

The environment I grew up in until I was ten years old was a small-town vibe. The town was truly peaceful. Virtually no crime. The people in the community were all kindhearted and safe types of folks. It was a dramatic difference compared to my original environment in Venice. The people my mom had me around were anything but safe, bless their souls, as most all of them were drug users and criminal deviants, including my mom.

My aunt and uncle agreeing to raise me was indeed a soul-saver for me. Even though, as a teenager, I would go on to become my own version of a madman, their early influence on me helped lessen the degree of that. I strongly believe that if my mom had raised me through my teens, I would have certainly ended up with teardrop tattoos under my eyes living amid violent gang activity. There is a high probability I may have been committing atrocious acts and using the same substances that stole my mother's soul.

For purposes of the story, Carrie would grow up to graduate college with a degree as a therapist, where she would eventually go on to work in the Air Force and become a Sergeant.

Barbara, Carrie, and me

One of many great Christmases   Barbara, Carrie, and me

⊛ Assurance from Beyond

As I was growing up, and through my first twenty-four years, for that matter, looming guilt followed me. In the back of my mind, I felt like I was on trial and always waiting for a judgment against me. I felt flawed. I felt like I had messed up. The subconscious feelings of guilt and inherent brokenness played out like a self-fulfilling prophecy through disciplinary issues as a young boy and through my teens.

Beyond that, at school, it was like I wasn't completely there. My grades weren't the greatest, but I also didn't rock the boat and get in a lot of trouble. I was lowkey and avoidant. As well, I was floating through most processes in a state of continual dissociation (checked out) from all I'd gone through in my first five years.

I'm not sure if anyone knew or understood the full extent of what I had experienced with my mom. My time with her and the experiences I went through I never spoke about with anyone, and it was never asked about or mentioned. It was as if my mother and that whole part of my life were avoided, like a taboo subject that no one wanted to talk about. When I asked the extent of the conversation was, "Tony, your mom is sick."

Once I grew up, I was able to gradually wrap my mind around my mother's situation. The comment, "Tony, your mom is sick," began to translate into the, at the time, heartbreaking realization that she had chosen drugs over our relationship and raising me. How having to accept that affected me is hard to explain. My broken sense of self-worth and emotional issues would ripple through my life beyond my twenties. My forgiveness towards her came when I grew to learn firsthand that addiction becomes a monster that almost transcends one's choice.

As I was going into the third year of living with my aunt and uncle, I was still pulling myself through depression. I remember the first day I ever contemplated not wanting to be alive. On that day, as I was getting ready for school, I remember hearing in my mind and heart a female voice that came over me that said, "Tony, today is not your last day here." This message came with a distinct feeling of peace throughout me.

Since that day, even as I went through immense stages of pain, trials, and tribulations, I have never again considered not wanting to be alive physically. This experience was my first encounter with a Guardian Angel. Many people have heard the voice of guidance from something beyond them at points in their lives, often in moments of emergency. This was one of many life preservers tossed to me through my life, from the other side.

My aunt and uncle would never press me about my emotions and withdrawn disposition. They showed me love and did everything required to take care of me. Emotionally, they let me be and let me work things out for myself. To this day, I thank them for that, and I thank God to the fullest that they did not put me on psych meds.

I only went to see a child therapist once in first or second grade. The meeting with the therapist led to naught. I completely stonewalled him and stared at him while he attempted to poke and prod me with questions about my feelings. I figured if my family wouldn't talk to me about my emotions and my past, then I most certainly wasn't going to talk about them with a stranger.

I am lucky I didn't end up part zombie, doped up on a cocktail of psych meds. Since becoming a professional in the mental health world, I see firsthand how psych meds (especially long-term) can have a disastrous effect on a person's body and brain, all the while keeping the original emotional problem suppressed and frozen in place. My aunt and uncle could have easily made me take a litany of medications, but they didn't. For that, again, I am so incredibly grateful!

My Aunt Barbara was of Christian faith, while my uncle was not. Steve was an open-minded, liberal intellectual. Barbara would take Carrie and me to church, and I enjoyed going. It was something I never resisted. It was peaceful and healing to my distraught psyche. I enjoyed the scriptures and anything about God. I remember always wondering and asking the Sunday school teachers who created God; what was before God? A question which is still yet a beautiful mystery to me, inducing so much wonder within me.

I remember one Christmas service at church when I had my first spiritual experience. I felt like I was in a type of deep peaceful spiritual trance-like state. A different type of glow emanated from within the candlelight. Light filled the room. There was a feeling of something beautiful and sacred in my heart. As I sat there and watched all the candles and listened to the music playing, I felt serenity. I didn't know what to make of this experience, but I still reflect on it often.

Around 11 years old, I noticed things about the church's message that didn't make sense to me. I couldn't reconcile how one moment they were teaching the Kingdom of Heaven is within you and talking about various principles of God's spirit, such as love, but the next moment telling me I was a born sinner and being made to feel guilty. The guilt-ridden implications of being a born sinner only compounded my shame stemming from feeling not wanted by my mom or grandma. I remember a few sermons specifically during which I could feel the heavy, dense layer of guilt in the room. When the sermon was complete, it felt like everyone was leaving with this somber stare in their eyes of self-condemnation. I concluded that the use of guilt while attempting to bring people closer to God was something with which I wasn't cool. Around 13 years old, I began deferring from the religion and instead held true to my connection to God in my heart.

It was also around 13 years old when I discovered the subject of the mind. This came by way of teachings from a man named Edgar Cayce. Upon one of my grandmother's visits, we were at a mall at the bookstore. She told me to go pick out whatever book I wanted and let me loose to search around. Of all the options in the entire bookstore, my attention was drawn to Edgar Cayce's book. It talked about the various levels of the mind and what he called the "super-subconscious mind." The level of language used in the book was a bit over my head, but I continued to power through it and read it. I remember rereading parts over and over, trying to comprehend it fully. I find it interesting foreshadowing when I think back on that book choice, considering the direction my life eventually took both personally and professionally. My work being oriented around the subconscious mind, the soul, and consciousness for healing.

⚙ Teen Spirit

As I grew into my teens, we gradually made our way from sparsely populated Atlantic to the more densely populated, yet still small, cities of Beaufort and later Morehead City. The sequence of these moves would increase my exposure to more people and kids to become friends with. Although I was guarded and reserved, I was always generally good at making new friends.

On the coast of North Carolina in a beach town, most of the "cool kids" were surfers or skateboarders. I gravitated toward skateboarding. At age twelve or so, I got my first skateboard. I would spend as much time on my skateboard as possible. This allowed me to develop friendships with other kids from the neighborhood who also rode skateboards. Subsequently, I began to come out of my social shell.

As I got to my teens, my aunt seemed caught in a difficult situation in her approach to raising me. She was a responsible woman and a healthy disciplinarian. She was also a social worker who knew my biological mother's early influence on me and the potentialities that come with that. At the same time, however, her disciplinarian side was coupled with a fun side, having experienced her own wild times as a teenager in her past.

As with most kids during this stage, a more rebellious version of me began to emerge. But with me, it had a dangerously high ceiling due to my early-life conditioning with my mom. I began showing more signs of her fearlessness and impulsivity.

I never really got into any serious trouble, other than once when I snuck out of the house with some friends, and we all got caught by the police throwing eggs at cars. I remember being in bad trouble and Barbara being stern about the punishment.

Through skateboarding, I developed friendships with kids that were years older than me. My friends were into all the usual things most teenage skateboarders were into at that time: smoking cigarettes, drinking forty ounces of Old English Malt Liquor, smoking marijuana, and taking psychedelics. We would ride around in my friend's 1992 bubble Honda Civic, which looked like a small spacecraft, listening to Cypress Hill, Ice Cube, and NOFX while riding from skate spot to skate spot.

By 15 and going on 16 years old, I had begun socially smoking cigarettes here and there and using marijuana. On occasion, I'd enjoy a 40 oz. of Old English. I never really liked alcohol though.

My first experience using LSD was epic indeed. However, being in eastern North Carolina, it wasn't the easiest to find. It was by far my favorite of all the mind-altering substances I had tried up to that point. At that time, it was one of the most unique experiences of my life. I remember my friends and me walking down the beach for what seemed like 9 hours straight.

Many of my friends had more freely allowing parents. Some of my friends had begun to sell marijuana in town, and they were doing quite well for themselves. In all, at that point, it was all innocent and nothing serious.

My aunt had begun to sense various shifts and changes happening in me. I was taking the counterculture road, but she never tried to shut it down and was still permissive. Permissive but strict. It was like being given enough rope to hang myself with. I am very appreciative that she allowed me the freedom she did. That allowed me to spread my wings just enough to find my courage. The freedom she gave me as well allowed me to develop friendships with people that would later be the conduits for great lessons and mighty opportunities for growth on a spiritual soul-level – which I feel massively shaped me and aligned me with my life's purpose and destiny.

Towards the end of my ninth-grade school year, someone broke into our house and stole our VCR. I have a sense that it was a friend of a friend I used to ride skateboards with. The police were called and they questioned me about the situation – to which I knew nothing about it. Tensions in our home grew to a red zone. Still, to this day, I do not know who stole that VCR, but it was a significant undoing of our household that was already a bit tense.

⊛ Split Decision

When the summer break of '93 came in June, I turned 16 years old. It was the end of the ninth-grade school year. Things between my aunt and I were tense. I was on summer restriction for my poor grades. Summer restriction at the prime of my social development was a hard pill for me to swallow.

After my birthday, two weeks into July, we had an intense argument. In reaction to the fight we were having, I decided I was leaving. First, I asked for my allowance of twenty dollars. Once I got it, I then packed two book bags of clothes and grabbed my skateboard and when no one was looking, I was gone in a mad, rebellious dash. I rode that skateboard out of there so fast I could've gotten a speeding ticket. I had never once opposed my aunt in this type of way before. I knew at that point if I were to get caught, there would be no tomorrow and I'd be toast.

I had no clear plan except to get as far away from there as I could – as fast as I could! I rode the skateboard to the nearest corner store and used the payphone to call my friends to come to get me. One of my older friends, Buddy, had a truck. I was terrified of my aunt somehow finding me there, so I hid behind the store until my friends arrived. Once they did, I jumped into the back of the truck, and away we went.

At that moment I was free, but I was freed into the struggles of a 16-year-old runaway. I had no idea how to survive, what to do, or where to stay. I slept under a bridge for a few nights. Rock bottom. There were nights I slept on the beach. That wasn't as easy or comfortable as I thought it would be. It was sticky, cold, and damp.

There I was, a teenage runaway with twenty dollars to my name. I wasn't eating much and went hungry most days. Most of my meals were Little Debbie snack cakes. I would have to eventually rely on shoplifting food from the gas stations and grocery stores to feed myself. My friends and I would go into grocery stores with only enough money to buy the loaf of bread. The sandwich meats and cheese we would have to steal.

I was fully dissociated in total survival mode and everything about me spelled *checked out*. I became someone who didn't speak much. The nights of being homeless echoed the loneliness I had felt emotionally for so many years after my mother surrendered me at 6. It was all a big feeling of *look at what you've done! This is what you deserve. Here's the failure that you are.*

I eventually ended up moving in with a friend named David Hardison from the local skateboarding community whose mom was cool with me living there. Their place was a small, one-bedroom home where two of my other runaway friends were living as well. I slept on a couch or the floor of the one-bedroom that the five of us were staying in. I was grateful to be brought in by them and to have a roof over my head.

◉ Just Trying to Survive

Going into the next school year I remained enrolled in high school. Of all my friends, I was the only one still in school. Before the school year began my Grandma Diane came out from California to see if I was okay. During her visit she gave me a hundred dollars. With the hundred dollars I bought an ounce of marijuana and flipped the money into as much profit as I could.

I decided to begin selling marijuana in school. Every day I would go to school with ten to twenty hand-rolled joints. Sometimes I would bring eighths- or quarter-bags with me for sale. I would usually skip the earlier classes and go right before lunch when all the kids who were potential customers were accessible.

The school was West Carteret High School. Of the two regional high schools in the area, West Carteret housed all the kids from the beach towns. The surfers and skateboarders outweighed all other social groups. I had a ripe market of potential customers to sell my product. Everything was working well for a while.

Although I was tenacious in my school marijuana dealings, I was still only barely getting by. I was making enough money to afford a little food and pay a modest amount of rent.

One day I arrived at school around lunchtime to sell my herb. On this day, I took a taxi to get there. I had the taxi drop me off a short way down the road from the school. I had two quarter-bags and about fifteen pre-rolled joints in my cigarette box. Little did I know I was being watched!

Upon exiting the taxi, I took a few moments to adjust the bags of marijuana into my shoes and proceeded to walk onto campus. Within twenty feet, the school security guard, Ms. Harris, walked up to me, grabbed my arm, and said, "Come with me. We want to talk with you at the principal's office." At that moment, I should have broken away and run — but I didn't, and fate played itself out.

The principal was a man named Mr. Lee. Being the past wrestling coach, he was a huge, strong man. I sat down in front of him.

"What do you have in your pockets?" he asked.

"Nothing," I said.

He motioned me to come toward him. I walked forward, and he tapped the box of cigarettes in my pocket, which I was not allowed to have at school in the first place.

"Pull them out of your pocket," Mr. Lee ordered, and I obeyed. When he opened the box, there were the fifteen joints I had on me, ready for sale.

Okay, I thought, *well, at least they don't know about the quarter-bags in my shoes*. But I wasn't that lucky!

"So, what do you have in your shoes?" Ms. Harris demanded.

Damn! I was caught red-handed.

I hesitated to answer. *She must have been waiting for me and saw me arrive down the road in the taxi and put the bags of marijuana in my shoes!*

They made me remove my shoes, and voila, there were the two bags of cannabis. The local authorities were called, and I was taken to jail.

As I was being transported to the county jail, I was more worried about my Aunt Barbara than I was about the police. My friends who were my suppliers of marijuana were concerned I would snitch on them, so they scrambled to get me out of jail as soon as possible. They had no reason to worry — I didn't have snitch in my blood. Throughout all my trouble with the law, I never turned state's evidence on anyone.

Once I was at the jail, I was given my one phone call, so I decided to call my friends. When I told my friends what happened they said not to say anything and that they were going to get me out.

Shortly after that, I was called out of the jail cell for what I thought was my friends bailing me out, but instead, it was my aunt and uncle! They looked at me with disappointment and scorn and said they were willing to bail me out.

I remember thinking to myself, *There is absolutely NO way I am going home with them*! If things were tense when I was living with them before, as generally a good young man, I could never imagine what it would be like living there after this happening. I declined their offer to get me out of there and waited for my friends instead.

Within a few hours, my friends posted my bond and I was released from the county jail. I was charged with my first two felonies. My charges were felony possession of a controlled substance with the intent to sell on school grounds.

It seemed like a huge situation over my head. I was the first of my friends to get arrested for serious charges. As I write this and reflect on it, I find it so interesting thinking that now that same plant has been made legal in most states.

The timing of my arrest couldn't have been worse. A few months before, the state had just passed stringent laws for selling drugs in school. I was kicked out of the North Carolina school system for my charges. The state judicial system wanted to make an example of me.

Once released, I waited about a month for my court date to roll around. In that time, I got a job at a local fine dining restaurant named A Taste of Class, which was owned by family members of the Chief Sheriff of Morehead City, Frank Galizia. I was the dishwasher. Frank was cool toward me, and they were all very accepting of me considering the trouble I had recently been in. It was a tough job. I sat there washing dishes for long hours.

✸ Boot Camp

I got a public defender to represent me on the day of my court appearance. On that day, I sat nervously in the Carteret County Superior Court with my Uncle Steve beside me. I was handed a 90-day probationary boot camp sentence with an accompanying three years of supervised probation by the State of North Carolina. It would take about three weeks to be sent to boot camp, and during that time, I was put on house arrest and wore an ankle monitor while I waited to be shipped off.

At boot camp, I stayed in line and played by all their strict guidelines. Somehow, I obtained a copy of the Tao Te Ching, which I read alongside the Bible while I was there.

It was nothing fun, but it could've been worse. While there, I got my GED, I did endless amounts of physical training, and, like most inmates in the system, I did free labor on daily work details. The work details were the worst part of it all. The boot camp had us doing jobs such as working at the landfills, cleaning the trash on the side of busy freeways, and clearing forests with swing blades and axes. The workdays were exhaustingly long, and if at any point any of the detainees acted out, we would all have to drop down and do push-ups on site.

While I was there, in boot camp, five of my friends from back home decided to move to Atlanta, Georgia, and leave behind the small towns of coastal North Carolina. Three of them had already begun their local town enterprise of selling low-grade marijuana back in North Carolina. They were sending me letters describing how exciting the scene was. The things they were describing were a way of life that I had never imagined before, especially coming from my sheltered life growing up in a little beach town of North Carolina. They had arrived in Atlanta right at the beginning of the rave era, when teens and young adults were going to parties using all types of substances while listening to electronic music all night. These "rave" parties were typically in large warehouses with massive sound systems.

Through letters, my friends explained how one of our friends named Brian, had all but taken over the underground black-market, designer-drug-dealing world of Atlanta. They talked about the money that was being made, the parties, the girls, and how fun everything was. As I sat in boot camp reading these letters, all I could do was imagine and marvel at it all.

Although what I was reading was alluring to my teen mind, I had no intention of ending up with them. I planned to follow the straight and narrow once I got out of boot camp. I knew I would be on probation, and I planned to move back in with my aunt, go to community college and get a job somewhere.

I went on to complete my ninety days in boot camp without any marks on my card for behavioral issues, which would have extended my stay there by extra days. Overall, my experience at boot camp was a beneficial one: I learned discipline, I studied spirituality, I was in great shape. By the time the program was completed, I could do a hundred push-ups continuously.

⊛ Then Watch What I Do

Upon completing the boot camp, my Uncle Steve came to get me. While riding home, it seemed very strange being back in the world. Steve was a man of few words, and he kept the ride home to the coast quiet and peaceful. He was always a very calm person. During the drive, my uncle informed me that in the ten months I had been away, my aunt and he had divorced, and he had left shortly after I ran away.

Moving back in with my aunt under her watchful presence was the decision made for me, and I was perfectly okay with it. I just wanted to get my life back together. I was fine playing by whatever rules I needed to.

I got a job washing dishes at a local restaurant my friend was working at. I also began to catch up with some of my past friends, but I stayed away from using marijuana. I had to report to my probation officer often, so I played the straight and narrow. My plan was to wash dishes at the restaurant and wait for the summer to pass, then begin community college. Although I had every intention to not rock the boat and do things right, fate was awaiting me right around the corner. A domino effect was about to be put in motion that would send me through a most perilous journey.

One evening after work, my friend Hunter invited me to go with him a few towns away and visit some of our other friends. The friends we were going to visit were brothers who lived with a very liberal-minded Vietnam veteran dad. He was the type of dad who would smoke weed with all of us and give us a safe place to be rather than driving around.

When we got there, I declined any offers to smoke herb with my friends. Unfortunately, Hunter ended up getting so high that he couldn't drive. I was getting nervous and told him it was super important that I be back to my aunt's house on time, before my curfew time. He was apologetic but adamant that he couldn't drive — there was nothing he or I could do in the situation. I was under his mercy to drive me home, so we hung out there until he was sober enough to drive me back.

I ended up getting back at around 11:30 p.m., about an hour and a half after my 10 p.m. curfew. I tiptoed my way into the house. I didn't hear anyone and figured I was in the clear. I went into my room hoping my Aunt Barbara hadn't heard me come in late – that was the last night I'd sleep on a comfortable bed for quite a while.

The next day I went to work, washing dishes at the restaurant on a day shift. I clocked out at around 4 p.m. and made it home at about 5 p.m. When I got there, all my stuff had been thrown out into the driveway. My aunt was livid and raging over me missing curfew the night before. As I tried to explain myself, her only response was, "If you can't live here by my rules, you can't live under my roof."

I stopped attempting to explain any further. A mix of survival-fear and cold, quiet, anger came over me, which was mixed with a big dose of confusion. The mix of emotions quickly morphed into a feeling of fuck-the-world, slowly pouring through me. It was as if the worst of my mom's fury had been fully evoked within me.

I thought to myself, *Okay, watch what I'm about to go do then!*

Instantaneously, I knew I was going to find a way to end up with my friends in Atlanta, Georgia, to join in on their clandestine underground black-market empire. But how was I going to achieve this? I had no clue, considering I was on probation and didn't even know what tomorrow would bring — or where I was even going to sleep later that night! Regardless, I knew that nothing would stop me.

In that moment I realized I had no mother, no father, no family members, and no guardians who had my back. I had no education, a job washing dishes, and a felony criminal record. The only thing I had going for me was some friendships that I hoped could help me – and a head-full of *fuck the world* ambition driving me.

My reaction in that moment created a version of me that was severely damning. I became an inferno of compromising insanity and dangerously unwise decision making with consequences that ripple effected through my teens, twenties, and much of my thirties.

My aunt let me use the phone to contact my friend Hunter to get me. I then called another friend named Justin, who was a runaway from home, who had moved into a shabby trailer down the road, to see if I could stay with him.

"Yeah, come over," he said.

Hunter came over and picked me up and helped me pile all my belongings, littered across the driveway, into his car, and we pulled away. That would be the last time I would see my aunt or speak to any family members for the next five-plus years. The next time I saw my aunt would be in 1999, while I was out on bond waiting to potentially go to prison for twenty years for my third set of drug trafficking convictions totaling twelve felonies.

After a short drive, I arrived at my friend's trailer in the woods. My room was small, scanty, and unclean. In the bedroom, there was an old hospital bed that was remaining from the past tenants, one of whom happened to be an older sickly person living in the room on medical bed rest. It was super uncomfortable, and the entire experience felt utterly upside-down and dismal. Justin saw me in, and it was super kind of him to do so — I had nowhere else to go.

I began to plot and scheme what would be my next moves. Most of my thinking was financial. I knew if I were to make it to Atlanta, I would need to figure out how to make enough money to get there. I would also have to somehow get my probation transferred from North Carolina to Atlanta. I began taking my dishwashing money to buy the local low-grade marijuana and attempted to sell it locally.

I also started using marijuana again, which was super foolish considering I was on supervised probation and getting drug tested. My disposition was of a blind rebellion containing the highest level of potential self-sabotage within it.

⊛ A New Life in Sight

Over the next few months, a friend of mine in N.C. had to drive to Atlanta for his new job, and he let me go with him. The short trips allowed me to get a firsthand view of my friends who had established themselves in the city. It was the fast life! My young coastal Carolina beach town mind was opened to a way of life that was an exciting new type of dangerous and fun all wrapped up in one. It was electric in nature that was nonstop full force. Upon seeing how it was all happening, I became set on moving to Atlanta hell or highwater!

During my short trips to Atlanta and back, while on probation still, I would bring LSD back with me to North Carolina to sell. My money gradually began to grow and so did my desire for moving.

Once I spoke with my probation officer about wanting to relocate to Atlanta, I told him that two of my older friends, who were a couple, both older than eighteen and responsible legal adults, were open to me coming there to live with them. I explained that they had already lined up a job for me where they worked. Surprisingly, he was completely open to allowing me to move and transfer my probation.

The condition of me being able to move was that I pass one final urine test. This was a risky ask due to my copious marijuana use at the time. I figured out the old trick of flushing my system with excessive amounts of water and Niacin, as well as drinking the masking solutions for passing urine tests.

On the days leading up to reporting to him, I was insanely nervous. My mind went in constant circles of fear about failing the urine test.

The day I arrived at the probation office for my test, I felt visibly nervous. So much so, I was surprised my probation officer didn't notice. The moment of truth was upon me. I was in the process of getting clearance from my probation officer to let me transfer to a city where my friends had become drug lords — and I had to pee in a cup after using loads of marijuana the week leading up to the final urine test to do so!

The situation was an extreme make-or-break moment. If I were to fail that urine test, not only would I be stuck in dead-end North Carolina, unable to move to Atlanta, but I would also be violating my probation, which would've led me back to jail for quite a while! The stakes were so high!

Upon being given the cup to pee in, I proceeded into the government building bathroom to seal the fate of my future.

As I patiently waited for the never-ending three-day window for the drug test results to come back, I was beyond nervous and worried. I had never overthought anything that intensely in my life.

When I finally got the call from my probation officer, he didn't mention anything about my test results. He only said to come to his office and gave me a date to report there. Although uncertainty consumed me, what I did know was that I was going to visit this man for the final time, one way or another.

I arrived with anxiety pulsing through my body and my heart beating like a drum! With my nervousness as hidden as possible, I sat down at his desk with the balance of my future resting on his next sentence.

"I am going to need the name of the people you are going to be moving in with and the address of where you are going to be moving to in Atlanta," he said.

I was about to cry from joy and relief! I tried to act as casual as possible and not give away my emotions so that the news of me passing the urine test seemed expected and like business as usual.

"You passed the test and are clean," he said. "Here is a form with all the information that I need so that I can get your probation transferred to the correct county in Georgia."

As I sat there and filled out the form, it was like a celebration parade was going on within me. I could barely hold back the smile. I filled out the form, handed it back to him, and he gave me a date that I could finally leave North Carolina to move to Atlanta. He told me to contact him before the time of moving so that he could tell me who my new probation officer would be in Atlanta. I was a free man in my mind!

Once I set my date to leave, I said my goodbyes to my friends and quit my job at the restaurant washing dishes. I got my final paycheck and made one last call to my probation officer to receive the information for who I was to contact at the Fulton County Probation Department.

My next step was to get to Atlanta, Georgia. The best way for me to get there was the Greyhound bus. I consolidated all my belongings into two book bags. I then got a bus ticket to the big city. I was off into a new world with a one-way ticket – and with no clue the perils that awaited me!

CHAPTER 3

❋ THE TRIALS OF DARKNESS ❋

⬢ Atlanta Madmen & the Psychedelic Mafia

Within five years of arriving in Atlanta, Georgia, I was a three-strike felony offender. I had accumulated eleven felonies for drug trafficking: amphetamines, ecstasy, and psychedelics, as well as firearms charges. I was facing twenty or more years in prison in my final offense, potentially charged as a career criminal.

I arrived in Atlanta, Georgia, around September 1994, still at the tender age of 17 years old. I was apprehensive knowing the level of danger involved in my friend's lifestyle, but I was also excited for the change and to establish my new life!

On the Greyhound pulling up to the downtown Atlanta central station terminal, I could feel the big-city vibe in the air! The first thing I noticed was the busyness of it all. Then next thing I noticed was the homeless people. I then noticed the pimps wearing feathered Fedoras. I was quickly met by hustlers trying to swindle me with the Dixie cups and acorn trick. The energy of financial opportunism and hustle was something I could tangibly feel.

Close to the time I was arriving in Atlanta, the local hip hop group OutKast had dropped their first album: Southernplayalisticadillacmuzik. There was a special energy in Atlanta at that time. Listening to

OutKast made it feel like the city came with its own theme music, which made the entire experience have an even more powerful impression upon me.

After gathering myself from the fourteen-hour bus ride, I called my friends to pick me up from the bus station. My five friends were all living in an apartment in Roswell, a suburb right outside the city.

Two of my friends, the couple, only smoked herb and drank beer here and there. My other three friends were a dramatically-different story. I came to realize very quickly that sleeping arrangements weren't all that important: the three of them never really slept.

Once we arrived at the apartment, I walked in, and there was a room full of people there that my friends were doing business with. There seemed to be a strange vibe in the room that felt alert and serious. I looked at the coffee table and noticed that there were lines of powdered substances lying there. It was crystal-methamphetamines on the table. The lines were so long they were spelling out words with them. Being an innocent boy from a North Carolina beach town, I had never experienced this breed of drug activity before.

My three friends who'd first moved to the city had taken over the city's black-market drug trade. Their central focus was rave and hippie drugs, also known as "designer drugs." The business was primarily oriented around federal amounts of ecstasy, LSD, mushrooms, boutique marijuana, and pure amphetamines. The amounts of substances were not like the ounces or quarter pounds of marijuana we had back in North Carolina. They had tens of thousands of ecstasy pills, tens of thousands of doses of LSD, pounds of methamphetamines, pounds of herb, thousands of pharmaceuticals, and slews of everything else you could imagine.

Although people in the scene were sometimes using heroin and cocaine, my friends weren't selling them. I was thankful for that, considering these were the two substances that had robbed my mother's soul. Being highly opposed to them both, I always told myself I would never use or sell either. Gladly, they weren't prevalent. Everything else was an open playing field, in a big-time way!

My friends' drug dealings were being done on a scale that was hard for me to wrap my mind around at first. There was nothing small about it. If I wanted to get a small amount of personal marijuana for myself it was next to impossible, but if I wanted fifty pounds of marijuana, it was more easily obtainable.

With business knowledge I didn't know my friends contained, they'd somehow met all the right connections of suppliers, brokers, distributors, and customers in the city. They had become massively respected in the drug trade world.

My friend Brian was the mastermind of it all. He had become the respected ringleader. The influence and respect he had, not only from my other four friends but from every other person I met or saw walk through our door, was visibly noticeable.

There were non-stop amounts of people they interacted with daily. It was overwhelming to keep up with, especially while being spun out on amphetamines and other substances for days in a row. As I integrated into their world, I began meeting all the people surrounding my friends, trying to figure out what was what.

My friends from North Carolina, who I had once known from skateboarding and innocently smoking weed, had become a vastly different breed of human. A breed of human I'd never seen previously or imagined. The skateboarding had become nonexistent. The only thing that was important was the relentless pursuit of getting and selling substances for massive profits.

They had this inner-city clout, swagger, and attitude about them, accompanied by loads of money! They were wearing all the newest urban gear and skateboard clothing. To my surprise, they were teens masterminding a million-dollar enterprise. My mind was partly blown, and completely seduced by it all.

I would do my best to figure out how to merge into their scene and ethos as quickly as possible. I followed suit and began sniffing lines of these potent methamphetamines up my nose. Within the first few hours of arriving in Atlanta and setting my bags down at the apartment in Roswell, I was going line for line with them. The first day in Atlanta turned into four days of being awake. I remember it all being so overwhelming in my green mind that I was pacing in circles and having to tell myself affirmatively repeatedly, *It's going to be all good, it's going to be all good.* After those first four head-spinning days, I finally got much-needed sleep.

⊛ Absconding

After starting off on the wrong foot arriving in Atlanta, I soberingly realized I still needed to report to my new probation office in Atlanta. They had been expecting me to call. Once I called, they gave me a date to report that was about two weeks away. I realized that there was a 100% chance I would fail a urine test with the number of drugs I was doing! At the same time, I had no intention of slowing down or playing the straight and narrow. All caution had been thrown to the wind at this point. I disregarded the probation date and kept on my clandestine way of life.

I hadn't eaten anything in about a week. During my second week in Atlanta, I finally went to the grocery store for the first time. Once I got food in me it wasn't much longer until another bender on methamphetamines began, this one being a multi-week venture.

The next two weeks passed and it was time to check in with my new probation in Atlanta. I was not in any shape whatsoever to do so, though. I'd been getting super high on amphetamines and smoking herb continuously. There was no way my probation officer wouldn't see through me. And there was certainly no way I was going to pass a urinalysis!

Right before I was supposed to report, I serendipitously stumbled upon a loophole. The couple who I was registered to live with decided to move to a neighboring county. They could no longer handle the drug dealing by our other roommates. So, I called my probation officer and told them that I was moving with them from Fulton County to Gwinnett County – although I wasn't. Things got a bit complicated from there. But it was the type of complicated that ended up working in my favor. The Fulton County probation office told me they would need to transfer my case to the other county to which I was moving. But because I hadn't officially reported to the Fulton County probation office yet, they would need to first send my probation papers back to the North Carolina probation office. Then North Carolina would send my paperwork to the new county I was moving to in Georgia. I was told to contact the probation offices in Gwinnett County in a couple of weeks, and all the paperwork should be sent over. I never contacted Gwinnett County, and there was never a warrant issued for my arrest. I never figured out why. Maybe because I was a minor when it happened. I decided to simply not worry about it any further.

My attention went back to the mission at hand. I was learning the ropes of the business. I was meeting everyone who was part of my new extended social circle and getting as high as possible in the process. I studiously observed how my friends moved through the streets. A strict code had to be followed to be a successful drug dealer – especially while also evading the police because of warrants being out for your arrest. As my understanding of how everything worked increased, I began plotting how to start making my own money from the situation.

The drug use was so continuous that the days and weeks would blur together. The next thing I knew, we were awake for close to twenty days, with only a couple of hour-long naps here and there. It was a form of pure insanity. When you stay awake that long, your thoughts and fears begin to project out of you visually as a hallucination. It is like you are living in a waking dream, or nightmare.

One night into this multi-week bender, as I was out of my mind, there were a bunch of local friends over at the apartment. Everyone was split into two-to-three people groups talking nonstop. My mind was blurring all the conversations into one never-ending sentence. It was the most discombobulating, head-spinning thing you could imagine. There's a term for this, and it's called being "spun." That night I learned what it meant to be spun. Although it was all in the name of recreational fun, the experience was terrifying. All I could do was sit there silently, doing my best to hold it together, eyes wide looking like a deer in headlights.

⊕ Crossing State Lines

My friends had established connections with the most important sources and customers in the city. That left me without much room to earn money within the local scene. The only thing I knew to do was to continue taking substances from Atlanta back to North Carolina to sell.

I never had a driver's license (I wouldn't end up getting one until much later in my twenties), so I convinced a friend to drive me to coastal N.C. to transport substances there to sell them. I was an absolute nervous, paranoid wreck being in the car, trafficking drugs across state lines. I would be so nervous during road trips I would just lean back, close my eyes, and pretend I was asleep throughout the drive. On occasion, I would take the Greyhound bus, which was much less stressful.

Considering my past in North Carolina, making moves back and forth from Atlanta was extremely risky. At this point, I had no other options. I had chosen my life path, and it was getting high and getting money. I was playing with the deck of cards that is fate. Even if I wanted to, I couldn't get a job because of the possibility that I had a probation violation warrant out for my arrest.

After a few successful trips, I generated enough money to start making moves in the Atlanta scene. Once I had the ball rolling, I rapidly gained more momentum. There was a level of responsibility and consequence involved that my 17-year-old mind was blindly not considering.

⊕ Hotel Hopping

Once my friends and I had moved out of the apartment in Roswell, we began living in hotels around the city. We called this "hotel hopping." It was most suitable for our lifestyle because it allowed us to never be in one place for too long. The motto was *stick and move*. There were so many people coming in and out daily that there was no way we could stay in one place longer than two nights. With that volume of people, all committing felonies, it simply wasn't wise to live stationary at one place for too long.

This began a five-year transitory state of being without a homebase. In a sense, I was homeless. It was an ever-changing environment from a night-to-night basis, rarely staying at one hotel longer than two days.

It was like being on a music tour but in the same city every night. And I felt like a rock star — 17 years old, no parental supervision, loads of money and substances, infamy, and staying high out of my mind! We travelled light, only owning book bags of clothes, book bags of drugs, and book bags of money.

The entirety of it all was a wild time in my mind – at the time, truly exhilarating! With the combination of being awake for days, plus dodging the police, making money, and possessing dangerous amounts of drugs, the feeling of nervous excitement was immeasurable! Regardless of everything, I learned to keep a cool head. I had to!

Besides the level of anxiety-inducing danger involved in drug sales, just the sheer number of substances being consumed was enough to make a person lose their mind. There were occasions where we'd have to evacuate a hotel and instantly move to a new one out of fear and paranoia because we'd be having collective hallucinations of federal agents, para-trooping down the side of neighboring buildings, seeing the SWAT team coming for us.

We were the epitome of fearlessly impulsive, which led to potentially compromising decisions being made. On top of being awake for days, with rooms full of drugs and money, we would use high-grade marijuana on top of it, which smelled for a mile. We would attempt to get rid of the smell by placing a wet towel under the hotel room door and over the smoke alarms – which didn't help much in all reality.

Marriott hotels throughout the city were my main stomping grounds. My favorite places to stay were the Embassy Suites, JW Marriott in Buckhead, The Marriott Marquis downtown, and the old Biltmore Hotel in Midtown. Atlanta was big enough to where I felt protected, while staying on the move. Living on the move was great fun because it was always a new experience. I grew to love living in hotels.

⊛ Level Up

For the first year of being in Atlanta, I tagged along with my friends, observed, and learned the ropes. The next thing I knew, a series of events happened with my inner circle, which would prove fortuitous for my position. Our main ringleader, Brian, got arrested in South Florida with thousands of ecstasy pills. Upon getting out of jail, he decided it would be best to leave Atlanta and move up to New York, where his family lived to avoid getting into more trouble. Before he left, he decided to introduce me to all his connections and his customers so that I could manage the local business.

Brian's partner, my friend, Barney, had also gotten in trouble and was in jail for an extended amount of time, so I was the next man in line. With the introductions coming from both Brian and Matt, I inherited both the ability to make money and respect with the Atlanta locals.

By this time, I had also developed close friendships with people who had grown up in the Atlanta scene. One of those people being a guy who knew everyone, named Matt. Matt, who was planning to go on the Grateful Dead tour, and knowing I was on my own, was kind enough to introduce me to a lot of resourceful people. One of the people Matt introduced me to was the person who became my main source of income and survival, the local ecstasy connection, Dusty. In a highly competitive business market, Matt's introductions proved to be one of the most selfless acts anyone had ever done for me. My financial livelihood was secured because of it.

Things in my social circle changed quickly. Although I didn't have my main crew of friends around me, it all came together perfectly. I began to survive and eventually thrive in the scene. My work ethic was 24-7. I began to make a name for myself. It took me a little bit to gain my footing, but when I did, I Really did!

I was 17 years old and my illicit business practices were jumping and active. I had my primary circle of connections and customers. At the same time, there were also other surrounding circles who all sold drugs and had their own network of connections and customer bases, but oftentimes they would overlap. It was an extremely competitive market, many of us knowing the same connections and customers.

The early- to mid-'90s was the era of pagers and pay-phones. There was no social media or internet. Your ability to make money was determined by how tenacious your work ethic and social abilities were. It was the money-driven drug-dealing era. This was when the music of Jay-Z and Biggie Smalls was making its beginning. Everything about our generation was "get money." As Wu-Tang put it, "cash rules everything around me," and that was very much so our mantra.

I would typically stay awake and sleep little in fear of missing financial opportunities. My mind remained ever-presently focused on getting rid of the various types of drugs I always had on me. In my mind, it was all about the next business deal.

Most of my original friends from N.C. all left Atlanta around the same time. A few of the new friends that I began to roll around with were locals who were older than me. Some of them were DJs and very connected in the electronic dance music scene. One of my closest partners was a guy named Mike G. Mike was a little older than I was, and he had transportation. I felt safe in the company of Mike because he kept a cautious headspace, and he knew the terrain. That was all crucial for my safety, considering I wasn't from around there, and that I was often high out of my mind, not paying attention to my surroundings. Having extra sets of trustworthy eyes around me was helpful.

As my resources and opportunities grew, so did my confidence and drug use. Although I was living from hotel to hotel, high as a kite, somehow, I stayed in control of myself and was able to conduct large money transactions. I walked around with a quiet feeling of invincibility within me. Everything in this beginning stage was innocent in intention: have fun, stay lifted, make money, and don't get caught!

⊛ Lessons and Integrity

As time continued, I worked hard and strengthened my foothold in the game. With my inherited relationships and new opportunities, I was able to live a life of plenty. A life of plenty and splurge I should say: I spent money just as fast as I could make it. These years of my life created a temperament of carelessness about money that I'd eventually have to work hard to fix and rewire later in my life.

I was a free spirit with my profits. I was always openly sharing with my friends and those around me. Saving money was never the goal or intention. I enjoyed being inclusive with my profits and substances — that is, until people began to steal and act shady. With the amount and types of substances we were using, very unfortunate versions of people often emerged. Our lifestyle was a ripe playing ground for learning through the darker sides of humanity.

I learned mighty lessons about integrity and money. In the world of fast money and drug sales, it was much to balance – while also being on lots of mind-altering substances. In the early stage of my career, in moments of desperation, I lacked integrity. I didn't like how that felt in my conscience and heart in the aftermath of those choices. Over time, this led me to become someone who always played fair when it came to business, money, and exchanges – regardless of how desperate I was when times were tough!

With these mistakes I quickly grew to establish a code of conduct: that the best policy is to be respectful to others and do good business. This helped me maintain success and keep unnecessary stress out of my world. There was no room for conflict considering how volatile the design of my life was. It was in the best interest of my freedom that I move through the world quietly – unnecessary problems and the attention problems bring could've easily led to prison!

I witnessed unfortunate disasters caused by people's envy and jealousy. Because I was doing well financially, I was faced with it firsthand, often. Jealousy reflects one's lack of self-love and choice to be pathetic. This taught me to be congratulatory to other people's success, happiness, and prosperity. Jealousy is a tower toppler; a ship sinker — some of the greatest things in existence have come crashing down because of it.

People began to noticeably change the more financial success I obtained. Knowing that I always had larger amounts of drugs and cash on me, people who I thought were friends started trying to use various manipulation tactics to take advantage of me. These people would try to purposefully get me extra high and mess with my head and see if they could cause me to make a sloppy mistake or freak out, thus giving them an opportunity to steal from me or get information about my business practices.

There were times where friends — people whom I thought I could trust – would steal from me in moments of their desperation – even when I'd be willing to share with them. Sometimes these were people I'd let stay in my hotel rooms because they had nowhere to live. After days of being awake and finally collapsing into sleep, I would wake up to find my bags had been searched through, and stuff of value had been taken.

On one occasion, a friend of mine I was sharing a hotel room with stole money out of my pocket while I was sleeping. When I woke up and confronted him about it, he said, "You got caught slipping — you deserved it." He never gave me my money back and acted like business as usual. As a non-confrontational person, and considering he was bigger than me, I let it go and took it as a lesson learned. But the lesson wasn't about getting "caught slipping," falling asleep with money in my pocket around friends I was supposed to be able to trust, in my own hotel room. The lesson was that I should be even wiser about who I should allow around me. When someone showed they weren't to be trusted, I quietly removed them from my active inner circle.

There were lessons around deception. There were times when people would finagle their way over to the hotel under the guise of wanting to talk about business, but in all actuality were just there to spy. They'd come over to supposedly talk, get high in the process, then pretend to fall asleep so they could eavesdrop, attempting to gain insight for their financial gain. A week later, I'd hear they had reached out to attempt to work with someone they had seen me serving at my hotel. The level of shadiness I witnessed was quite sophisticated. It all made me value trustworthiness and integrity.

Through all these types of situations, I was forced to learn the importance of necessary boundaries. I learned the difference between a family-friend and a frenemy: people who were seeming friends but were plotting against me with the wrong intentions. I became highly discerning with when to cut ties and move on from friendships without attachments to the past.

The human experience is one of learning through error. Life is about evolution and sequential growth and improvement. What's most important is that you're evolving forward from versions of yourself in the past. I'm grateful to God I had the opportunity to learn through an abundance of mistake making.

⚛ Psychedelic Psychological Warfare

In that my business practices primarily oriented around the combination of psychedelics and amphetamines; I was right in the middle of two diametrically opposing forces. Psychedelics would bring forward and enhance one's soul light, and ice-amphetamines would in large rob people's soul light. When the combination of these two substances were mixed it could be dangerous, spiritually speaking.

Because of the nature of the substances that I was dealing – specifically the crystal methamphetamines – as my network grew, I began doing business with super intense, psychologically-burly people. Charles Manson types. I was swimming with vampire sharks in the deep end of dark, cold waters.

While already being up for days on amphetamines, the folks in mention, would challenge me into taking gargantuan amounts of psychedelics with them to see if they could make me lose my mind. The abstruse amounts and combinations of substances would be followed by head games on top of it. It was a warped psychological chess match. I couldn't tell if I was being tested to see if my mental fortitude could withstand it, or if they were trying to mentally overpower me for humor or ego points.

On some of these earlier occasions, things got severely strange, but I always held it together to a large degree. Not being of weak mind, their attempts to break me down were futile.

Although intense, these early-stage experiences were spiritually innocent, and vanilla compared to what was awaiting in my near future.

❀ Violence

With all the potential danger involved in my environment, somehow, there was virtually zero violence. Since my childhood, watching my mom get in fights, I always wanted to avoid violence. Thankfully, it's never been a theme in my life.

I can't speak for the entire city of Atlanta, but in the '90s, to me everyone wanted to work together in the name of one primary objective: making as much money as possible without the police catching on.

After 1995, although guns entered our scene and everyone around me carried them, fortunately they never had to be used. They functioned as a preventive measure more than anything.

Instead of guns as a form of street justice, people who acted sideways were dealt with by unknowingly being given gargantuan amounts of LSD. LSD can sometimes put people in a highly-vulnerable space of self-reflection – a moment of truth of sorts – it makes you look at the dark spots in yourself that need to be addressed. They'd be left to think about what they'd done in the most concentrated manner imaginable – most oftentimes leading them to change themselves afterwards.

I am grateful to The Creator there wasn't gun violence and death in my experience of the drug trade. My guardian angels were working overtime and they deserve all the appreciation I could ever give them. In the everyday world, not to mention in the drug world, people get murdered for petty cash all the time. Here I was always walking around with large money and hundred thousand dollars' worth of substances on me, and never once was my life threatened.

❀ The False Light

By the age of 18 years old, I had become well known throughout the entire southeast scene. I was one of the main decision-makers of a large network of drug dealers. I was a respected and successful figure in my world, but I was empty in my heart. I remember reflecting on myself at times with deep disappointment, thinking that my only self-worth and value was the drug connections I had.

My environment gave me a first-hand experience and understanding of what I call the *false-light* – the material light of this world. At the time it was ego-fulfilling and exciting, and it taught me about worldly power and influence.

The deeper my desire for money grew the further I drifted from what's truly important, and the emptier I felt. At a point in time, nothing was sacred in my mind other than making money. I was a materially-driven, drug-addicted, drug dealer, with a head full of past traumas – my soul had gone dim.

The unseen benefit of my emptiness was reflection. I began questioning what *was* truly valuable in life. Although the coming years would be a continuation of madness mixed with survival-fueled materialism, after a few jarring wake-up calls from the universe, and a handful of faceplants, my eyes eventually opened. I came out of it all with the knowing that outer wealth without inner wealth is nothing but a box in wrapping paper minus the gift inside. I discovered that true power is peace. And that the love-light within you is the ultimate treasure of life. One's worth isn't found in the amount of *valuables* accumulated: Our worth is based on our innermost essence as God first birthed us. What is valuable on this earth is the value you bring to others' lives.

❁ Strike Two

At around the two-year mark of my clandestine life in Atlanta, I had my second major run-in with the police. My business partner (who was also my connection) and I were attempting to trade a half-pound of amphetamines for twenty pounds of commercial marijuana through an associate of mine. Undercover police were unknowingly setting up our customer who was conducting the trade. Once the deal got busted, the cops ended up tracing his pager back to our hotel room.

As we waited throughout the night for news about the proceedings of the deal, at around 4 a.m., the police came busting through our hotel room door. As they entered, I completely froze in place. I was in shock and paralysis when they came through the door. The police ransacked the room, and luckily, I only had a small amount of my personal drugs on me. All our other product had been sold earlier that day.

That was my first time getting arrested for something serious. There were implications of the case that almost made it be picked up by the feds. During it all, one of the worries sitting in the back of my mind was if I was going to have a warrant out for my arrest from my previous North Carolina probation. Thankfully, it never showed up. Somehow it had fallen through the cracks.

Being in jail while detoxing from long-term use of copious amounts of methamphetamines was an absolute nightmare. The first night sitting in the single-person holding cell in Roswell City Jail, I felt broken and as alone as a soul could feel.

I went on to spend about four months in the cozy confines of the Roswell Jail. While there, I saw the true colors of many *supposed* friends. Many of the people I called on to help me get out wouldn't. I learned they'd been envious of my success and wanted to benefit financially from my being away. One of the few people who attempted to get me out was my friend Abraham. His efforts were unsuccessful because he wasn't a legal adult who could sign my bond.

While there in Roswell Jail, in a broken and humbling situation, my commitment to being a drug-dealer was concrete. Changing my ways was never a consideration in my mind. There was an older mild-mannered gentleman who was in the same jail pod as I was. He was a disciplined, Christian family man who kept to himself and was usually doing push-ups or reading his Bible. He was there for insurance fraud. One day, about a month into me being there, he came up to me and began speaking with me about leaving behind the world of drug-dealing. With deep sincerity, he went on and on. I informed him that I had no plans to change. He explained that continuing to do the same thing would surely lead me back to jail in the future. I gave him his moments to say his words of wisdom and then I informed him that I was in too deep, and it was all too much fun to change it. Bless his heart for trying, but there was no getting through to me.

After around two months in the Roswell City Jail, I was transported to the nightmare that is Fulton County Rice Street Jail. Rice Street Jail was a cold and grimy place — a place no one would ever want to be. Soulless.

While in Rice Street, I tried to use my time as constructively as possible. I read the Koran and revisited the Bible. I appreciated the opportunity to read of the wisdom from both books – but that wasn't going to change my commitment to the drug game.

I was never bothered or bullied by anyone while in jail, and no one tried to pick fights with me. I was always respectful. Whether in jail or the free world, it's all the same when it comes to relating to others — come in peace, be real in your heart, and approach people with respect.

After six months, which felt like years, in Rice Street, my bond amount was eventually reduced. The reduction in bond made it easier for my friends to get me out. Once I was released from jail, we went back to the hotel room where they were staying. I was back to the familiar ever-changing life of hotel living.

I did my best to hit the ground running. Instantaneously I was going line-for-line of ice-amphetamines with my tribe of madmen and women. After being away for so long, it took me a bit to fully figure out what was going on in the scene. In my mind, there was no other choice but to continue what I'd been doing before. I eventually regained my momentum and reconnected with everyone.

There were multiple people who had capitalized off my arrest. Many past customers had been moved in on by other competitors. The whole experience was a classic example of "One man gathers what another man spills."

Once my court case came around from the arrest, the past charges had been reduced to felony possession of the drugs that were found in my pocket on the night of the arrest. Because this was my first offense as an adult, I was given first offender's probation.

The court case was on a Friday, and I was the last case the judge saw that day. Because my case was so late in the day, the probation department was already closed by the time I got my sentencing. Consequently, I was instructed to report to the probation department the following Monday to get assigned a probation officer. I had no intention of showing up that following Monday. In my mind I was just in too deep to be looking a government official in the face once or twice a month, while potentially taking drug tests. I continued to pound the pavement and psycho-swing drugs out of my hotel rooms with an attitude of "catch me if you can."

⊛ Catch Me if You Can

After facing my charges in court, and not showing up for my probation assigning, in my mind I was on the run again, skipping out on another probation. Armed with a gun, a pager, and bags filled with drugs and money, it was business as usual.

My world felt like the Olympics of drug dealing. My friends and I would have multitudes of hotel rooms all over the city. Everything in life was spontaneous and based on impulse. Organized chaos.

My circle was connected with the best of the psychedelic drugs. But beyond the psychedelics and designer, chemical-based drugs, I was also connected with the Mexican cartel. This allowed me to obtain hundreds of pounds of Mexican marijuana at a time. Having access to a market outside of my familiar business circle allowed me to diversify my portfolio in a way that gave me a well-roundedness in my clandestine money-making ventures.

When doing business with my Mexican connections, I'd usually be picking up huge loads of marijuana at a time. Generally, I was always on high alert, but when I'd be picking up loads of marijuana in these small suburb towns in Atlanta, my paranoia was on max! Looking back on it, I can only shake my head in disbelief at how noticeably suspect I was. Imagine a young skinny teen in oversized raver clothes, dark sunglasses and a visor, carrying a ten-millimeter handgun in a shoulder holster, walking through a Mexican apartment complex with three huge duffle bags packed to the brim with pounds of marijuana.

To be as bottom-line as I was financially, I had personal code in my business dealings. Beyond my own personal aversions because of my mother, there were certain substances that just seemed like an expedited prison sentence on a platter. My Mexican connections would always try and get me to sell kilos of cocaine, but I just wouldn't do it.

Although cocaine wasn't any less virtuous than selling methamphetamines, I didn't view amphetamines as bad yet. I hadn't been around it long enough to see its long-term negative effects on people's lives. It wouldn't be until I changed my life that the reality hit me of how badly I was affecting people's lives for profit.

Here I was, 18 years old, neck-deep in a world of potential danger, that I didn't want to acknowledge. I had grown up way too quickly, in a line of work with people whose lives had taken a very wrong turn at some point.

To be so young, I was serious about business and capitalizing on every opportunity possible. Being high and making money was virtually all I ever thought about. I was being fueled by a combination of opportunism, materialistic thirst, survival fear, the fear of missing out on a potential drug deal. I didn't deviate away from my pager, the payphone or the hotel room phone, and my Rolodex. That period of my life was highlighted by an undying dedication to shallow, material self-servitude.

⊛ Luck or Divine Intervention?

Through luck — or divine intervention — there were so many times things could have gone extremely south but didn't. Having illegal substances on you 365 days a year, for consecutive years, offers ample room for the sister named fate to catch you in her clutches.

One time, a group of three of my partners and I were staying at the Sandy Springs Inn. We had been up for days and had a cornucopia of drugs on us. I had eight ounces of methamphetamines wrapped up in eight separate pairs of socks. My friends had vials of liquid LSD and mason jars full of high-grade marijuana. One of my friends, Barney, was meandering through the hotel and decided to try and exit out a prohibited door that set off an alarm. The police were called, and they arrived at our hotel room door — they could tell we were high as kites. As I sat there coming to terms with the fact that I was in front of the police, I looked like I'd jumped out of my body with fear. One of the officers specifically looked at me and said, "It looks like that one's seen a ghost."

Brian, whose father had been a police officer in the past, was calm and more comfortable in the situation. He asked to speak with the officers alone in our conjoining hotel room. Five minutes or so later the police officers and Brian all returned. When they came back into the room to search around, the police officers were very chill, but nonetheless they lightly searched through our room. Luckily, they didn't find the half-pound of methamphetamines in my bag! Though my heart did skip a few beats once they made it to my bags. They did find and confiscate the marijuana we had in mason jars. The police also found the vials of LSD, which they made my friends dump in the toilet. Somehow, whether it was divine intervention or Brian's silver tongue, the police left that hotel room, and we didn't go to jail. If they would've discovered what was in my socks I would've gone away for many years. To this day, I'm still baffled by it – and so grateful to God!

This was just one of MANY similar close calls where divine intervention and luck joined forces on my behalf – including my final run-in with the law at 20 years old.

⊛ A Visit From an Angel

In this stage of my life, as you've read, I wasn't a religious or spiritual-minded person at all. I was worldly – purely. My sole focus was on making and spending money while staying high. Even with me being a secular materialist, strange paranormal occurrences began happening.

One Sunday, I had paranormal communication with what I could only consider an Angel. Three friends and I were hanging out at a hotel. Everyone was doing their own thing, and the next thing I knew, I noticed a glowing, circular light appear in the upper left-hand corner of the room. It seemed to come out of nowhere. But it wasn't like a light from a lightbulb. It was an otherworldly type of Light that was transferring a feeling of peace and loving presence into my heart. At that time in my life, peace and a loving presence was something foreign to me. I remember it being such a comforting feeling, and the only thing I could gather was that it was an Angel I was in the presence of.

As I sat there, partly in astonishment, staring at this Being of Light, I asked it what my purpose on earth was. I then received a telepathic type of reply that said, "To help save your mother." I continued to sit there in amazement, not sure what else to do or ask. A few minutes later the Angel was gone, yet a feeling of deep profound peace continued to reverberate through me. I sat and pondered the whole experience deeply.

As far as the reply I received, the only thing I could conclude at the time was that saving my mother meant through financial means. I figured I should try to save enough money to buy her a home outside of Los Angeles and relocate her away from the drugs and streets of Venice. I wasn't fully aware that drug addiction of her caliber didn't work like that. The irony as well: I was so deep into my lifestyle, and oblivious to my wrongdoings, I was blind to the fact that my plan was to make enough money selling drugs, which fuel addiction, to try and help get my mom away from drug addiction.

This visitation with the Angel this day lasted for about 10 minutes. This was my first visual experience of something of a nonphysical nature. It was a deeply emotionally-moving experience because of the feeling of love and care that it brought into my heart. Something my soul had been starving for deep down. The unexpectedness of it made it even more impactful on me. It happened during a time when I was just a young, rebellious teenager with no spirituality in my life whatsoever.

✸ Brooke

Throughout all these years, I was often in the Atlanta underground-rave clubs. One of the places I would often go to was called Skylab. I was never a dancing type of guy. I more so would go to the clubs for business networking purposes.

Personally, I wasn't the most social of people. I was an introvert with an awkwardly-distant vibe. I was always in my own head high on drugs, typically amphetamines, pharmaceuticals, and psychedelics. Day or night, indoors or outdoors, I wore dark black sunglasses everywhere I went. It was rare that I would ever come out of my shell to introduce myself in public to anyone new.

Though, there was this one night out where the stars were aligned for destiny. While at Skylab, I noticed a group of girls there together. One of them stood out to me especially. She was around 17 years old, and her name was Brooke. She was a smiley Pisces with pretty, long blonde hair and big, starry eyes. As the night went by, I wanted to go up and talk to her but was having a challenging time mustering up the courage.

Luckily, as the party was ending, her friend's car battery had gone out, which gave me some extra time to approach her and try to talk to her. Once I finally introduced myself, I didn't have a permanent number I could give her because I lived from hotel to hotel, so I gave her my pager number. Knowing that wasn't a homerun, I was adamant about asking for her number. However, she was a little resistant to offer it up. So, I continued to ask until she finally gave it to me. The number she gave me was the number to her parents' house, where they lived out in the rural country areas of Georgia.

Since making it to Atlanta and establishing myself in my career, I hadn't put any thought into women, a relationship, or intimacy. My 24-7 focus was always money and survival. Yet, there was something that seemed magical and destined about Brooke. All I could think about was being with her. I was determined to know her. At the time, she was still in high school and had a job working at a local hair salon in a small town located about an hour from Atlanta.

After that night, I went back to my life living in hotel rooms. I called her house often, trying to contact her and talk. I would leave messages on her parents' answering machine. Being that I never slept, I would often call late at night. Sometimes her mother would answer, half-awake, and talk to me.

Her mother (a person who would become one of my strongest support systems eventually) was dealing with a daughter who, at the time, was gaining her autonomy as a teenager. In that, her mom was experiencing the leave-the-nest syndrome. She was an incredibly involved, caring, and loving Italian mom, and she was always open to speaking to me. Looking back on it, from a privacy standpoint, Brooke wasn't too thrilled about me talking with her mom, but I was determined to get closer to her however I could.

The next time we would see each other was at the next big rave party. At the time, I was living at the Biltmore Hotel in Midtown Atlanta. When she finally arrived at the party, my friends and I were dealing with a sketchy situation with someone at the club who we thought was a snitch. We ended up having to leave the venue in a rush. So, I asked Brooke and her friend to ditch the party and leave with us. Reluctantly, her and her friend came with us.

Later that night at my hotel, she kissed me for the first time. That would be the beginning of my longest relationship to date.

We remained together for five years. As together as we could be in the face of my disconnectedness. Although she was an amazing girl, I couldn't fully open up to her for the better part of the first two years of our relationship. She stayed loyally by my side through a lifestyle of Absolute madness for many long years. She wasn't into drug use the way my friends and I were. She was a pure-hearted person — in hindsight, on what seemed to be a mission from God to keep me safe! She loved me wholeheartedly even in the face of lifestyle and drug habits. While most women would've been out of there, she stuck with me and loved me unconditionally.

At 17 years old, Brooke ended up dropping out of high school to live with me from hotel to hotel. There I was in the most precarious and sometimes dangerous environments, with absolute wolf sharks and hyenas of people hovering around me, and then there was Brooke, like a human angel, so innocent and pure in spirit.

When I would finally collapse into sleep, after being on multi-day methamphetamine benders, she would stay by my side and make sure everything was okay. For days, while I slept, she would be there beside me just watching television. Funny enough, there were times when I would wake up, to find she had manicured my fingernails. She was the most nurturing and caring person I'd ever known.

Within the first few years of our relationship, I regretfully cheated on her multiple times. Nothing came of it, and I concealed my misdeeds until a year after our breakup in 2002.

To this day, I know that if Brooke hadn't been by my side, I wouldn't have made it through the insanity that was my life from 17 to 22 years old. I wouldn't have made it to where I am today, helping people, either. Her love was a shining ray of light that was the only thing connecting me to a thread of my heart while traversing through the darkest night of my soul.

Brooke and I - 1995

⊛ Souls Turned Unholy

After 1996, with certain friends within the scene, things started becoming a different type of dark – on the spiritual level. When I say "dark," I mean literally, not figuratively or symbolically. Also, I don't mean "dark" as in "bad," because we were selling drugs and such. When I say "dark," I mean the unholy version of dark — like the Robert Johnson story.

There would be times we were staying awake for weeks on mixtures of strong amphetamines, pharmaceuticals, and psychedelics. This combination of drugs coupled with power and money-hungry people, led to a wrong turn for a handful of folks in my scene. It led to otherworldly temptations! For those of a weaker constitution, things went south, in a soul way.

For this handful of brothers, I'm not sure if this was due to some type of entities that found their way into their fields that were influencing their minds, or just karmic darkness carrying over in their souls. Regardless, the next thing I knew, people were talking about warped, dark, demonic stuff. I noticed changes in friends who used to have light in their eyes. The light which went missing. Even in my unconsciousness, I could clearly see and sense the shifts in these particular people.

Things getting otherworldly was the last thing I saw coming. I was young, surfaced, and materialistic. I thought we were all just trying to have fun, make money, spend money, and hang out. In my mind, I was content with things being just and only that. What used to be an environment for having fun suddenly became a feeding ground for spiritual stuff that I'd never encountered. When people in my surroundings began talking about demonic forces, evil spirits, and souls, I found it all lame and unnecessary. I did my best to completely ignore it and block it out. It was not an element I wanted to entertain. All of it was completely out of my scope of understanding.

I'd been exposed to, and knew how to deal with, people being deceptive, dishonest, and manipulative, but this version of dark was simply wrong on a whole other level. I eventually discovered that these people, whom I was once close with, had made pacts with dark supernatural forces for money in exchange for their souls. Then to add to the insidiousness of it, they were trying to, as covertly as possible, find recruits to convince others to do the same. It's as if they were soul hunting. Trying to feed off spiritually weakened innocent drug-addicted people.

Around this time, there were people getting arrested who began working with the police to get reduced sentences. It was the most alert time in my life. I had to be concerned with thieves and robbers, people trying to steal my business connections, people trying to set me up with the police, and those who were taxiing demons around coming at me sideways on a spiritual level.

Thank God throughout this time I had a guardian angel of a girlfriend, Brooke. She, and just enough remembrance of love for God in my heart, became my saving grace.

As I noticed these people speaking in spiritually-wicked tongue, I began to gravitate more toward people in the scene who were good-hearted and weren't about the dark realm type of things. My friend Kyle was one of those friends I became closest with. My friend Ryan was another one. They both had pure hearts and were real people of kindness. I never had to question either on a spiritual level.

Even though I changed my immediate inner-circle, I still had a dilemma. I used and sold methamphetamines, which required me to intermingle with these other darker associates to meet my needs. Some of these people were my connections and suppliers of the substances I sold. I was in darkness's web, and it was of my own participation.

I grew to realize that the forces working through some of these people were particularly interested in me for whatever reasons. I had a target on my back. A series of sequentially more revealing experiences began unfolding, all leading up to an outright attempt at my soul.

On one occasion, it was a dark, cold night in Georgia, and I had gone to meet one of my amphetamine dealers. George was his name. As I arrived, he came out to the front of the house to meet me. It was just the two of us standing there, smoking a cigarette. The next thing I knew he was speaking to me in this strange double-talk, veiled way of speaking. While doing so with this twisted, warped stare in his eyes.

As he finished his spiel, he looked at me with a sinister grin, a deep gaze, and a seriously-dark tone said, "Now, Tony, walk with me. Will you walk with me?"

I got an eerie tingle down my spine and just looked at him like, *What the fuck you talking about, man?* In all the years I'd known this guy, he'd never spoken that way, with that use of words, or with that style of language, adding to it, while trying to eye me down as if he was attempting to look into my soul.

I had an intense feeling of resistance within me, to which I said, "Nah, I'm good, I'm going to stay out here for a little bit and check my pager. I'll come inside a little bit later." He continued to stare at me and again say, "Walk with me, follow me," but was saying it in a manner where the look in his eyes and his tone of voice meant something other than physically walk with him back into the house. I looked up at him, stale-faced him, and I didn't budge. He finally shook his head, turned around, and walked off by himself. I didn't make an issue of it, or speak on it, but I took note.

I would go on to have three further experiences with this guy, two of which were blatant. It was as if a grooming was taking place. George incrementally showed his cards gradually.

The next occasion, I was visiting him and one of his associates to pick up product. We had been in the kitchen area for a little while before we decided to go to the living room. As we walked out of the kitchen area, he began talking about how they'd been praying to Satan. When he said this, I looked at him with a blank stare, and replied, "What are you talking about?"

"What do you mean?" he asked.

"What the fuck are you talking about?" I repeated.

He looked back at me with this devious, devilish smile and said, "I don't know what you're talking about. I didn't say that." At that point, I didn't try to push the conversation any further.

I shook my head, "Whatever, man."

On another occasion, I had let him stay at my hotel room after the rave party ended. It was a Sunday morning. George woke up from being asleep in one of the beds and with the most sober normal face, the first thing he says to me is, "I sold my soul for ten thousand dollars."

I just turned and walked away and said, "I'm sorry to hear that, man."

I kept an internal log of all these experiences. In hindsight, I should have just cut him out of my life (which is what I would recommend everyone else to do in a situation with this type of person), but I've grown to realize that there were reasons why I needed to go through these tests and trials.

Another of these types of situations happened one morning when he had been sleeping on the couch of a friend's place that we were both staying at. He woke up, looked at me, and mentioned that spirits were entering his body and leaving and taking turns coming back in. I just looked down, shook my head with no response, and walked away.

The finale of these experiences with George occurs in the fall of 1997.

❀ The Invasion & Exorcism

I preface the next part of the story by saying that throughout all the years, and the multiple hundreds of occasions utilizing psychedelics, only three of them stood out. These three experiences were full-blown supernaturally spiritual. Profoundly serious from an otherworldly perspective. I remember every nuance of these experiences perfectly. They were all way beyond my understanding at the time. As I've grown through the last two decades of studies of metaphysics and the astral realm, I now know very clearly what was at play during these experiences as a teen. The best way I can describe these experiences is psychic attacks by dark entities. Two of these occasions ended with me strapped down in an ambulance, being taken to the emergency room.

The first of these three occasions, the most intense and terrifyingly humbling one, occurring in September of 1996. I had been staying at a house with my close good-hearted hippie friends. At the time I was in an unhealthy place within myself – but I wasn't using methamphetamines at the time due to a drought.

The previous days before this experience the weather was overcast. The dark ominous tone in the sky had been a perfect match for the strange energy I'd been noticing around me. Before the night of this encounter, for days in a row, I'd been experiencing what I can only describe as forced thoughts of violence, which were uncharacteristic of my normal thinking. These thoughts of violence towards others kept entering my headspace. They seemed like they were being projected into my mind from an outside source.

I kept having to shake these thoughts out of my headspace with a perplexing response of, *What is this?* Although I was a gun owner at the time, I was never violent and I'd never in my life had thoughts of violence toward anyone. Now, out of left field, I was getting these thoughts about hurting my roommates. I was so perplexed by this, I even mentioned it to them. At the time I knew nothing about astral entities and their ability to attract into and taxi around in people's fields, while telepathically projecting disturbing thoughts into one's mind.

My roommate and friend, Matt, happened to have twenty pounds of psilocybin mushrooms. On this night, we decided to have friends over and make mushroom tea. We pushed the limits and made a highly concentrated batch.

Before the tea was prepared, we were outside on the back porch. The sun had gone down, and the cold Georgia air had ushered in the night. As we stood there on the back porch, I saw a jet-black figure with horns, standing about three feet tall. Once I noticed it, it swiftly moved across the backyard – without making any noise. It was a shade of black, darker than the night. The moment happened quickly so I brushed it off and proceeded into the night.

The batch of tea contained a little over an ounce and a half, which would be equivalent to around forty-two dried grams. We boiled it down into about a three-cup size (24 oz) of concentrated tea. We placed the batch of psilocybin tea into a Victorian goblet and proceeded to pass it around between the five of us. As the five of us passed the goblet around, it soon became three of us. Then the three of us became just two of us passing this tea back and forth until it was all consumed. By the time we were done, it was after midnight.

After about an hour of enjoying the night with my friends, the feeling within me rapidly turned into an extremely uncomfortable, dark, supernatural vibe. The feeling was unlike any experience on psychedelics before – after hundreds of times of taking them. I had experienced "bad trips" before, but this wasn't that. Things started feeling a strange type of serious. I had a sense I was in uncharted territory. An undertone of something horribly wrong permeated the energy in the air. The CD playing at the time, a Grateful Dead song called "Estimated Prophet," began skipping and creating a warped bouncing sound to the song. This continued in the background for an extended amount of time.

The presence of evil was in the room with us that night, and it attempted to make me its welcomed host. This was about to be one of the most spiritually-defining moments of my life – a moment that would blatantly reveal the reality of the forces of both darkness and Light.

As I sat on the couch, noticing this deeply concerning feeling in the air, I looked down at the three necklaces I was wearing. One was a cross, another an astrological necklace on black thread, and the third, a hemp necklace. Two of the necklaces began aggressively twisting around the cross necklace – by themselves! Fearfully I pulled the necklaces off my neck and tossed them away from me. The best way I can describe it is, things began to feel unholy. I didn't know exactly what to make of it – or how to respond. I was growing more concerned by the moment. A feeling of panic began to build within me.

It was late at night, but I had a strange sense to call a friend of mine named Ian, thinking that maybe he'd know what was going on.

Much like me, Ian was a troubled young man. He was someone who came from an unfortunate family background with a drug-addicted mother. As a child, he had been disappointed by the Christian Church and Jesus not helping him or his family. Because of this he carried a rebellious undertone of transgression against anything having to do with God – and he was never shy at vocalizing his disdain.

In my moments of growing panic, I picked up the phone and called Ian.

Sure enough, he answered. The tone in his voice was dark. He almost sounded like a monster of sorts when he answered. Throughout my time knowing Ian, I had called him hundreds of times and he'd never answered a phone call from me like that – not even jokingly. His tone of voice so perfectly coincided with everything else that, in my mind, it confirmed that he somehow knew what was going on.

As I attempted to begin the conversation, I was noticeably a bit timid. I was desperately attempting to suppress my growing terror.

"What's going on?" I asked him.

"I don't know, Tony. What is going on?" Ian responded in a serious voice.

I began to apologize for calling so late; for a fleeting moment I had a hope that the reason he sounded so monstrously angry upon answering the phone was because how late at night my call was.

What came next was the most bone-chilling response that multiplied the terror of the moment in the worst of ways.

"It's not me you have to apologize to Tony. Now it's God you have to apologize to," he said.

His words dug the dagger of confirmation even deeper into my soul. At that point, there was a melting panic within me. I hung up the phone. I felt time stop. Something on a different level of wrong was happening!

Although the feeling of terror heightened, there was no escape. I began to sense that the whole situation had been prepared by dark forces that were way beyond my understanding or experience. It felt like I was in a trap – a *gotcha* moment; like I had been hunted.

Sitting there petrified, I began to feel like my hair was falling out. This was followed by a sensation that my teeth were dissolving. The next thing I noticed was that a layer of dull grey darkness had been cast over everything in the room. The next thing I noticed was the love-light in my heart was gone. As I sat there, I felt like I would never feel love again – for eternity! The feeling within me was a desolate, alone feeling so deep in my soul. It was the saddest, most empty feeling you could imagine! It was despair that could never be measured.

The next thing I noticed was that a second set of eyes appeared in my head. It was like I could see them overlapped in front of my eyes, like

I was seeing with two sets of eyes. I closed my eyes and could still notice the second set of other eyes there.

Next, I mentally heard a definitive voice say, "Now you are one of us."

It was by far the most soul-traumatizing moment of my life. I became frozen in a state of shock as to what was happening. This was something serious – it was the presence of a dark entity that had entered my field!

This thing within me began to induce horrible visions in my mind. One of them was of me walking into a church and the entire congregation immediately and simultaneously turning and looking over their shoulders at me with scowls on their faces, as if I were being exiled from the church. The looks on their faces were as if they were all simultaneously giving me the forbidden eye to leave, that I wasn't welcome there.

I remember Brooke was asleep on the couch beside me while my other friends were on the couch or laying on the floor. There was no one to turn to – but I had to do something! Within me was the feeling of the deepest sadness, aloneness, and terror, all at once, all throughout me.

The words my friend had just spoken, "Now it is God you have to apologize to," flashed through my head. I went into desperate prayer to God. With my eyes to the heavens, I begged for help, hoping that somehow this hostage situation would end – and hoping I would feel love once again. At this point, all my friends became aware of what was going on, as I sat there asking for forgiveness and for God to please help me.

After what seemed like a few minutes of this, a largeish size circular figure of Light appeared in the upper left-hand corner of the room. It was around three feet in circumference. It was an Angel. It was visually similar, appearing as a large orb of brilliant, beautiful Light, located in the same upper left-hand area of the room as my experience a year or so previous.

This Angel told me that God loved me. It then asked me to tell everyone in the room that God loved them, which I did humbly, one by one.

Next, the Angel asked me to tell God the same. Then it asked me to ask each person in the room to express their love for God. They all did, except for two people. After this, I could feel this dark force, which had been the second set of eyes within me, lifted out and removed. The next thing I knew, the feeling of the Light of love returned to my heart. I had just experienced an exorcism by way of an Angel.

Suddenly, and in perfect orchestra with the sequence leading up to the moment, the CD finally stopped skipping. The song that played was still "Estimated Prophet." It was a truly sacred and beautiful moment. The feeling of relief that I felt I could never put into words.

The length of the entire episode felt like an eternity! I was exhausted! A little while later the sun rose, bringing with it morning. Being able to feel and know love again was the most amazing feeling ever!

Brooke woke up a short while later after sleeping through the whole episode. There was no way for me to even find the words to explain to her what had just happened, so I didn't even attempt to. We left the house and got a hotel where I could sleep for a few days while coming to terms with what had just occurred.

The experience gave me an extreme firsthand lesson about the spirit world and the nature of astral entities. I knew of the forces of Light and dark in a way like never before. The entire thing deeply strengthened my relationship with The Creator. My allegiance to the Love of God became unshakeable.

Although I continued using and selling drugs, the experience changed me internally and I was noticeably different in my soul – in a loving way.

These things helped open my eyes to the spiritual side of existence, which eventually guided me onto the path of the healing arts.

After this occurrence, I stopped spending every waking hour inside the hotel room, glued to the phone, trying to drum up drug sales. Instead, I would often go and sit at spiritual bookstores and read. I didn't have any clear direction of what I was looking for or studying, but I was open to learn and grow deeper in my understanding of spirituality and God.

✸ LSD Therapy

In the spring of 1997, I attempted to stop using methamphetamines. My desire to get away from that substance resulted from a growing distaste for the people connected to it. I was so far into my use of it I was clueless as to how to break the addiction. At this point, I had been consistently using the most potent form of the stuff for years. I had become seduced by it socially, neurologically, and psychologically. Whenever I attempted to come off it in the past, I would end up sleeping for weeks straight – and I would always feel exhausted – a condition which is called adrenal fatigue.

I brainstormed ways to get off amphetamines. The only thing I could think of was to trade it off for another substance. It couldn't be marijuana or alcohol because it would deepen my need to sleep for weeks, thus maybe becoming months, while my body recalibrated.

I needed to be alert enough to still make money and keep up with the competitive nature of the regional drug trade.

Using pharmaceuticals to get off amphetamines was not an option either. I had developed a strong disdain for people around me, friends, or business associates who used them because of how mistake-ridden and zombie-like people would become on them. They would cause horrible decision-making that was a potential liability for everyone involved — decision-making that could result in people going to prison for a long long time!

At the time, I had massive amounts of LSD coming from the production of William Pickard. I would get around 20,000 doses at a time, which were two raw grams of crystal LSD. After laying the LSD on perforated paper, I would always have around 100 to 200 extra doses leftover. Those extra doses were for my personal use.

Considering how much LSD was around, and in my possession, I thought to try and see if it would help offset the withdrawal symptoms from stopping methamphetamine use. I decided to use just enough to be functional. Nowadays, people call this *micro-dosing.*

Sure enough, it helped keep the horrid effects of detoxing from being completely incapacitating. Although my body developed a tolerance to it, taking between three and ten micro-doses a day would usually be perfect for me to have a gentle glow while also allowing me to be aware enough to be mindful of my decision making. I would go on to use this approach for around six months.

I effectively detoxed from amphetamines and was feeling good. I was only using and selling LSD then. As strange as it sounds to me now, at the time, LSD was one of the only substances that I took pride in selling. From a moral perspective, it had more of a positive effect on people than it did a negative.

The months rolled on and I had found a good groove and version of myself – then suddenly, two unfortunate things happened simultaneously. First, the flow of LSD coming to Atlanta from the West Coast came to a stop, causing me to run out of my supply. Additionally, the purest amphetamines that had come through the city in a long time showed up on the market. And it was all around me. It was a recipe for my disaster.

I was given an opportunity to obtain a large amount of it for a price that my then business mind couldn't turn down. Aside from my financial reasoning, my plan was to avoid using it. For quite a while, I stuck to that plan and only sold it.

✺ Escape for My Soul

Not everyone in my social circle was on the same page as me about not using methamphetamines. Eventually, the peer pressure and the memories of staying awake for days and making money caught up to me. I ended up back on the multiple-day train, sniffing line for line up my nose.

Because we had such a high demand for LSD, instead of waiting on it, one of my partners went directly to San Francisco to force our financial hand a bit. As my friend arrived back in Atlanta with the grams of freshly-laid acid, we set off to get things moving. The first order of business was to try out the product.

I was already upside down from being awake for about three to four days on amphetamines. Although intense, it was a combination of substances I had experienced before, so I didn't think anything of it. At the time what I failed to take into consideration was that I was a person that was right smack dab in the middle of a holy war. The combination of fresh, strong, acid mixed with being awake multiple days on amphetamines would prove to open a gateway to disastrous darkness.

On this night, my friends and I were at the old Refrigerator Factory Lofts located at the end of 17th Street in Atlanta. It was 1997, the biggest song on the radio was Biggie Smalls' "Hypnotize." As the acid kicked in, this song began to play, and a strangely-warped stretching of the music notes began, like the distortions in the music on the night when the entity attempted to enter my field the year before.

As the LSD began to take effect, one of the guys I was with in the loft began giving me cynical looks. He had a devilish grin on his face. Next thing I knew, the feeling in the room started getting weird and eerie. He asked me *what was wrong* with a deceptive look in his eyes. I could feel an uneasiness in my gut. I decided to leave the loft and head toward the parking lot where some of my other friends were.

As I walked outside, moving at a quick pace, I began hearing horrifically evil laughter raining from the sky. It sounded as if it were coming from all around me. My feelings of uneasiness quickly turned to terror and fear!

I was wearing a necklace pouch containing several types of stones and crystals. I looked down, and the pouch of crystals was winding up and creating an upside-down noose around my neck. My other necklaces began to feel like a mix of steel wool and barbed wire on my neck. I removed the pouch of crystals from my neck and threw them as far as I could. The horrid demonic laughter continued to reign from the sky.

My fight-or-flight response escalated as the sounds of inescapable demonic laughter poured from every direction in the sky. All I could think to do was run. As I did my friends began to chase after me, including the original guy from up in the loft.

I ran from the parking lot to the opposite side of the street, where I saw a MARTA transit bus coming toward a bus stop. The bus was full as it pulled up to the bus stop. I got on the bus, shaken, and made my way to the back of the bus. The laughter reigning from the sky had finally subsided. I was on this bus and deeply relieved to get away from the previous scene.

I fumbled around and attempted to pull the money out of my pocket for the bus fare. I was so discombobulated that I couldn't get the correct money out of my pocket.

As the bus turned on to 17th Street, the driver looked at me in the rearview mirror and said, "Sir, are you going to pay the fare?" Everyone was looking at me as I stood there in the aisle, frozen with the fear of spiritual death upon me. I couldn't respond, so the driver pulled the bus to the side and asked me to get off.

I stumbled my way off the bus. As I got off, I looked back, and I could still see the lofts in the distance behind me. My fear grew. Not only was there the darkest, sinister laughter projecting from all around me in the sky, but I also began to feel the presence of otherworldly forces around me. Screaming, "Help me!" I began to run as fast as I could to escape, doing my best to keep my oversized raver jeans up on my hips as I ran down 17th Street.

My friends were still chasing after me, which made the situation even worse! One of my friends looked like he had six-feet-wide bull horns protruding from his head. They were all screaming my name. I continued trying desperately to escape. There I was half out of my body, eyes the size of tennis balls, running down the road, pants falling off me and foaming from the mouth due to dehydration.

As I ran, my screams went from "Help me!" to "Jesus, please help me!" at the top of my lungs. In this type of situation, all I could think about was escaping at all costs – even if it meant ending my own life to get away.

As I have grown and learned through the work that I assist Angels in now, field of consciousness-clearing, I understand the tendencies, agenda, and primary objectives of these entities. One of their primary plans is, unfortunately, to influence you to off yourself and commit suicide.

As I approached the 17th Street bridge overpass that crosses above Highway 400, my impulse was exactly that: escape at all costs, even if it meant throwing myself off the bridge. Luckily, the bridge had a gate with an inward-curving angular top. This made it impossible to climb up and jump off.

It was around midnight, and there were very few cars on the road. As I stood there looking deranged with fear, the police rolled up and pulled right in front of where I was standing on the sidewalk of the bridge. Their car's headlights were directly on me. My eyes were huge with fear. I had no shirt on, my oversized pants were falling off my hips, and I was still screaming "Jesus, help me" at the police car. There were two police officers in the vehicle, and they wanted nothing to do with the situation. From within their car, they looked at me for about ten seconds to assess the situation. They then put the car in reverse and drove away.

The police pulling up caused my friends who had been chasing me to go the opposite direction quickly. Once the police pulled off, I felt even more hopeless and terrified. I continued to run another hundred feet down 17th Street. All I could think was to escape even though I had no plan or direction as to where I was going. I only knew I wanted to be as far away as possible from the monstrous laughter I had heard.

The next thing I knew, my friend Dusty saw me on his way home from the club with his girlfriend. He happened to live close to where I was on 17th Street. He jumped out of the car and yelled my name.

Dusty, mentioned earlier, was one of my primary financial resources and someone I trusted wholeheartedly. I was receptive to him and didn't feel the need to flee from him. He grabbed me and told me to sit down. He then called an ambulance, which took me to Grady Hospital.

Thank God the police were not the ones to apprehend me that night because I was ducking probation and had a large amount of methamphetamines in my pocket. I couldn't imagine also going to jail that same night, on top of everything else.

At the hospital, strapped to the bed, I had another eerie experience. Two medical personnel came in to give me the shot of Thorazine. While doing so, I noticed one of them looked like Dracula.

They obviously knew why I was there and that I had been freaking out. One of the doctors walked into the room and had a book in his hands that had the word "soul" in the title. As he was talking to the other doctor about the book, he kept looking over at me as if he was talking to me, too. Still in fear of everything that had just occurred, I thought to myself that the doctors were also in on this conspiracy for my soul. My natural inclination was still an impulse to escape, but I had to submit to the fate of the situation because I was strapped down to the hospital bed. The doctors gave me the shot, and I faded into sleep.

I woke up the next morning with no shirt on and the drugs in my pocket from the night before still there.

I had no pager on me or phone numbers. Thankfully, Dusty had given the hospital his house number for me to call when I was released. He and his girlfriend picked me up and took me to their house to regroup and gather myself. Once I got there, I called Brooke to come pick me up. I was so relieved to still be alive!

⚘ No Price for My Soul

After the traumatic experiences I'd gone through, I decided to put down the psychedelics and methamphetamine use. I'd been focused on just making money and spending time with Brooke. I had been sober and away from all drugs for months.

It was late 1997 and Brooke and I were staying at a friend's apartment – one of my longest spans of time not living in hotels, in years.

One morning I got a call from George saying he needed to come over and talk to me about *business*. At that point, his once kingdom had toppled and he was living in a shabby motel with a few of his cronies, all of them having graduated to intravenous amphetamine use.

When he came over, I could tell he'd been awake for days. He sat down on the couch in the living room and was silent. His energy was serious and stoic. Sober, I sat down in the chair across from him and waited for him to start talking. I asked what was up and what did he want to talk about. But he said nothing. He sat there looking at me for about 30 seconds, then simply closed his eyes. Suddenly, I could see this holographic projection-like image appear in front of me. It was in full color and clear as day. What projected in front of me was a demon-looking entity, spinning a wheel-of-fortune-like wheel, like the one on the game show *Wheel of Fortune*. The wheel spun round and around as this monstrous beast-like looking thing stared towards me. This continued in silence for about a solid minute. The next thing I heard was George saying to me, "Everyone's got a price, Tony. What's your price? What's the price for your soul?"

"There's not a price," I said with a deadening seriousness. Instantly, the projection in front of me vanished, and he opened his eyes. He looked exhausted, depleted, and defeated. He laid down on the couch as if to take a nap.

I stood up, feeling the power of God's Spirit within me. Like I was wearing a knight's armor. I walked to the bathroom and threw water on my face. I walked out and said, "You're gonna have to go. You're not welcome here."

He asked if he could stay a little while longer, and I told him I needed to get on with my day, but I'd call him a taxi.

That was the final episode and one of the final times I would ever see this person again. What came of his life? I don't know exactly, but nothing noteworthy.

The ultimate betrayal is when someone tries to purposefully sway you for your soul, away from the Light of God. My hope is that George isn't still attempting to spiritually prey on the innocent and unsuspecting.

Of all the unfortunate things I witnessed in these years, from people dying of overdoses and drug addiction to people going to prison, the most tragic thing I witnessed was people losing their souls for the attempted gain of money and power. To me this was the most foolish of misfortunes. Every one of these people ended up crashing and burning and ending up at zero.

The forces of darkness are liars and thieves. They use weak humans like carriers, eventually leaving people in further despair of emptiness. Of the people I have seen that took that route, their lives ended up as shell-like shambles of what their potential in life could've been.

If the bottom line and your goal is wealth in this material world, you never have to compromise your soul to do it. Utilizing your God-given ingenuity, sincere effort, creativity, and consistency, the ability to create abundance and become successful is highly achievable. In doing so through integrity, you can earn self-respect and long-standing respect from others. Your soul's true resources and inheritance from God deem any need you have obtainable without compromising your Light.

One of the most important messages I hope to share with others who are desperate or in a place of weakness is this: always maintain your soul! Nothing of this temporal world would ever be worth the treasure, which is your soul essence. You are of God's Presence, creatively extended into, unto, and as you. It is the element of your divinity in this world. No matter how grim or desperate times get, hold true to your soul from a spiritual and an ethical standpoint.

I'll say it again — anything you may ever want or need materially on this earth can be obtained through your effort, belief, intelligence, diligence, prayer to The Creator, and patient persistence!

With devils dancing around me, while addicted to drugs, materially driven, and at my weakest, I stood strong. Regardless of my lawless life and poor values, I never bent spiritually. I never compromised my soul. I remembered God's Love in my heart and held true to that.

Although there are far less treacherous ways to grow spiritually, these blatant experiences rooted me in my commitment to the Light of God and to learning the soul's sacred path of awakening. Through these trials I developed a value for truth, love, and beauty. This is when the wings were earned which carried me to the eventual work I do today.

◈ Meeting a Master

In 1997, my close friend and partner in crime at the time, Matt, told me an astonishing story about a profound man he had met at a store called Mother Earth's Adornments in Little Five Points. He told me he was a teacher named the Cosmic Son. My friend had a noticeable wondrousness in his eyes while telling me about his meeting with this man.

I could also tell his tone of voice was different. Usually, my friend only had that type of enthusiasm if he was talking about an enormous potential drug deal on the horizon. I was intrigued, and something in my heart told me I should go to meet this man.

When I finally met Son (whose birth name was Josiah Osuagwu), I saw a gentle-looking man of African descent. He was in his seventies. He stood about 5 foot 8 inches tall, with grey hair like Einstein's. He was a small man with towering energy. The look of light, love, and wisdom in his eyes was enchanting. The best way to describe him was astonishing — like a real-life Yoda in an older Nigerian man's body. He spoke excellent English, with a loving and kind tone, in a slight African accent.

I walked up to him, and he looked up at me with what seemed like interdimensional eyes. In the sweetest tone, he said, "Hello, I am Son. I am pleased to meet you." He motioned me to have a seat.

He began to speak to me more about his work and explained that he taught physical and souls in Spirit about the laws of The Creator of All.

I mentioned to him that my friend had told me about him. He responded with, "I see, very good. I am glad that you came."

He pulled out a blue piece of paper and began to write something for me, which read in underlined words at the top, "The Cosmic IAM." Underneath that, in the body, he wrote:

"O' Creator of All, that is All, please place me in Your Absolute and Eternal Light, Presence, Wisdom, Knowledge, Truth, and Justice. I am always an inherent part of Your Presence and Purpose, O' Creator of All. Grant me to know who and why I am what I am. Teach me Cosmic Destiny and Citizenship. I accept the Blessings of all of Cosmic Presence and Existence. I accept the Peace, which is Your Pleasure within me. I claim The Creator that is All for my worship!"

At the time, I didn't know the magnitude, value, and importance of the words written there by him. That moment was my first step onto the path of conscious reunion with The Creator.

Son and I talked for a while longer that day, and then our time came to an end. I was mesmerized by this man's wisdom, grace, and love. There was an ancient feeling about him, and it was a true honor to sit with him that day.

Here and there, I would go back to visit Son in Little Five Points. The times when I would go to see him after being awake for days on substances, he would send me away, with a pure and loving, "Come back at another time."

During one of my final times ever seeing Son in that early version of myself, one of the final things he said to me was, "You will not find the completion of your destiny by socializing at the party." He looked at me so deeply when he said this. I was 18 years old at the time, and I would not see Son again until I was 23 years old. That being after many abrupt but necessary life changes had occurred.

Our reconnection came after I had made a complete 180-degree turn in my life. At the time, as a sober version of myself, living in a monk mode during the first stages of realization spiritually. I became his caretaker and took him into my home, where he taught me as his student and furthered his work with The Creator of All.

⊛ Strike Three

By the spring of 1998, at 21 years old, my tower crumbled and came crashing down. I faced my third and final run-in with the police – after one of my best friends, Abraham, snitched on me. This placed me in the three-strike offender category with twelve felonies on my record for drug possession, sales, trafficking, and firearm possession by a convicted felon. This arrest came with the greatest potential ramifications.

By this point in my street career, I'd graduated to a more serious status. I'd become more focused on saving money instead of blowing it as I got it. My plan was to continue and grow and eventually become the biggest LSD dealer on the East Coast. Leading up to my arrest, I had every ingredient in the recipe to systematically make that happen. I was at new heights and doing great financially before the police kicked in the door to my apartment.

One of my driving motivations was to get my mom a home somewhere away from the Los Angeles area, where she had spent thirty years feeding her hardcore drug addiction.

At the time of my arrest, I was living with Brooke and two friends, one being Kyle. This was one of the first permanent places I had settled into throughout all my years in Atlanta. It happened to be the third year of my relationship with Brooke. She had put up with the transient life of hotel-to-hotel living, with no permanent home for years, and she wanted stability and normality. So, we settled down and got a nice corporate apartment. After only seven months of living there, the most life-changing, serendipitous disaster found me.

The week before the police stormed our home, I started to get an eerie feeling that something bad was about to happen. I felt like people were watching me. Yet I couldn't tell if I was just being paranoid because of the level of business I had been doing, or if it was because I had been using methamphetamines again. In this case, it was all the above.

One March night, while working with the police as a confidential informant, Abraham decided to offer up my whereabouts and set me up in a controlled sales case. Abraham was naturally a loose cannon type. He was someone who had a beautiful heart, but at the same time was volatile and could become quite emotionally unstable. At the time of the occurrence, he was under the influence of a combination of methamphetamines and pharmaceuticals, which didn't help his cause.

Abraham was a close friend who I had to distance myself from after his arrest a year earlier. I did so because I felt there was something off about how quickly he'd gotten out of jail. Although I didn't know for sure, I just wanted to play it safe. I knew he was a little vindictive toward me because I didn't try to help bail him out of jail. That mixed with his general volatility made for a dangerous recipe.

There had been an extended amount of time since I had seen him. I decided to open the door for him to come back into my life. This invitation was coming at the height of my career selling drugs – a time when the stakes were the highest and while I was making more money than ever before. All seemed good until it wasn't. That's when he turned state's evidence against me. As mentioned earlier, I sensed something a little weird in the air, but I never saw *this* coming! To add insult to injury, the day he made the controlled sales case to set me up, he brought mushrooms with him and gave them to my roommate and me.

Before I discovered he was the one that told on me, he had already helped gather the money to get me out and was the one who signed my bond!

As disastrous as it all was, it could've been far worse. Just one week before, Yannis, one of my partners in crime, and someone who had a massive collection of firearms, had gotten into a huge fight with his wife. He was afraid of the police being called, so he asked if he could keep all his guns at my house and stay for a bit until everything cooled off. Kyle, my roommate, happened to be out of town, so I knew there was an open room. For the better part of a week, that room was a storehouse for what was at least thirty guns, ranging from handguns, automatic rifles alongside bulletproof vests and ammunition. If the police had entered my apartment just one week earlier, I wouldn't have seen the light of day for a long time.

When the police initially busted down the door, they were in full SWAT riot gear. There were about fifteen or more of them that entered my home. They found a cornucopia of substances and my 10-millimeter handgun – which made the situation far more severe. In Georgia at the time, possession of a handgun by a convicted felon came with a five-year mandatory minimum sentence.

There was LSD in the freezer, 10,000 pills throughout the house, amphetamines in my pocket, mushrooms my assailant had given me, and 180 Rohypnol in my pocket. As well, there was a shotgun in my roommate Kyle's room. There were also 5,000 Rohypnol in my closet in a Timberland jacket that the police didn't find. If they'd found those, I would've been extra-charred toast.

When the police entered, I froze! I knew the moment that I heard the door crash open that I was unbelievably screwed. It was a sinking feeling that is hard to explain in words.

Friends of mine who were at my place tried to escape out of the windows. Brooke was raising cain, and her hotheaded Italian side was on full blast towards the police. Everyone was apprehended and eventually taken to jail.

At one point, they pulled me to the side and said, "Look, we are going to find everything anyway, so just tell us where everything is."

"I'm just visiting. I don't live here — I'm from California," I told them, but they knew I was lying.

Luckily, my name was never put on the lease of the apartment because I was living on the run. My name not being on the lease of the apartment eventually helped four of my felony charges to be dropped. Luckily, the situation was judicially confusing. The night the police raided my place, I had friends and multiple customers from out of town in the apartment. My roommate Kyle being out of town also made it more complicated because he had a shotgun in his room, while as well there were drugs hidden all over the house, some of which were even in my other roommate, Gwen's room.

One of the felony charges that eventually got dropped was the possession of a firearm by a convicted felon. This being because it was not on me, and my name wasn't on the apartment lease. Brooke, being the best girlfriend, a man could ever have in his corner, was willing to take the charge of the handgun to lessen my sentence if she had to — though I would've never let it come to that.

The day before, we'd taken most of my money and put it in a safety deposit box in Brooke's name. They found the safety deposit box key in her purse, and while we were in county jail, they tracked down the bank and confiscated the money.

The arrest was my third, and like the previous two, I never told on anyone, and that wasn't going to change. The police didn't even try to ask me to rat on anyone. Every encounter with the police I was terrified, but I never turned state's evidence.

Although what Abraham did, to many, would be considered the ultimate act of betrayal, it all led to the most profound positive change. Positive change I couldn't have ever imagined. I forgave and appreciated him as a brother then and now. As I marvel at how the path under my feet has unfolded, compared to where I was, I realize what he did was truly an act of divine intervention.

❁ My Pact with God

Sitting in DeKalb County jail, I had the sober realization that I wouldn't be given a bond because of the probation I had skipped out on from two years earlier in the neighboring county. Luckily for me, because the two counties were not communicating efficiently, the police struggled to find the files for my Fulton County probation – which I had never checked into.

While sitting in the jail cell leading up to my bond hearing, I prayed from the depths of my soul. I said with complete conviction to God, "If you please help me get a bond and get out of here, I will change my life completely."

On the day of the bond hearing, while sitting in the holding cell at the county jail, before making it to the courtroom, one of the arresting officers tried to question me about who my probation officer was from my arrest in Fulton County years prior. I told him I didn't have one, which was completely true. This frustrated the officer immensely. As he sat there staring at me, I could tell his desire to drive the stake even deeper was growing by the moment.

At my bond hearing, the arresting officers did everything they could to ensure I wouldn't be given a bond. They called me a flight risk. They told the judge that multiple counties had been trying to apprehend me for years, and since no one from my circle would tell on me, they hadn't been able to find me. Then they said that I violated my earlier probation.

"Where is his warrant?" the judge asked. But the arresting officers couldn't produce an answer.

"You have had more than a week to find all of this information, and you could not," the judge said — and he granted my bond for $50,000, to the disgust of the arresting officers.

❀ The Aftermath

After receiving a bond, I was only in there for a short while longer. With the help of my friends, including Abraham, Yannis, Dusty, and Kyle, Brooke raised the money for my bond. As mentioned, my friend Abraham was the person who signed the paperwork for my bail bondsman! To add an extra layer of bizarre to that situation, somehow, the bail bondsman allowed him to sign me out without him having an I.D. on him, and he even used a fake name. It's all truly mind-boggling looking back on it.

When I got out, we first went to the DoubleTree Hotel in North Druid Hills. From there, Brooke and I got a room at the Biltmore in Midtown. This is where we stayed until I gathered my footing.

I tried to figure out my financial situation first. At first, I was counting on the money that Brooke and I had put in the safety deposit box, thinking that it was still there. I knew I would be able to use it to pay for both of our lawyers. However, we couldn't find Brooke's purse containing the safety deposit box key. When Brooke went to the bank to retrieve the money, she was informed that the police had seized the safety deposit box. I was doubly crushed! I had no money and had street debts at this point.

I then remembered that there were still 5,000 Rohypnol in my Timberland jacket hanging up in my closet that the police hadn't found. Our plan was to immediately go back to the apartment and recover them and get any other valuables that may have been left behind.

The twist is that by the time I bonded out of jail, two of my customers that were at my place the night of the raid, had gotten out quickly. Once released, they decided to go back to the apartment and retrieve their belongings that were left behind. While there, they also decided to ransack the place and steal everything of value that was mine or my roommates' — including the 5,000 Rohypnol pills inside the Timberland jacket.

When I learned what they had done, and that my primary source of funds to pay my lawyer was gone, it was an extreme insult to injury. I remember standing there for about five minutes, with my head dropped, shaking my head in disbelief.

The two above-mentioned customers who had stolen our belongings had also begun eating the Rohypnol pills they had stolen from me, which blurred their decision-making.

The next twist was that Abraham was in touch with these two. Apparently wanting to help serve justice again, he offered to help us get our belongings back. We devised a plan to convince my past customers that he wanted to buy the Rohypnol they had for sale.

The plan was to trick them into coming back to Atlanta and take as much of our belongings back as possible. As we put together the plan, we decided it would be the wisest decision for me to remain in the hotel room, considering I had just been bonded out of jail and was facing eight felonies.

The two culprits then drove back down to Atlanta to sell a portion of the 5,000 pills they had stolen from my apartment to Abraham. Yet, when the two of them arrived to make the sale, they were met by Abraham, Brooke, and Yannis. As these two, now thieves, entered Abraham's apartment, they were met with the reality of the situation. Although they were never seriously hurt, the night ended up being an awfully long one for them. Brooke obtained as much of our stuff back as possible, which was around only a third of what they had stolen.

About a day or so after, I received a call from one of the two guys apologizing for what they'd done.

With the resources we recouped from the thieves, I was able to muster up part of the money we needed for lawyers. But it was short by a lot. This meant that I was going to have to make illicit moves to drum up the money for our legal fees.

Making money wasn't the easiest thing to do, considering all my connections viewed me as "hot" and a liability to work with after my experience with the police. They knew it was a possibility I had eyes on me. In the world I was living in, getting busted was like you had leprosy. People wanted to keep as much distance away from me as possible.

At this point, we had no money, and I was looking at eight or more serious felonies. Brooke's job as a hairstylist was almost in jeopardy. We'd been evicted from our apartment. And all my connections to make money were keeping their distance from me. I was crushed with barely any fight still in me.

Luckily, Brooke was able to maintain her job at the hair salon. We stayed at a weekly hotel. While we were there, I drew upon every resource I had so I could come up with enough money for us to survive and pay for our lawyers.

⊕ Overdoses, Prison Sentences & Suicides

By the time my involvement on the frontlines of the drug trade was done, I was looking back at a wake of disaster. But it could've been much worse, for it oftentimes is, in that world. Through the years of my involvement, I witnessed and participated in many people's addictions, especially to crystal methamphetamines. At the time it was such a part of my social ethos, that I didn't acknowledge it was a bad thing. Unfortunately, many of the same people I was selling methamphetamines to continue to use it to this day. A little piece of my heart breaks in the knowing of that. Atoning for this and doing what I can to tip the scales is why I work so feverishly to help people in my life personally and professionally.

Thankfully, there were never any overdoses on the substance I sold. Nonetheless, I had family friends who passed from heroin overdoses.

Two of them specifically being Revere and Little Jay. Both beautiful brothers gone too early.

By the time the dust settled in 1999, most everyone I'd been closely associated with had ended up in state or federal prison. By the grace of God, although I went to probationary boot camp twice and spent a solid fifteen years on probation, I never went to prison.

I say a huge prayer for anyone who has ever ended up in prison for extended amounts of time. As well, I have tremendous respect for anyone who can come out of a situation like prison and create a new course for their life and a new version of themselves. Prison stains people's souls in a way that isn't easy to shake off.

Young men and women that are inner-city youths, hear and see hip-hop artists glorifying a life of crime and fast money, but they never take the time to research the statistics to learn what percentage of drug dealers end up going to prison. The numbers are staggering. The next thing you know, their youth and potential is gone, and they're being shipped away to live in a cage for a decade or more. I was lucky beyond understanding.

There were only three drug-related suicides during my tenure in the streets living a life of crime. One was a friend who died from throwing himself off a ferry boat into the San Francisco Bay while on a massive amount of pure LSD. A friend told me his final words were, "They're trying to get me, God, save me." His experience mirroring the previously-stated things I went through multiple times: the experience of astral entities trying to invade one's space while being way too open and vulnerable under the influence of large amounts of psychedelics.

At this stage in my life, I do everything I can to display my limitless appreciation to God and my guardian angels for helping me to get through the gauntlet that was that stage of my life, without going to prison, losing my soul, or leaving the earth.

CHAPTER 4

❀ SENTENCED TO AWAKENING ❀

❀ The U-Turn

Upon my release on bond, Brooke and I spent around four weeks at a weekly hotel room, preparing for what to do next. During our time there, we were eventually able to gather enough money to move into a small apartment in midtown Atlanta. I was grateful we had a place to live, but I was dumbstruck by all the conflict we were wading through.

Once we settled into the new place, as promised to God while sitting in the Dekalb County Jail cell, I began making fundamental changes. I stopped selling drugs and made a vow to stop using methamphetamines and pharmaceutical chemicals. I threw away the pager and Rolodex, both of which I had been glued to for the last five years.

Though I remained friends with some people from my past, I walked away from my illegal business involvement with everyone. It was immensely challenging to leave behind who I'd become in the streets. Especially considering how ingrained it was in my persona for financial purposes. There was a point when I genuinely believed I'd be selling drugs for the rest of my life. The only world I'd known for survival, I dismantled piece by piece.

I got a job at Panera Bread on Peachtree Street. It was humbling to my ego, to say the least. I went from feeling like I had the world in the palm of my hands, running a million-dollar-a-year, tax-free, underground enterprise to pushing a broom at the bakery and taking payments for customers' muffins.

The allure of fast money remained around me in ways. Kyle, being one of my best friends, moved in with us, while still actively being in the drug-trade. At one point he was getting bulk amounts of LSD sent to him in the mail to sell. I eventually had to ask him to move out because it was just too much on my nervous system.

The unconscious pull toward using methamphetamines was also greatly challenging to resist. I had to consistently reinforce my vows and commitment to change to myself and to The Creator.

Most of the people I used to roll with weren't supportive of my changes. Once partners in crime would make sideways comments toward me about my decisions to change. One comment I remember distinctly was, "Have fun being broke for the rest of your life." These kinds of comments and judgments added insult to injury and all too often.

Regardless of people's side talk and the fact that I was on unfamiliar shaky ground, I found the strength within me to tune out the negative comments. If I was going to move in the right direction and change my life, I had to stay focused and determined as to honor what I knew was the right path for me.

It was autumn of 1998; I was 21 years old, looking down the barrel of a potentially very lengthy prison sentence. I had no high school diploma, no college education, and was coming out of a five-year stage of personal madness and drug addiction. But beyond it all, I was just incredibly grateful to not be sitting in the county jail, with the chance to grow and come to terms with a new way of living.

I had a commitment to God and a head full of curiosity about spiritual growth and healing. My desire was sincere. Regardless of how unfamiliar being on a healthy path was, my heart was determined. I made a list of all the areas of interest and topics I wanted to study and learn about. The three main things on the list were rudimentary but sincere: meditation, cleansing my body, and the process of enlightenment. When it came to my spiritual growth, I had a healthy head-start from my past experiences mentioned earlier.

I researched natural ways to detoxify all the chemical drugs out of my system and purchased the *Handbook of Natural Healing*. I researched various liver detoxifying herbs and supplements and began to take them. I also began practicing vegetarianism. For the spiritual aspects of my growth and healing, I had a healthy head-start from my past experiences mentioned earlier. I also began practicing meditation and I read a book called *The Seat of the Soul*, and another called *The Celestine Prophecy*.

❀ A Course in Miracles

By this time, my friend Ian had moved from Atlanta down to South Florida. There, he went through his own personal spiritual awakening. This led him to begin studying the *Bhagavad Gita*. He also began to learn from a spiritual teacher named Mother Rytasha. He developed new friendships with spiritually-minded people. One of Ian's new friends was a gentleman named Manny. Manny was a student of a book called *A Course in Miracles*.

When Ian and I spoke, I let him know I had begun making changes and was trying to better myself. He shared with me various important insights he had gained while on the spiritual path. I was a bit taken aback by the conversation. This was someone that just 3 years previously was running through the city with me as misfit drug dealers. When we finished the conversation, he took it upon himself to send me a copy of *A Course in Miracles*. This would end up being one of the most beautiful life-altering gifts anyone has ever given me.

A Course in Miracles is an in-depth spiritual study manual about Christ consciousness and reunion with God, yet through a psychotherapeutic approach. It's written with Christian terminology. Me being raised in the Methodist Christian Church, the terminology and language of the book didn't bother me. The knowledge and insights it expressed were on a whole different level than anything I'd ever read. After just a day of reading it, I realized it was outlining the process of the path of enlightenment. A form of death and resurrection process, on the psychological level.

I proceeded in reading it, discovering it was a book on achieving the peace of God through learning what we *are* spiritually. And learning to discern between what we *are* and what we *aren't*. I found it profound immediately. It felt like I was swimming in the deep end. As I sat and read its words, I could feel a combination of deep peace and serenity within me.

It was a big book in size, so I had plenty on my plate for what seemed like a long-term study. And it became just that – a long term study. It would take years of consistent reading and study for this book's wealth of wisdom to sink in fully. As it did, it profoundly changed me. What affected change within the most was the knowledge of our innermost nature as sacred immortal spirit. This was foundational in the building of the rest of my life.

Throughout my twenties, I went on to studiously read the main text three-plus times. I also completed the 365-day workbook three times over. The workbook was a study manual, requiring reflection and contemplation of daily lessons. It is something that I still read and listen to out of appreciation for how much it has helped me and how beautiful it is.

A Course in Miracles prepared me for and facilitated tremendous self-healing and growth. Its wisdom led me back to an all-encompassing love, true peace, and remembrance of our Reality. From the very beginning, I credit it with helping me to rid myself of my remaining addiction to methamphetamines at the time.

From the Christian religion, my understanding was that spirituality, or religion in this case, was for becoming a good virtuous human; avoiding hell and going to heaven through accepting that a man named Jesus died for my sins – because I was born as a sinner. Whereas Christianity was more focused on one central figure being the representative of what is holy, *A Course* directed attention more towards witnessing unto what is holy within others. From *A Course* I was taught what we are truly were spiritual beings, eternal in nature, of God's Spirit, and that we *all* are the child of God. It began this process by first bringing attention to the error, of this world's psychological and perceptual programming, which casts a type of veil over our mind's awareness of what we are.

By far, the first most difficult idea for me to wrap my mind around (especially with the stage of life I was in) was the part where it spoke about how beautiful and beloved that we are in God's eyes — as Its children. Up to that point, I felt like a tired washed-up drug dealer. My sense of self was not framed in beauty at all. Even from childhood, I felt broken and disposable. I felt like not even my mom or dad wanted me. I had a very guilty, darkened view of myself, feeling inherently bad and unworthy of love. My early exposure to Christianity played on that and furthered it by leading me to believe I was an ugly duckling born sinner and that there was only one child of God. As a teen, I had grown to see myself as an addict and a criminal-minded drug dealer. Coming out of that phase I then added an extra layer of guilt onto my feelings about myself, for being someone that created addictions for financial profit. In that I felt like someone deserving to go to prison for doing the wrong thing for a long time. The last thing I identified as was a beautiful and beloved child of The Creator.

The teachings of *A Course in Miracles* held an uncompromising central message: this temporal experience isn't what we are – that what we *are truly* is what we *are eternally*. That being what we have always been, and what we forever will be.

A Course taught how to develop eyes that see spiritually, or vision, which comes from one's mind being awake to the innermost Light of God that we are.

This temporal world of human "reality" is a type of vivid, collectively agreed-upon illusion. A collective sleep. A sleep where we're dreaming the dream of separation from divinity in the flesh. This dream being something we have all agreed upon before physicality was ever created. This collective sleep and perception that we are flesh — which is what most consider "reality"— isn't our true reality whatsoever.

I also learned that the thoughts we think while under this sleep state, are not our real thoughts whatsoever. That our real thoughts come from the mind awake to its truth: the mind we share united with God, direct.

A Course also used the term "ego" in a way that seemed strange to me at first. I always thought of the word "ego" as an overt sense of superiority or being braggadocious. Instead, *A Course* referred to ego as the collection of ideas and beliefs we hold about ourselves, oriented around the central reference point that we are a temporary, physical body. This flesh-oriented sense of self-acting as a script is the antithesis of our reality as Spirit.

My studying started to peel back the layers and I began seeing differently. This way of seeing was challenging for me and something I naturally resisted at first. Who I was as a person named Tony that I'd always identified as, oriented around the central premise that I was a physical body, was what was familiar – and that's all I'd ever known. The narrative of my past seemed like my everything. At first, I didn't know what I would be without my past perception of myself. The idea of divorcing the structural and foundational perceptions of myself, and others, was a somewhat fearful notion.

Another idea that was new to me from *A Course* was how it spoke about the word "sin." From what I'd been taught in traditional Christianity, we are "born sinners" — by default. That we are human-being sinners, and that sins were actions that don't meet the guidelines of behavior expressed through the Ten Commandments and the Bible. In contrast, *A Course* taught that what is truly *sin* was an error of misperception; a misperception causing us to deny our divine nature and oneness with our Creator. That sin was seeing or perceiving ourselves incorrectly – as beings of temporal-flesh, bound to death.

A Course explained that once our minds enter spiritual sleep and forgetfulness, all our subsequent actions and decisions are simply chain-reaction errors. That actions that would popularly be considered "sinful" are instead just errors spawned from the misperception of not knowing what we are.

People are capable of the most heinous acts when they're asleep to their divinity. In spiritual sleep, most people live from a place of animalistic survival impulses and fear. People operate with greater self-regulated governance, guided from the Light in their hearts, when they live in witness of and remembrance that we are Spirt: immortal-sacred-divine and one with each other and our Maker.

Another difference I noticed in *A Course* was the use of the word "forgiveness." Forgiveness typically refers to recognizing a person's wrongdoing, then pardoning them. *A Course* instead expressed forgiveness as seeing beyond a person's errored misperception of themselves as temporal and separate from God. Instead of being a pardoning judge and jury of violation, *A Course* suggested forgiveness being not joining others in their view of themselves which their misdeeds spawn from. *A Course* went further with this by teaching that attacking, holding responsible, or defending against actions that come from a person's sleep state is to validate their illusions of mind. This causes us to join them in the dream realm: to fall asleep within our own self.

From my studies, I grew to realize, very clearly, that God sees us for what we are before the physical. The Creator sees us according to Its original design of us in eternity and Spirit. To truly honor The Creator, it's of the utmost importance to see our brothers and sisters accordingly.

I found that compassion and getting over someone's wrongdoings is much easier when we remember that there is an existential spiritual identity crisis at the root cause of their trespasses. This expression of forgiveness is akin to the verse in the Bible when Jesus says, "Forgive them, Father, for they know not what they do." *A Course* added to this idea, teaching its readers to forgive others, for *they know not who or what they truly are.*

I learned that we are all part of an extended family, connected in Spirit, with our Maker. Learning to see people through this lens of knowing established a deep feeling of togetherness and love within me for all others. This is seeing others without an agenda. It took me a while for this way of seeing to integrate. It was very foreign to me, especially from my past work line as a drug dealer, where I most always saw people as potential resources for self-driven, financial security, survival, or gain.

Through studying *A Course*, I began to cultivate the ability to listen and live in guidance with the "Inner Voice" of The Creator within. There was a stark difference between life unfolding through inner guidance versus making decisions from hard-headed self-determination. The idea of making decisions based on inward listening to The Creator's Voice was incredibly challenging for me, being someone who traditionally only considered my own plans and desires, exclusively. As well, being an overthinker, I always wanted to be in control. This step took me a while and it required much surrender and trust in the beginning. Then it finally dawned on me, the endlessness of all that The Creator orchestrates simultaneously in nature and existence. I realized that if The Creator of everything that exists, seen and unseen, wanted to guide my part of It, that It knew better than I did. Even then, it would still take me a while to integrate that knowing into my outer material world decision making.

The uniqueness of these teachings didn't end there. *A Course* also spoke about intimate romantic relationships in a way that was head-tilting to me at first. It explained that a typical human relationship, or "special relationship," between two people, who are asleep spiritually, is a container for reinforcing each of their self-deceptive illusions and misperceptions of themselves. *A Course* explained that conditional, "special" love is the antithesis of what Love *truly* is. It explained that the Love of The Creator is all-encompassing. That God's Love is an inherent characteristic of a heart and mind awake to our oneness and kinship. *A Course* went on to explain how relationships undertaken by two people awake and in the true perception of each other are a vehicle for both of their souls' liberation and graduation spiritually.

❀ As Promised — My Pact with The Creator

As months unfolded, I sat and studied. I continued to grow internally. I changed. Layer by layer, I began releasing who I once thought I was from my mind. That came with moments of serious uncertainty and fear of the unknown. It was a death of sorts happening within my beliefs and concepts that once constructed my self-identity.

I found myself being completely disengaged and fully uninterested in having conversations about the past. My emotional investment to my past, emptied. I wasn't into reminiscing with friends of the past or preserving perceptions about my past identity. A further and further distance came between people of my past and me.

I received dismissive and condescending comments from people who used to know me in the past who weren't supportive of my change. I would hear the lines, "Who is this person?" and "We want the old Tony back." People I considered friends weren't the most receptive to me initiating conversations with them about the things I was learning. They would often blankly stare at me or change the subject. People wanted to pander to a version of me that I was laying to rest. I learned a great deal about the process of walking on your own path in life — that sometimes that path is a solo mission.

As I had promised to The Creator while sitting in the holding cell of DeKalb County jail: step by step, I changed my life from the inside out. As I embarked on my spiritual studies, I noticed that my proclivity for spiritual matters was naturally higher than everything else I had ever attempted to learn. For the first time in my life, I began to feel a deep peace within me.

I was steadfast in learning and continuously contemplating. I structured my daily life in a way that supported the time needed for my studies. I disengaged from hanging out with friends recreationally and retreated into a monk-like mode. I filled my mind with studies of *A Course* and natural healing, and I also practiced meditative stillness and contemplation.

Aside from my spiritual growth, I really wanted to get the chemical drugs completely out of my body from the past. I began reading about herbs for detoxification. I then applied the things I was learning for the internal cleansing of my body. Besides using herbs and fasting for cleansing, I also decided to become vegetarian, then vegan.

During this time, my heart began to open with love and compassion. I naturally began developing empathy and kindness for others.

Across the road from our one-bedroom apartment, there were railroad tracks and a slight mountainous area. Upon the top of the mountainside lived two homeless men. One Thanksgiving, instead of going with Brooke to her parent's house and having a traditional Thanksgiving dinner, I felt the desire to buy a turkey and sides for the two homeless guys. I took it to them and hung out with them while they ate.

As my heart was opening and I was finding peace, I also became more aware of the total nightmare that was my previous five years. As I reflected on those years, I felt great remorse for the monster I had become in the name of money. I hadn't just sold methamphetamines, but I made it look like it was the coolest thing ever. I had influenced and hurt people by creating addictions for profit, and I found myself deeply wanting to right my wrongs. I really regretted my actions.

My guilt was something that I eventually had to come to terms with. Realizing all of this, I asked God to please show me how to help more people than I had previously hurt.

In all of this, the guilt from my past ways began to morph into a disdain toward money. I didn't want to think about it. I resisted money and turned away from it. This dissociation towards money grew and would end up leading to various imbalances, lack of stability, and challenges in the future.

Another thing I noticed as I embarked further into my new path was that unresolved child and teen conflicts of abandonment, rebellion, and anger issues — all which had been suppressed by drugs, were beginning to come to the surface for healing.

Here I was at 21 years of age, with So much to process at once. My inner world was dismantling, awakening, and healing, while my outer world was leaving behind a past life of crime and fast money. As well, my body was detoxing from drug addictions and substances I had abused for years. The cherry on top was the looming reality that I was potentially about to be going to prison for twenty-plus years!

⊛ Family, Five Years Removed

The year leading up to my sentencing brought clearing and healing from my past. Part of this healing was around my relationship with Barbara and my biological family. I had not seen or spoken to any family members in over five years up to that point.

While I was awaiting my court sentencing, my grandmother flew out from California to visit me. It was good to see her after so many years. Although she could tell something was troubling me, I never told her I was potentially about to go to prison for a long time. I didn't want her to be concerned about me.

I was also able to visit my Aunt Barbara in North Carolina with Brooke during this time. I brought with me a copy of *A Course in Miracles* to give to her. Unlike my grandmother, I explained to Barbara that I was awaiting a court sentencing, and I might be going to prison for a long time.

My Aunt Barbara was doing well, and I was happy to see her. Toward the end of the visit, she expressed emotions and tears about our past. This was a first for me to see from Barbara — I'd never seen her cry before. She showed me love and remorse for the past. I told her that everything unfolded as it was supposed to, and if I hadn't gone through everything I did, I would've never found myself on the path back to God. I told her everything was going to be all right and that I loved her. She went on to marry a great man for her named Joe. They've built a great life together.

I remember that during the visit, one of the days, Brooke and I decided to go to the beach. It was a weekday in fall, so there was no one on the beach. She and I sat there on a sand dune staring out into the ocean as the waves rolled in—both of us silent. I felt like the sound of the waves, and the wind were carrying me into a trance. I had no clue what was about to happen in my near future, but I remember feeling deeply at peace with whatever was going to happen. In that moment, I was serene, in my soul, and I felt like everything was going to be okay. It was a moment in my heart which I can still remember like it was yesterday.

Brooke and me – 1998

⊕ Escaping Shadow Forces – Part 3

In the year leading up to my sentencing, although I had made tremendous progress internally, my worldly life had become quite uneventful and a little boring – especially compared to my past!

Around the end of 1998, there was a movie about psychedelics called *Fear and Loathing in Las Vegas* that was just coming out. At this point, I had been away from all forms of substances. Around the time of the movie's release, The Grateful Dead was also performing in Atlanta. I was still friends with people that were touring with the Grateful Dead. There was always a constant that came with them: psychedelics. One of my friends wanted to visit me before I potentially went to prison for a long time. While visiting, he gave me a small bottle of liquid LSD.

Considering my past with psychedelics up to that point, you'd think I'd defer. Hindsight being 20/20, taking LSD at this point was not the most intelligent decision. Not just because of the terrifying astral experiences in the past. But also, I was out on bond, actively in the process of getting my life together.

Knowing that I might be going to prison for a long time, I wanted to let loose one last time and have some fun. I figured since I was in a good headspace, and the LSD was clean and from reputable friends, I'd be fine taking it. I decided that I would take it with my friend Todd the night of going to see *Fear and Loathing in Las Vegas*.

I dosed two gumdrops with the liquid LSD. I then gave one to Todd and took one myself before arriving at the movie theater. When we arrived at Phipps Plaza in Buckhead, we all stood in line for a while to get tickets. The wait was longer than normal because so many people wanted to see the movie. When we finally got to the ticket window, we were informed that the movie had just sold out. By this time, the acid had just begun to kick in, majorly. From a dosage perspective, I wasn't sure quite how much I'd taken, nor how much I'd given to my friend.

As we drove home from the movie theater, there was a sequence of things which triggered an off-vibe. I began growing uncomfortable. Brooke was sitting in the back of the truck. I looked over at Todd, who at the time was beginning to peak. He looked super serious. The situation started feeling jaggedly off.

I began getting that familiar feeling of something eerie in my space. It was like I could feel strange forces were hovering around in my field. It was like the otherworldly experiences in similar times before. *Oh man, not again,* was my thought.

We made it back to the apartment, and the sense something was just inherently wrong within the atmosphere continued to build. All I could think to do was leave the apartment. I was entering an adrenaline-fueled state of flight. I left through the back door, and while trying to get away I lost my footing and tumbled down fourteen metal stairs onto the sidewalk. Brooke began chasing after me. I took off running toward Piedmont Road, which is a major street in Atlanta. She caught up and tried to stop me, pleading, "Tony, Please stop and pray with me."

I began seeing visions in my mind that looked like exhausted men, in this black and red hellish realm, swinging pickaxes at what seemed like granite rocks over and over. It felt like they had been stuck there captive for eternity, making no progress.

Trying to escape, I fought Brooke off me and continued to run toward Piedmont Road near the MARTA train station. As I approached Piedmont Road, there was a major train/bus station there. Brooke continued chasing after me screaming my name. Noticing what was happening, a MARTA train station police officer tried to apprehend me. I was fading in and out of these horrific visions in my mind. The police officer tackled me and tried to hold me down. I punched him in the face, which peeled him off me.

Like the time on the 17th Street bridge, my impulse was to escape at any cost. I ran into oncoming traffic on Piedmont Road and jumped in front of a car. My shoulder blade hit the upper-right portion of the windshield on the driver's side, which threw me into the air, spinning around like helicopter blades! The impact knocked me partially unconscious! The terrified driver stopped, as well as the rest of the traffic. As I laid there, it felt like time had stopped as well.

By this time, the MARTA police officer, Brooke, and a nearby motorist apprehended me and held me down until an ambulance arrived.

Once I was strapped down in the ambulance, my instinct was to flee from whatever was causing the visions in my head. I had so much adrenaline running through me that I was able to break the straps and try to escape from the ambulance. The paramedics then double-strapped me down while proceeding to take me to the emergency room. Once at the hospital, they pumped me full of Thorazine, and I fell into physical sleep.

The next morning, I woke up and left the hospital with Brooke. I was sore and relieved to be alive. After all these types of experiences, I felt vulnerable and humbled to be alive. I began to cherish the simple things in life even more.

This experience was the final of its type. I realized that it had happened too many times. The substances were creating gaps in my auric field of consciousness, allowing disincarnate entities to mess with me by inducing horrific audible or visual phenomenon, leading to potentially life-ending attempted escapes.

❀ Facing Fate with a Touch of Grace

While the months crept forward, my court date drew closer. The sorting out of everything in my case was a very slow-moving process. It felt like an eternity. The time between my arrest and my final court appearance was lengthy, longer than a year and a half. Over that time, the district attorney and my lawyers went back and forth to settle on what my final charges would be.

Things gradually started looking better for me. My lawyer got the district attorney to drop all the charges, other than the controlled sales case and the felony possession of substances I had on my person the night the police raided our home. Of the substances in my pocket, they decided to drop the felony charges from "intent to distribute" to "felony possession for use." The gun charge was dismissed because my name wasn't on the lease of the apartment, and it wasn't on my person. However, it all still looked ugly, considering this was my third strike for drug sales and distribution charges.

While awaiting my court date, I remained sincere in my efforts to continue to grow. It was both a magical and terrifying time in my life – I was waking up spiritually and awaiting a long prison sentence all at once. Regardless of what was to come of my court case, I knew I was on the correct path and that I was honoring what gave me the ultimate solace.

One day, when Brooke got home from work at the hair salon, she mentioned that a woman named Ariel had approached her at work. The woman was a psychic, but at the time, Brooke had no clue who she was. Brooke mentioned that the woman approached her and asked her how she was doing.

Brooke, always with a smile and cheerful disposition, responded, "Oh, I'm good."

Then, Ariel looked deep into her eyes and said, "No, how are you *really* doing?"

The woman proceeded, "I am a seer, and I know what recently happened to you and your boyfriend. You're going to be fine, but your boyfriend may be in serious trouble. Because he's been in trouble in the past and it will factor into the judge's decision."

When Brooke told me this, there wasn't an increase or decrease in my personal level of concern. I had already conceded to going to prison for a long time. But I was relieved to know that Brooke would be fine.

⊛ My Sentencing

Around September of 1999, I got a phone call from my lawyer telling me that there was a warrant out for my arrest for failure to appear in court. I was totally confused by this, considering my lawyer hadn't notified me that a court date was set for me. He informed me that I would need to turn myself into DeKalb County Jail and await my new sentencing date.

After checking him for not informing me of my court date, he told me that he'd done this on purpose so that by serving time in the county jail before my final sentencing it would hopefully decrease my punishment. I thought it all to be a strange approach, but it made a bit of sense at the time. I had no choice but to turn myself in. I explained everything to Brooke and decided I would turn myself in on the following Monday night.

On Monday night, I had my final home-cooked meal for a while. I then grabbed *A Course in Miracles* and a piece of paper containing my family's addresses and contact information and headed out the door. I hopped on the bus toward the "terror dome," the DeKalb County Jail.

When I checked into jail, they let me keep *A Course*. I was then processed, step by slow-moving step, into the general population of the jail. My court date wouldn't be for another three months. As I waited, my lawyer pulled another fast one on me that I never saw coming. Nonetheless, it would be nothing short of Brooke pulling off a last-minute miracle, which helped me through the situation.

As I spent the next few months in DeKalb County Jail, I remained in observance of my vegan diet. I traded all my meat dishes with other inmates' vegetables and fruit. Unsurprisingly it was limiting being vegan and eating healthy in county jail.

While awaiting my sentencing, I kept to myself and continued my studies of *A Course.* I would read around ten hours a day. The internal progress I made at the time was deeply furthering. My understanding, progress, and commitment all grew. A deep peace, like a glow of serenity, grew within me. In a way, being in the highly isolated environment of DeKalb County Jail, able to study and reflect, was of tremendous benefit to my growth.

As time passed, I decided to write a sincere letter to my judge, Gail Flake. I intended to explain what had led me to that point in my life and all the trouble I found myself in. I spent two days writing it and sent it to my lawyer to send to her before my sentencing date.

As my court date approached, Brooke worked tirelessly to keep up on visitations and made sure everything was the best possible scenario at my sentencing. I had Brooke contact my lawyer's office because I hadn't heard any updates from him.

Her lawyer, Michael Mann, who worked in the same law firm, informed her that my lawyer had decided to leave town for two weeks on vacation, which meant that I wouldn't have representation on the day of my sentencing. She also informed me that my lawyer had never sent my letter to the judge.

Speaking with Brooke over the jail payphone, we were both perplexed. My lawyer was attempting to get my court case rescheduled again to a later date to increase my time spent in county jail and potentially reduce my final sentence. I wasn't open to sitting through another continuation of 3 to 6 months — I wanted to get it all over with.

Brooke drove to the law firm, ready to break down the door. She first fired my lawyer, then she pleaded for her lawyer, Michael Mann, to represent me in my case, and he obliged. The courts made Brooke sign a conflict-of-interest consent form, and her lawyer was able to represent me. He got my case pushed back another week so that he could better prepare.

In that week, a miracle happened, which dramatically reshaped the fate of my near future. The district attorney, who had been overseeing my case for the previous year and a half, met his resignation date and decided to go into defense attorney work. The person who replaced him to become the DeKalb County District Attorney happened to be a woman who was close friends with my new lawyer. The way things unfolded couldn't have happened any better for me!

When I arrived in the courtroom, Brooke was there with her mother. Her mother had been so lovingly supportive of me through all of this. I looked around and saw my new lawyer, the new district attorney, Judge Gail Flake, and all the rest of the inmates in orange awaiting their sentencing that day.

The district attorney and my lawyer pulled me to the side and told me that the judge had it out for me since I had been in trouble so many times in the past (exactly as Ariel had said). The district attorney asked me if I wanted to spend a year and a half in a divergence program at the county jail or if I wanted to go to prison — not an easy decision! I didn't want to spend another year and a half at that county jail in a drug rehab program. Not only because I was over being there, but I also honestly didn't have a drug problem anymore. I also didn't want to go to prison – at all!

Then, out of nowhere, it just came to me and out of left field I asked if I could be sent to a boot camp, with probation and community service added to it. The district attorney and my lawyer looked at me sideways. They were puzzled and surprised that I would choose something as rigorous as boot camp. Somehow, they didn't know I'd already been through the program in North Carolina. I knew what it entailed, and I knew I could do it with my eyes closed a second time. The two of them spoke about it and concluded they would give it a shot.

When it was my time to face the judge, I was called up to stand in front of her. My lawyer read the short, amended version of my letter of explanation to the judge, but she wasn't overly impressed. The district attorney then said her part, stating what she felt was the state's recommendation for me. Their recommendation was 8 years' probation, three years' intensive probation with five more years supervised probation, five hundred hours of community service, a fine, and three months of probationary boot camp.

After the sentence was read, the judge cocked her head down at an angle and eagle-eyed me through her glasses, which were slid slightly down the bridge of her nose.

"Mr. Torres," she said, "I was strongly considering trying you as a career criminal and three-strike offender. Since you turned 16 years old, you have gotten in trouble for distribution of drugs three times, once every year and a half. I am going to accept the district attorney's sentencing guideline, but If I ever see you in my courtroom again, it will not be pretty for you. You will not see the light of day for a very, very long time." She then read my sentencing of the state's recommendations for my punishment and proceeded to give me boot camp, extensive probation, and community service.

I was so relieved that I didn't have to go to prison. Most of my closest friends and past partners in crime were already in the prison system by this point. Brian had moved back to Atlanta, began using heroin, and, in a drug-induced haze, ended up wrecking his SUV into a woman driving and killing her. At the time of the accident, his truck was filled with automatic weapons and various substances.

Yannis and a few other friends were indicted for involvement in an international MDMA/ecstasy-trafficking ring and went to federal prison.

After turning state's evidence on me, Abraham had gone on a tear of madness, kidnapping, and armed robbing local drug dealers in the Atlanta area. He eventually got sent to state prison. While he was there, I wrote to him a few times and sent him a study companion book to *A Course in Miracles*, called *A Journey Beyond Words*. He ended up getting out of jail a few years later, and shortly afterward, he passed away.

⚙ Boot Camp: Round 2

I ended up having to wait another two months in DeKalb County Jail before it was time for me to be shipped to boot camp. Overall, I had been in county jail for five or so months. I continued to study *A Course* as well as other books on Eastern Spirituality. I was tenacious in my reading and contemplation of all matters. There were no distractions. It was a highly concentrated time for my internal progress.

When the day came for me to be transported to Treutlen Boot Camp, I couldn't be any more ready. After being in the concrete county jail with little to no sun nor outside time for the previous five months, as crazy as it sounds, I was eager to have a bunch of drill sergeants yelling orders at me and screaming in my face.

My main concern was if I was going to be able to keep *A Course* with me and continue my in-depth studies. At this point, I had so much momentum, and I hoped that going to this new facility wasn't going to sabotage my focused efforts. At that stage, I was about halfway through the 365-day lesson plan.

On the six-hour transport to the boot camp in Soperton, Georgia, the DeKalb County bus first made a stop by the state prison to drop off the inmates who had been sentenced to prison. I couldn't help but feel relieved this wasn't my last stop. "Relieved" doesn't even explain the feelings within me. I felt as if I had been salvaged, knowing I wouldn't be spending the next ten years there as I had originally expected. For the entire time I awaited my sentencing in 1998–1999, I had submitted to the fate that I would be spending my twenties and part of my thirties in that state prison.

As we finally pulled up to Treutlen Boot Camp, there were two others who were coming along with me. We got off the bus, and as is the norm with probationary boot camps, I was met by marine drill sergeants screaming in my face to "break me in." One of them looked at me and started degrading me for how long my hair was. He got right up in my face, two inches away from me, and said, "Boy, you look like you could smoke a joint the size of your arm. Look at that hair — you look like a girl! We're going to have fun shaving all of that hair off." At this point, I knew to keep my mouth shut, take it all like a grown-up, don't talk back, and follow commands.

As we approached the intake desk, the other drill sergeants kept making references about not being able to bring in any personal items with you — my one fear! To me, it was upsetting thinking about not being able to have *A Course* with me that entire time.

As I made it up to the intake officer, he told me to put my belongings on the desk. He immediately picked up *A Course*. He opened it to a random page, looked down at it, and read a few lines. He then looked up silently and stared at me for about five seconds ... then, he closed the book and put it in with the rest of my belongings that I was allowed to bring in with me. My soul took a deep exhale. I was so deeply thankful!

The next three months entailed living with a shaved head, waking up at 4:30 a.m., doing extreme amounts of physical training, jail labor, and studying *A Course*. We constantly stood in straight lines, like soldiers, and marched everywhere we went.

The work details, like my first experience at boot camp in North Carolina, weren't enjoyable to say the least! We would be in the middle of nowhere picking up trash on the side of the road, clearing old forests, and working at the sewers and landfills. While working, I'd go on autopilot, keeping my head focused on my studies from *A Course* and the New Testament of the Bible.

Maintaining my way of eating at boot camp was next to impossible. I couldn't trade food with other inmates the way I was able to in DeKalb County Jail. There was no way to be vegan. It would've required way too much trading of food items to pull it off. Trading food requires too much communication and talking with other inmates would lead to infractions. Infractions added extra days onto your time. I knew what to do and what not to do since I had made it through the program six years earlier with no infractions and zero time added. This time was no different, and my goal was to achieve an on-time release date of exactly ninety days again. I kept my mouth shut, didn't talk back, did everything asked of me, and was able to complete the program in precisely ninety days.

Although my body was in boot camp, and my behavior abided by the mechanical flow of their regimented days, I remained one-point minded and centered in my spiritual studies. The central theme of most of my studies during that time was around tuning your way of seeing for witnessing the sacred Light within other's eyes. Through this I began feeling a deep resonance of togetherness with others, a sameness of essence, and in this I found a deep peace and serenity within my heart.

One day, while in meditative contemplation, there was a word that kept coming to me. The word was FOCUS. But with it was an inner dictation of multiple acronyms associated with it. The acronym was: From One Connected United Self, or From One Creator United in Spirit. This proved extremely helpful. I could simply remind myself FOCUS. This acronym of FOCUS has always served to help bring me back to center and vision when needed.

As I was completing the 90-day boot camp, I was a different person. By way of the last 8 months of my spiritual training, I'd changed in my mind. I felt an illumination within my heart. This period of solitude and lack of social distractions was the most advancing growth-filled months of my life. My focus on my studies was unbreakable. With tremendous gratitude for it, I found the strength to remain focused and disciplined while in the highly challenging environment of incarceration.

The importance of discipline when advancing on the spiritual path is paramount. During this time of being in jail, I blocked out all distractions, and treated it like being in a monastery. With how things are in modern-day times with handheld devices, technology, and social media, I wonder how the future generations of souls scheduled for awakening will find the discipline and distraction-free time required to honor the great inner work.

By the time of my release from boot camp, Internally I was a different man. I had no clue what direction to take once I got back out in the world, but I was at peace in my heart.

CHAPTER 5

 INTEGRATION

⊛ Head in the Heavens, Feet in the Western World

Upon my release from boot camp, my years of intensive probation were just beginning. Alongside the probation, I had a sizable amount of community service I had to complete. Regardless, I was glad to be back in the free world — but I was quickly reminded of the reality that it certainly wasn't free!

I found it difficult to find a job when I got out. I was twenty-two years old with a criminal record consisting of eight felonies. I had no driver's license or car. Neither did I have a college education or any legitimate vocational training in anything. I hadn't discovered any inherent talents outside of my proclivity for understanding spirituality and metaphysics, but that wasn't going to be translating into my bills being paid. I was distant towards money in general and the challenge of financial survival constantly pulled and nagged at my resistant mind.

Aside from reacclimating to the responsibilities of the world, as well, I had changed over the last year. The changes were in a way that Brooke didn't know how to wrap her mind around. And admittedly, I was still in the process of fully wrapping my own mind around it. At the time I couldn't yet fully express or teach what I was learning.

Through all we had gone through and made it through, I had reverence and respect for her, yet we were growing apart. Our relationship was about to be met with layers of insurmountable and unavoidable divide.

Brooke had been shouldering all the bills the entire time I was gone. It was straining for her, waiting around a year for my return. In the beginning, all my efforts to get a job led to naught. I applied at multitudes of restaurants. Every job I applied to rejected me. The worldly pressures were continuously building, and I started to get increasingly concerned.

Although my soul had found true peace, the world and all its demands were unescapable. In the Western world, bills and financial responsibilities didn't just go away when you were on a spiritual path. I wasn't living in the Himalayas, and I wasn't going to go to live in a monastery or an ashram. I was smack dab in the middle of the Atlanta metropolis. I had to figure things out like a grounded, financially responsible man the best way I could.

At this stage of my spiritual evolution, I hadn't yet developed trust and surrender to guidance for my financial material world affairs. My focus had been exclusively on the inner world of Self-realization. Although *A Course* had introduced the idea that God is willing and capable to guide us through any worldly situation or choice on earth, it hadn't fully sunk in yet. In hindsight, I would've saved myself a decade of time and energy by bringing my worldly concerns to The Creator in prayer and meditative listening for guidance.

I wasn't yet able to relinquish the control of major decisions when it came to the material world of finances – especially when I was in survival mode.

By this time, a past friend named Billy had established a vast enterprise in the Atlanta area. He continually had hundreds of pounds of boutique marijuana. Upon seeing my struggles, he offered to give me as much as I needed to sell to get back on my feet financially. The option was by far the most immediate — as well as the most idiotic — I could have chosen, especially considering I was fresh out of boot camp, on intensive probation, and had just been cosmically-pardoned by God, as well as the judicial system.

The stress mounted from not knowing how to pay my bills and survive financially – I needed to pull my weight. As my survival pressures mounted, Billy's offer began to feel more like a blessing sent from God, than it did a mistake. I began to rationalize me selling marijuana as being ok and vanilla compared to the danger involved in the substances I used to sell. The dangling carrot of opportunity was presented to me, and I was in dire need.

I decided to take Billy up on his offer. I kept my involvement on the low end, but it was foolish, nonetheless. For every hundred-pound load Billy got, I would piggyback off it and sell four or five pounds to people I knew from the past. At the time, it seemed like nothing, but given the situation I was in, it was blisteringly dangerous.

⊛ Breaking Point

When Brooke discovered I was storing pounds of marijuana in a duffle bag in the house, she snapped. She was livid and confused. She hit her breaking point, and understandingly so. Around the winter of 2001, things had all but completely fallen apart between us. Although we were living under the same roof, she had moved on.

One morning as she was getting ready for work, the house phone rang. When I answered it, a guy on the other side of the phone asked to speak to her. The person calling was a guy I'd vaguely known of from years before. He had harbored a romantic attraction to her for years, and they'd run into each other recently at a club. I honestly knew it was for the best, but at the time I also felt betrayed. Having another man calling the house phone to speak to the woman I was still sharing a bed with didn't sit well with me.

I thought about the matter throughout the day while Brooke was at work. I decided I would move out immediately. Later that night, I informed her of my decision, though I didn't have a concrete plan on where to move. My only viable immediate option was to move in with Billy, who had just gotten a house with his girlfriend in West Atlanta. It was a large house with an upstairs area that wasn't being used.

⊛ Social Discernment

Although Billy was at the height of his drug-dealing career at the time, I trusted I would be fine. My optimism was blind and overconfident, for there was still a real element of danger involved. Billy always had hundreds of pounds of marijuana and a dangerously large amount of psychedelics – not to mention, hundreds of thousands of dollars.

I had no business being around people still living a life of crime in any way. Regardless of the danger of my environment, I felt universally protected. I knew I was on the right path spiritually and that I'd honestly made core changes in my focus, intentions, and determinations in life.

While being on the path I was on, I remember making the conscious decision to see and relate to people from my knowing of what we all are, more than relating to and judging others because of what they do. The indwelling immortal Light of Christ is all of us united, beyond anyone's role in the world. I didn't want to turn away from people not on the same path of consciousness as me. However, I would have to eventually learn the importance of the wisdom of discernment practiced socially. There were certain people that by being around them in any social capacity, it was simply an act of self-disrespect to my freedom– I especially had no business intermingling in their illicit dealings – financial survival challenges or not (a lesson that I'd be dangerously met by twice in the coming future).

⊛ To Know

I eventually got a job at a Jamaican restaurant called Bridgetown Grill. While working at the restaurant, I remained focused on my lessons from *A Course* and continued applying its lessons. The job at the restaurant was an immediate legal solution for earning basic living expenses and keeping my probation officer appeased.

Alongside my job waiting tables, I continued to moving pounds of herb here and there. Financially, I began to find stability finally.

At home, I was either studying or teaching myself to make vegan food in the kitchen. I had become very content with spending my time alone and reading. I was very inwardly reflective and contemplative. I had little desire to deal with the world.

I utilized all my time to reflect and apply my devotional studies of *A Course*. The time I spent traveling on the train was especially useful for this. On the train I could read, contemplate, and not have to think about all the things you must think about while driving.

During two of those train rides specifically, while working with the 365-day workbook of *A Course*, I had consciousness-altering experiences. The first came from an exercise where you ask The Creator, "What would you have me do? What is your will for me?" After doing so, I sat there on the train patiently there for a while, with a clear mind and an open heart to hear. Then, within my heart and mind, both simultaneously, a clear, direct voice spoke and said: "Share with others where you have been, where you are, and where you are going."

At the time, I knew where I'd been, and I knew where I was in the process of awakening to Self, but I had no clue where I was headed, and I surely didn't yet know how to share any of it with the world. As life proceeded forward, the instructions from this day would remain in the back of my mind as a guiding force. That eventually became one of the main motivating forces for the writing of this book.

The other of the two mentioned experiences came as well while doing a lesson in *A Course* having to do with seeing the formlessness comprising all form; seeing beyond the veil and helping to open the eyes that see *truly*. *A Course* guides the student through experiences referred to as "Light episodes." These Light episodes function as gradual glimpses into seeing the Light of the beingness of God. These lessons begin by guiding the student through the process of withdrawing your perception from your personal past identification and association you've constructed to define the world around you. This is coupled with consciously seeing things through the knowledge that all form is truly the direct Presence of God's Mind and Light manifest.

As I sat there on the MARTA train, riding along, following the instructions of my lesson, the next thing I knew, form, as it is normally seen and perceived, wasn't there anymore. It's as if it had vanished or been replaced, and all I could see was Light surrounding me. After about forty-five seconds of this experience, I began to panic a little bit. Within a few moments, the appearance of form around me returned. After this, I understood that what we see around us is only a small percentage of the whole reality, which form is a part of. The experience, although brief, was astonishing in a beautiful sense – and a little bit mind-bending. It was humbling to observe and experience. From there forward I have moved forward with the firsthand knowing that while it seems like we live in a physical world, we're actually living within the Mind-Body of our Creator.

❁ Cleanse the Past

Aside from spiritual growth, I was also extremely focused on cleansing all the chemical toxins and drugs out of my body from the past drug use. To accomplish this, I found a naturopathic doctor named Yakov Koyfman. Dr. Koyfman specialized in full-body multi-organ internal cleansing.

Dr. Koyfman had an office far from where Brooke and I lived in Sandy Springs. Having no car, I had to take two buses and two trains to get to his office for appointments. Usually, the trip was two hours there and another two hours back. I was unconcerned with the gauntlet of travel required to get there – I was determined to have my past completely cleansed out of my system.

Throughout my visits to Dr. Koyfman, I learned about juice fasting for cleansing purposes. My process with him began with colonics. At first, the whole idea of it seemed crazy to me. Going into the process like a much-needed medical procedure made it easier. After the very first colonic, I felt like I was in the Garden of Eden. Colors were brighter and more vivid; I felt lighter and less stressed. After a series of colonics, I did a liver/gallbladder cleanse, stomach cleanse, intestinal cleanse, and blood cleanse.

I was putting significant effort into increasing my understanding of physical health and conscious eating. My body began detoxifying all the chemicals and drugs from my system that caused horrible skin problems. As a teen, I also developed severe allergies to certain foods and digestive and eliminatory issues.

For years I had felt chronically tired. As I went deeper into physical body improvement, I discovered this was something called adrenal fatigue. This was caused by my teenage use of methamphetamines and nicotine, on top of my stressful, anxiety-ridden lifestyle.

I knew if I continued to cleanse my body, learn more about nutrition, and apply the correct health principles, I would eventually get my body back into perfect working order. My soul and mind were at a great place of health, but my physical health was far from optimal.

⊛ Raw-Living Foods

One day, as I was reading one of the local conscious living newsletters, I came across multiple articles about a way of eating called "vegan raw-living foods." This was new information to me at the time. Up to this point, I had been juicing and eating a bland cooked vegetarian, macrobiotic diet primarily: rice, steamed vegetables, and soy. I began noticing more little snippets of information about the vegan raw food movement. The more I saw these articles, the more they grabbed my attention. I decided to investigate it more deeply.

In the early 2000s, the vegan, raw food movement exploded throughout the country. Its growth was especially prominent in Atlanta. I found out about a raw food delivery service run by a kind-hearted, mad-scientist-looking man named Brother Bill. Brother Bill would go around to the local raw food restaurants and establishments and deliver the prepared food to you, similar to DoorDash. I decided to call and order a plate of "vegan raw-living food" from Brother Bill.

When I got the food and began to eat, I was impressed – it was amazing! The flavors were pronounced and rich! Beyond the flavors of the food, I discovered that the *real* experience of this food existed in the energy and vitality it gave to my body. It was a type of physical feeling that I'd never felt from food before! It felt as if it ignited a glow within me. I knew at that moment I was onto something. I decided instantaneously that I wanted to learn as much as possible about the vegan raw food movement and begin cooking and eating this way all the time.

Right around this time, my great-grandmother passed away and left me an inheritance. I used the inheritance to purchase all the raw food kitchen tools I needed, such as blenders, food processors, and a food dehydrator. I quit my job at the Jamaican restaurant. I decided to dedicate my time teaching myself how to make this cuisine.

I dedicated significant time to reading raw food preparation books and going to all the local vegan raw food cafes to try different recipes. I spent long hours at health food stores and farmer's markets, getting the products and supplies to put to work in the kitchen.

One of the raw food restaurants was located right down the road from our house in the West End of Atlanta. They were Ital Nyabinghi Rastafarians, who owned a restaurant called "Iternal Life." My friends and I would spend hundreds of dollars at a time on gallons of freshly-made Irish Sea Moss drinks and raw food.

The other group I grew to learn from was the Hebrew Israelite community in the West End of Atlanta. They had a restaurant called "A Taste of Life." All the food there was excellent. Everyone I met in these communities was always genuinely kind and gracious to me. It was a blessing to be around multitudes of people living a health-conscious lifestyle.

I learned more about their food preparation with every visit to one of these restaurants. I would do my best to mimic the recipes in my kitchen at home. I continued to spend my days and inheritance money, learning the ways of vegan raw food preparation. Before I knew it, I had developed a knack for making great dishes. I was very motivated by the fact that this way of eating was beneficial to my personal health and the health of others.

⊛ Ariel

Around this time, I also decided that I wanted to begin a conscious-clothing T-shirt company called "Divine Mind Clothing." I planned to design and sell T-shirts with conscious slogans and logos on them. I thought that putting conscious slogans onto T-shirts was a great way to plant spiritual seeds of wisdom in people's minds.

I had a small amount of money left from my inheritance and money that I'd saved from selling cannabis. However, I didn't have enough to move forward with the company, so I borrowed money from my surrounding friends to purchase a small screen-printing machine.

For the artwork I wanted to use on the shirts, I arranged a meeting with Ariel. Ariel was the psychic woman who had approached Brooke a few years earlier at the hair salon, who gave her the message about our court case. She was not only a gifted, highly intuitive psychic, but she was also a prolific artist. I was hoping to commission her to do some of the designs and artwork for my shirts.

Ariel and I met at Houston's on Peachtree Street. She brought her portfolio of prints and artwork. We talked for about thirty minutes about various things, including my breakup with Brooke and my desire to start the conscious T-shirt line. She showed me her art portfolio and seemed open to working together.

As we concluded our meeting, Ariel paused and looked at me with lasers in her eyes and said, "Tony, for you, nothing truly good will ever come from things not meant for you." This was something that stuck with me throughout my life as a major lesson. Earning money from things like cannabis sales may work for others, but it wasn't going to work for me in my life. She spoke her words with emphasis. We parted ways, and that was the last time I ever saw or heard from Ariel.

⊛ The Wakeup Call

Transitioning from my past life as a big-time drug dealer into my life focused on the spiritual path, I had a severed relationship to money. At the time, I thought turning away from money was the righteous thing to do. Although money was a necessity, I really didn't *want* to care about it. This translated as a dissociated carelessness towards it. To add to it all, I also had an irrational optimism that everything would be okay. The combination of all this kept leading me to moments of desperation – usually coming at the first of the month. Those moments of desperation would lead me to consider resources that weren't wise – which could've led to massive self-sabotage. Once a person sabotages themselves out of survival desperation, the result is that a person's situation becomes even more desperate and challenged.

Once I began living with Billy, there were hundreds of thousands of dollars around me and infinite resources. Although I was cautious, my surroundings caused me to become increasingly relaxed towards the potentially-dangerous consequences of my modest involvement of cannabis sales. Although this door had initially been opened out of desperation and necessity, as time unfolded, I got a job and didn't need to use those resources – but I became complacent with it and continued to go to the wrong well. And by doing so, I would go on to get a massive cosmic wakeup call, consequently.

Upon one of the loads of cannabis that came into town, Brooke's brother, Robbie, asked me for twenty pounds. Robbie was a close friend of mine and someone I fully trusted. He told me one of his friends had twenty pounds lined up to sell to a customer they knew, and they just needed to take it to them. I gave them the benefit of the doubt. My friend Billy consigned the twenty pounds to me, and I turned around and gave the twenty pounds to Robbie.

Robbie and his friend went to deliver the twenty pounds. While doing so, they got robbed of all of them. We all suddenly had a genuine problem on our hands.

When the two of them came back with their tails between their legs to report what had happened, I was in utter disbelief. It was at this point when I was made aware that the source of the marijuana was connected to a serious no-nonsense group of people. I was told that I was responsible for repaying the $70,000 quickly, or there would be real implications for everyone involved.

My stomach sank to my toes. It was a smack to my soul, which left me dumbfounded and extremely upset with myself. A sobering moment.

Luckily for me, Billy and his friends decided they would help me get out of the situation. The plan was that with the next load that came to town, I would have to sit in a local hotel, receive the whole pack of one-hundred pounds, and they would divert all their clientele to me. All the profits made from this would go toward quickly paying back the $70,000.

It was a perplexing task of extreme pressure – and one I couldn't get out of. I *had* to sit there in a hotel with duffle bags full of high-grade marijuana and sell it all, to people I barely knew — or didn't know at all. It was a karmic cold dish of reality. There was no way around it, so I did what I had to do.

At that time of my life, I simply was no longer built for that type of situation. It was one of the heaviest, most stressful moments of my life.

By the grace of God, everything went smoothly, without hiccup. I sold all one-hundred pounds in three days, and most of the $70,000 debt was paid back within a weekend. After that, I walked away from all of it.

Again! – all of this is a sound lesson for those making self-sabotaging decisions caused by limiting beliefs, fear, or survival needs. Moral of the story: Short-term decisions made from desperation can often lead to long-term consequences that are even worse than your initial problems were.

For anyone coming from a world of fast money and living on impulse, my other advice to you is to learn how to use forethought and be okay with earning things the long way. Sure, doing things the long way is challenging, sometimes it seems like an insurmountable mountain.

It may involve going back to school or training yourself in a new skill, getting a second job, and/or barely getting by. Regardless, earning things, is the most enriching and rewarding to one's soul.

Every time I have ever prayed and asked to be shown the way forward, ten times out of ten, it has always been clearly revealed — and what came with it was the support needed to move forward in that direction effectively. But you've got to trust and not remain reliant on old ways of doing things.

⊛ The Cosmic Son

Around the spring of 2002, I began wondering about my first teacher, Josiah Osuagwu, The Cosmic Son. This was the man spoken about in a previous chapter who had introduced me to The Creator of All and Cosmic consciousness. I set off to find out what had happened to him since the last time I had seen him back in my crazy days of 1997. Through her radio show, I figured out how to find Adamah, Son's student and past caretaker.

When I got ahold of her, she mentioned that when she ended their lease at the shop, Mother Earth's Adornments, Son couldn't move with her. He became displaced and lived at a state-run transitional facility for the elderly. When I inquired more deeply, she told me that she'd gone to visit him and he seemed physically unhealthy, probably because of the quality of the food at the facility.

My instincts were to get him out and bring him to live with me at the house. The place I was living was a larger-sized house with plenty of room, so I was sure it would not be a problem. A small room adjacent to mine upstairs would be perfect for Son. I shared the house with Billy, his girlfriend, and another roommate named Todd. Billy and his girlfriend were rarely around because of traveling, and due to his day job, Todd was only at the house at night.

Brooke and I were still in close communication, so I asked her to give Adamah and myself a ride to the transitional facility to get Son out of there. Brooke also knew Son from the past, and she agreed to help without hesitation.

I had made up my mind about bringing Son to live at the house and didn't even think to ask my roommates if it was okay with them. I just went and did it. We got to the facility where Son was located, I signed him out to my custody, and we drove him back to the house.

Although he had a roof over his head at the facility and lived in a safe, controlled environment, I thought it was horrible for Son to have to live in a place like that, with nowhere to go and with no family or friends around him. Looking back, he didn't care much or have anything bad to say about the place. As long as Son was able to do his spiritual work on the inner planes, uninterrupted, he didn't care much about his physical surroundings.

Originally, although naïve, my feelings on the matter were simple: Son was a person I respected and cared about, who was in a situation I viewed as not optimal, so I wanted to help. In hindsight, it wasn't the wisest thing to take him from where he was, considering I didn't know what my own future would hold and the general lack of stability in my life. I had projected my own values as judgments of his situation, which led me to pull him from a place of safe certainty into my world of potential future uncertainty. I learned a major lesson in that.

Although everything went well while Son lived with me, taking care of another human was a big responsibility. And it all fits with a particularly important lesson Son eventually taught me: "never begin something that you're not prepared to see through."

When we got Son back to the house, he was incredibly grateful and settled in quickly. He minded himself and continued to do his work.

Once Billy found out about me bringing a 72-year-old spiritual master to the house to live with us, at first, his reaction was, "What exactly is going on? You did what?" However, once he met Son, with his twinkling eyes, his white Einstein hair, and his gentle, loving demeanor, he warmed up to him immediately.

Billy, along with his friends, were often under the influence of psychedelic drugs, usually LSD. They would sit and listen to Son, like tribesmen sitting around a campfire listening to the wise man of the village.

Son would go on to receive and express prophetic visions about Billy's future and prison — unfortunate realities that would come to fruition within a year.

Son had graduated with degrees from Indiana State University and the University of Pittsburgh. He was highly educated from the worldly perspective, but he was far wiser spiritually than he was educated.

Upon graduating, he decided to renounce the world and its ways. His primary motivation being because he wanted to discover The Creator of All and learn of Its Wisdom. He wanted to discover why the organizations of the world didn't contain the direct, miraculous hand of The Creator— knowing that if they did, the world wouldn't be in its current state of darkness.

Son began to meditate upon the discovery of The Creator of All devotedly. Through his meditation practice in 1977–1978, an internal process unfolded within him. It was a meditation system used for merging with, and being guided by, the Light of existence. Son explained that his conscious awareness merged with the Light of The Creator and was then transported through the layers of manifest existence. This guidance through the layers of the manifest continued unto arrival at the aspect of The Creator, which he explained as the "unmanifest," or non-formed presence of The Creator.

During this experience, he received revelation through direct communion with The Creator. He went on to teach about The Creator and Cosmic Consciousness to students for more than ten years.

Son explained that after this experience of meeting The Creator, he began to be guided through existence to places in existence where he was called to teach. I gathered that this was like an extreme version of non-physical astral travel guided by The Creator for specific purpose. Son would teach the Laws and Wisdom of The Creator throughout noncorporeal, astral, and spiritual dimensions of existence to beings, leagues, and legions of beings who had fallen from the Light of God's Plan and Design. He mentioned that some of these areas of existence were under a type of battle/war involving creation's will versus Cosmic-Will and The Creator's plan.

He taught me that this earth was intended to be a center and symposium for souls to learn the process of what he termed "Cosmic Wisdom." The way he used and defined the word "wisdom" was "the knowledge of The Creator's perspective and point of view and desire for any part or process of Itself in creation." He expressed this as being achieved through bringing an inquiry into prayerful meditation, then receptively, and sometimes patiently, listening within to The Creator for response.

Meditation can and should be used for receiving the knowledge of The Creator's point of view, perspective, and Will on the specifics of one's life. Son taught that this expression of Wisdom was how existence was intended to be lived – not an ability and right exclusive to a select group.

He referred to the word Wisdom in contrast to its opposite: self-will, or as he called it, "self-determination." In this case "self-determination" being the process of determining everything on one's life without conscious guidance from The Creator's perspective and input on matters of one's life. I learned that knowing and doing according to The Creator's Will and Plan for things places us on the path of Destiny rather than fate. He explained that we are citizens of the Cosmic Whole of existence and not just a small division of the earth. He expressed that by constructing one's life through Wisdom of The Creator's Will, it harmonizes and attunes you to the unified Destiny of The Whole Cosmic.

While learning from Son, I was also still studying *A Course in Miracles*. The two teachings complimented each other perfectly. I was deeply at peace within my heart and spirit and had made significant progress in my studies. Son lived comfortably upstairs in the room beside mine. He spent every day and night in meditative travel, doing his work for The Creator.

I tailored the design of my life to support my studies and training. Discipline was natural for me because I valued what I was doing. I had zero distractions from romantic relationships. After breaking up with Brooke, I was celibate until I was 27 years old. Throughout this entire stage of my life, I had no interest in the romantic area. I simply just turned it off.

While studying under Son, I was taught things that were more so on a Cosmic level of things. Though mostly on this vast scope of existence, it was also grounded and applicable to living one's daily life in communication with The Creator.

What I learned from Son about existence as a whole and the nature of The Creator was profound. He gave me a copy of his writings titled, *The Cosmic IAM*, which he composed after his previously-mentioned unification experience in 1977–1978. He expressed that this wisdom was directly revealed to him by The Creator of All Itself. I have included his works below. The following excerpt details the nature of The Creator in Its manifest and unmanifest forms:

⊛ Part I

1:1 - O'Ever-present Cosmic Supreme Being, I am an immortal part of you, and you are The Creator over all, in all, for all, with all, from all, unto all, about all, and throughout all.

1:2 - You are the Infinite and Eternal Cosmic Supreme Being and Creator over all individual intelligences, individual great spirits, individual great goddesses and gods, individual divinities and principalities, and individual great avatars, saviors, prophets, saints, and generals.

1:3 - You are the Supreme and Absolute Allness of Cosmic Reality.

1:4 - You are the inherent and succinct beginningless and endlessness of unmanifest Omnipresence. You are full capacity and the entire essence of Cosmic True Being.

1:5 - Your wheel, O'Ever-present Cosmic Supreme Being, is the primal motion by which, and towards which, all things are progressively driven in the fulfillment of your never-ending Cosmic designs and purpose.

1:6 - O'Boundless Ocean of Will, it is by your direct Presence and capacity as Cosmic Supreme Intelligence, and within your very living and boundless Body-Cosmic, that all creation is conceived, involved, evolved, revolved, convolved, and resolved.

1:7 - The diversity of your creation is an infinitude and you have made all things abundant in both reality and potentiality.

1:8 - O'Most Loving and Beloved, raise me to become truly and fully conscious as a Cosmic citizen: a living intelligent, loving, and potent part of you.

1:9 - Your capacity is everywhere present throughout the seen and the unseen. By your capacity, O' Boundless One, all creation is upheld and unified within the perfect integrity of your Cosmic purposes and plans.

1:10 - You have created innumerable heavenly mother and father goddesses and gods, great spirits, intelligences, chieftains, divinities, elementals, angels, lords, and ladies, to organize, administer, and magnify your glory throughout your countless super-spiritual dimensions, corporeal worlds, grand-universes, systems, galaxies, constellations, and kingdoms.

1:11 - Your infinite Spirit is the soul of all and everything. By your Infinite Light, the Spirit is formed, illuminated, and caused to be intelligent soul.

1:12 – You are the direct writer and revelator upon the souls of all things, of universal and Cosmic significances, values, and destinies.

1:13 - You are, O'Most Wonderful One, The Creator of our own beautiful local heavens and earth, and the suns and firmament local thereto.

1:14 - The powerful, wise, and high-raised heavenly father-mother gods and goddesses are your sons and daughters of superior accomplishments and superb organic progression in adept love, duty, and honor.

1:15 - You have placed them before humans and ex-humans as examples of heights attainable by all who abide devoutly in the Light and Love of thy Will and service.

1:16 - Is not to raise humans and ex-humans to goddesses and gods, O'Ever-present Cosmic Supreme Being, the labor of thy Light, the blessing of the earth, and the destiny of both the higher and lower heavens?!

1:17 - O'Ever-present, to truly discover you is to become conscious of my own true Being, identity, power, and purpose. To call unto you is to call upon my own soul, upon all your creatures throughout infinite creation, and upon All the Cosmic for support and love. To love you truly is to serve everyone and All things.

1:18 - O'Ever-present Cosmic Supreme Being, you are the very Infinity and Eternity and Totality of manifested and unmanifested reality.

1:19 - You are the Boundless Ocean of Cosmic Will, and capacity within which resides and flows Cosmic Intelligence, Cosmic Power, Cosmic Law, Cosmic Life, Cosmic Spirit, Cosmic Matter, Cosmic Energy, Cosmic Labor, Cosmic Light, and Cosmic Love.

1:20 - You are the Supreme and Absolute Being of all Beings, seen and unseen, by humans or by angels, and by gods and goddesses.

1:21 - You are absolutely the Presence of all presence, the Substance of all essence, the Life of all life, the Intelligence of all intelligences, the Purpose of all purposes, the Love of all love, the Joy of all bliss, and the Ultimate Parent-Reality of all fathers and mothers.

1:22 - O'Thou Infinite and Loving Verity, you are all and everything! Surely, you are the absolute and indivisible unity of Cosmic reality, diversified within Its own inalienable integrity of eternal wholeness and oneness.

1:23 - In both Cosmic and local omnipresence, you are Perfect, Ultimate, and Absolutely Supreme. In duration, you are both all times and timeless eternity.

1:24 - Certainly, you are beyond all qualifications and degrees or any names that any beings might choose to call you. Indeed, no one other than you, yourself, spans your Cosmic infinitude to comprehend it all.

1:25 - You are the Ultimate Reality of non-ultimate beings, and you are the only Ultimate Being there is and that there will ever be.

1:26 - You are Creator within and over all considerations, forms, ambiences, units, substances, categories, and significances.

1:27 - O'Ever-present Cosmic Supreme Being, it is marvelous and wonderful that we are all inseparable and imperishable parts of you.

1:28 - To call upon your support is to call upon everyone and upon all things throughout All of existence.

❀ Part 2

2:1 - O'Ever-present Cosmic All-Person, your direct Cosmic parenthood is the very womb in which all beings and things are conceived, and from which nothing can be delivered.

2:2 - You are all at once, the Cosmic crucible, and smith of all forms, and ambiences of spiritual, corporeal, and unmanifested creation.

2:3 - Your direct Presence is both all things and the capacity that upholds all things. Within your administration of adversary judgments over all the innumerable visible and invisible, corporeal, and spiritual-super-universes, galaxies, and worlds you are Creator – and they are all living and moving parts of your substantive Presence. You are their immediate and Ultimate Parent-Reality forever.

2:4 - Yes, you are The Creator in the smallest of the smallest, in the greatest and the loftiest, in the right and the wrong, and You are forever blessing and upholding all in thy essence, will, and love.

2:5 - Certainly, all Beings and things are points in and of the direct Presence of your Omnipresent Body-Cosmic.

2:6 - You are Creator over all local and heavenly fathers and mothers of all living things, including all gods and goddesses, saints and saviors, gurus and avatars, the knowing-ones, plants, animals, minerals, and diverse orders and sublimities of spirit.

2:7 - Throughout all heavens and all worlds, no matter what their harmony or chaos may be, you are the Ultimate Parent of All of creation. Yes, you are Creator and Father-Mother of the presiding goddesses and gods of our own local earth and heavens and their local systems and firmaments.

2:8 - O'All Encompassing and Wondrous Womb, am I not perpetually, and ever sustained, nourished, renewed, and reborn in you – and you in me?!

2:9 - O'Cosmic IAM, am I not of, in, and ever with, that, that you are?!

2:10 - O'Ever-present Cosmic Great Spirit, you are Creator of and over all individual great spirits and souls.

2:11 - Spirit is only the soul of things in Your Cosmic Reality; but you are everything. Your immeasurable reality is in totality unnamable by any finite class or genders, and for that reason has been called infinite and eternal by the wisdom of your Presence in folks and gods.

2:12 - Yes, you are both Creator and embodiment of all and every unit state, form, function, ideal, and category of creation or consciousness, and you are all consciousness comprehending.

2:13 - Sure, it is your direct Presence which capacitates and configurates Itself as diverse states of consciousness in order to meet the requirements of thy purposes, harmony, and love.

2:14 - Your Presence is the true alchemy, essence, vitality, and substance of all beings, and of all things.

2:15 - O'Being of beings, no one can be without being in every way a part of your Being.

2:16 – O'All at once, your substantive Presence is the very matter, mind, essence, capacity, intellect, power, process, performance, love, ethic, and integrity of every entity.

2:17 - Your Presence is the eternal abidance that is in eternal progression.

2:18 - The distortion of thy Presence and Light is the sorrow of creatures. The so-called *evil* is only due to creation distorting the harmony of the Light of your direct Presence – and there is no evil otherwise.

2:19 - Your Presence is my own very presence and to worship you is to witness to your Presence in my own soul, everyone, and all things.

2:20 - To embrace you, must not my own Being extend with love through all things, all places, and all conditions?!

❀ Part 3

3:1 - O'Ever-present Supreme IAM, you are the Macro IAM of all micro IAM.

3:2 - You are beyond all highs and heights, and Creator over all glory and exaltedness.

3:3 - Humanity is not only your glory, but you have granted it the destiny of multiplying and magnifying your glory.

3:4 - The intelligences of grand-universes and superlative inter-dimensional and intergalactic systems; the goddesses and the gods of Nirvana, and of the lower heavens and earth, are all your manifest glory for the magnification of thy created glory!

3:5 - Yes, you are Creator in and over all triune-beings, lords, lord-gods, goddesses, avatars, masters, gurus, saviors, prophets, saints, adepts, generals, and their multitudes.

3:6 - Yes, all resident humans and ex-humans of earth involuntarily represent thy Presence, or otherwise, denying the same.

3:7 - By the distortion of the Light of thy Presence, chaos and inharmony as the "devil" are acted out by elements of free will in creation. Your organic reality is without inherent devil or evil.

3:8 - O'Ever-present IAM, to perform in your Illumination is to live perfectly and at one with all things!

3:9 - You are, O'Ever-present Boundlessness, the Eternal Wholeness and unity that is beyond phenomenal diversity and aggregation.

3:10 - You are the Infinitude that is Absolute and All-Inclusive, beyond and above all arbitrariness, all thoughts, all postulates, all ideals, all dimensions, all coordinates, measurements, and all genders, known and unknown in the microcosm.

3:11 - It is your dynamic and abiding Presence which grants all consciousness, all abilities, all grounds, all motion, all purposes, and all significances to all entities and identities in creation. It is your Presence which allots true responsibilities, consciousness, and enlightened self-expression that they might choose to pursue.

3:12 - You are the Supreme and Cosmic administrator and counselor within all, throughout all, and over all.

3:13 - You are looking at the world through the eyes of the smallest insect and through the vortices of the grandest universes.

3:14 - You are the giver of all and the receiver of all, and the most Loving and Beloved. Indeed no one can serve you without you or offend you without you – neither can anyone love you without you!

3:15 - All things, without any exceptions, happen or fail to happen within your Infinite, Eternal, Living, and All-Intelligent Body-Cosmic.

3:16 - O'All Love and Supreme Wisdom, how great and joyful I feel knowing I am an immortal child of yours and knowing that the children of The Creator are surely destined to become real goddesses and gods.

3:17 - What best ways are there to speak of the highest truth than to speak of thee; to apply to the highest love than to apply to thee; to seek power and potency than to seek in thee.

3:18 - O'Ever-present Veracity of Cosmic Reality, your Presence is the highest and lowest common denominator of all beings' ideas, conditions, and significances. Your Presence is the substance of the tangible, subtle, and unmanifested.

3:19 - O'Cosmic Supreme Being; O'Light and Life of all microcosm, is not all consciousness the mode of flow of the essence and capacity of thy direct Presence, proceeding and progressing towards thy purposes?!

3:20 - O'Cosmic IAM, is it not thy Will to motion power, love, wisdom, thrill, form, and beauty, which is called consciousness?!

3:21 - O'Most Instant and Beneficent counselor of all, you are the Supreme Knowledge and Absolute knower.

3:22 - No beings, no matter what their order may be, can add one iota of intelligence and substance to their stature, form, or worth, without taking from thee and giving the same unto thee.

3:23 - You are the True-Self of all selves. There is no god or goddess, or any great spirit and intelligence, or any human or ex-human, or any character of elements, or any material or subtle worlds, anywhere, which stand upon their own grounds, breathe their own elements, float within their own atmosphere and essence apart from that which derives from the reality of thy direct Presence.

3:24 - You are the common ground of all reality and all possibilities. You are capacitor, the upholder, and the upheld.

3:25 - All so-called co-creators are mere parts of your own Cosmic Entity under your impetus and command – neither can they produce any elements that were not already in existence as part of thee.

3:26 - You are the circle without periphery and the cycle without ending.

3:27 - O'Thou Beginningless and Endlessness, you are the All-Central, and I thrill in the realization that I am an immortal and inalienable part of you, and that you are the Eternal and Boundless Whole of me.

✹ Part 4

4:1 - O'Everywhere Present Supreme Cosmic Reality, I am a part of your Living, and you are the Whole of my living; I am a part of your Intelligence, and you are the Whole of my intelligence; I am a part of your Consciousness, and you are the Whole of my consciousness; I am a part of your Labor, and you are the Whole of my labor; I am a part of your Capacity, and you are Whole of my capacity; I am a part of your Spirit, and you are the Whole of my spirit; I am part of your Substances, and you are the Whole of my substances; I am a part of your Proceedings, and you are the Whole of my proceedings: I rely upon the Whole of you, and you rely upon the part of you that I am. Are we not together Absolutely one as the Infinite and Eternal Cosmic IAM?!

4:2 - O' Light of my life, is not all progress the march of your creation from one applicable and accomplished destiny unto others?!

4:3 - The waters, the earth, the air, and the fire elements are corporeal qualities of the substance of your direct Presence. You have formed them in the construction of our local stars, sun, moons, worlds, and their residents - you have breathed your dynamic Spirit into their forms to elicit living souls in them.

4:4 - Yes, your Presence is both spirit and the manifest physical and the unmanifested; it is light and shade, night and day, and sound and silence.

4:5 - Color, thoughts, faith, conscience, research, reason, desire, feeling rejoiceful, order, attention, beauty, power, freedom, and spontaneous awareness are all acts of thy Will within the capacity of thy conscious Light.

4:6 - Within your all-knowing and all-thinking and all-doing Self, you have created and made each and every individual human being heir to both our male and female Cosmic faculties and all the glories attendant thereunto.

4:7 - From one life and world unto endless life and worlds of eternal progression – through the worlds of being human unto heavens of being ex-humans – defying the portals of death and emerging past ethereal planets and planes, visible and invisible – you are the rule, the ruler, and ruled, all by your own direct Presence.

4:8 - Your limitations are the limitations in the nature of your developing creations. Faults are the faults of creations distorted light of intelligence and abused imagination.

4:9 - All beings participate as elements of your Cosmic Reality and proceedings.

4:10 - O'Thou Creator of All, to know you is to know everything truly. But the distortion of the Light of your Presence, by your creations, is sorrow, illusion, and the very "devil."

4:11 - Thou art that absolute Cosmic administrator and Supreme counselor, and every order, hierarchy, and government of the seen and the unseen, of the animate and the inanimate, and of the mobile and stationary, is directly within your Cosmic administration.

4:12 - You are the land and its people, and the heavens and their spirits, and your ways of progress are the same for all things and beings.

4:13 - A corporeal particle of creation, existing in your Light, is far more joyful than a heavenly god or goddess in darkness.

4:14 - The abuse of your Presence in things, as things in places and in times, O'Creator in and over all, is the very meaning of chaos and hell; but is not the love and practice of your Presence real peace and harmony?!

4:15 - Are not your creatures desiring you with your own desires, looking for you with your own very eyes, and forgetting that the children of The Creator can only be goddesses and gods and should model their lives accordingly?!

4:16 - O'Most Harmonious and Most Beloving Governance of all, is not true independence conscious dependence upon thy Omnipresent Will?! Is not true individuality being consciously aware of oneness with thy Infinite Spirit of Love and Light?!

❀ Part 5

5:1 - Everyone, no matter what may be the system or order to which they belong, no matter whether or not they accept a name for thee, or whether they worship idols made of thy matter, or otherwise chosen from amidst thy innumerable and diverse ranks of heavenly entities: gods, goddesses, lords, builders, gurus, and ex-ambassadors of certain worlds, practice thy light each moment they live by their highest applicable truth.

5:2 - Truth, O'All Veracity, is the highest applicable knowing concerning your Presence and its inherent conjunctions and proceedings.

5:3 - To honor you is to truly honor my soul, everyone, and all things all at once!

5:4 - Is not the worship, magnification, and acknowledgment of the Whole the only salvation from idolatry?!

5:5 - By your Life and Light, all thoughts are formed, and all minds organized – neither can anyone's ideals and ideas cause any original things to come into existence.

5:6 - Human thinking is merely holding the Light of thy Creative Intelligence upon creation.

5:7 - Do not entities use, or otherwise, abuse, thy direct Presence, calling the use *good* and the abuse *evil* - although your Presence is only Love and the Way?!

5:8 - You have put your thoughts upon free-floating corporeal substance and produced material physical states and forms, worlds, stars, atoms, and universes, and by your direct presence you have sustained their motives.

5:9 - O'Boundless Boundary of all bounds, O'All One, you are the Positive and Supreme monitor of all levels of diversity.

5:10 - You forever transcend and encompass all good or bad, up, or down, yin or yang, saint or devil, male or female, right or wrong, and true or false. Is not "duality" for the souls who hesitate to rise above two-in-one to perceive infinity and eternity of diversity in the one?!

5:11 – What, O'Absolute Wholeness, is duality but the passing conjecture in the fixation of your imagining and thinking entities of creation, concerning the working of your events, cycles, products, and conjunctions, by reference to their own illusions and separate desires and will?!

5:12 - Surely, you are Infinite and Eternal Unity without divisions, vacancy, vacuum, or any chasm, demarcation, zeros, sects, sexes, likes or dislikes, and or any emptiness.

5:13 - Cosmic is the perfect integrity of the fullness and unity of your direct personal Presence as Infinity and Eternity of Absolute and Supreme Being.

5:14 - Your Supreme Presence, as Infinity and Eternity of Absolute and Supreme Being, is without duality, religion, color, and ideology, for or against any parts of elements of itself. All parts of thy Supreme Being are charged alike in the Breath and Light of thy Omnipresence Reality.

5:15 - To see, rise, and express your undistorted Light is your uniform Plan, Prayer, Will, and Command for all orders of creation.

5:16 - Your very person is the undistorted Life and Light, and your Harmony is upon the universes and the atom.

5:17 - To those who seek and rise to conscious affiliation, responsibility, and honor in the expression of love in thy Body-Cosmic, You have graciously capacitated to the ever-exulting level of Cosmic citizenship, conscious evolutionary development and progression, conscious immortality, and conscious daughterhood and sonship, or goddesshood and godhood.

5:18 - O'Substance of all selves, your Presence is All things linked and unified, apart and together – it is the gathering integrity of all entities and forms within formless Omnipresence of your Being and capacity.

5:19 - O'Ever-present, you are the One Truth that Totally, Absolutely, and Purposefully aligns, regulates, harmonizes, embodies, and unifies All truths.

5:20 - O'All Truth, all diversity is within your indissoluble Cosmic Unity and Integrity. Certainly, you are the Fullness of all the power, substance, and potency there is and that there will ever be.

5:21 - You have foreseen all the future because you are all the future there will ever be. You know all of the past because you are all the past there was ever; the fullness of all the present is the now-currency of your Cosmic Omnipresence.

5:22 - In your Body-Cosmic, and its worlds-beyond numbers, O'Most Loving and Beloved, you have provided just and orderly ways and means of progressive evolutionary qualification for eternally grading, posting, honoring, and elevating your created souls, from one plane of conscious adeptism and sublimity to endless other planes.

5:23 - Your infinite Cosmic cycles have set the tone for the eternal procession and progression of your Reality.

5:24 - You are personally the music and the dance, the player and the spectator, the believer and the unbeliever, the passive and the active, the theist and the atheist, the illuminated and the occluded, the servant and the served.

5:25 - For those who choose the path of your conscious Light, your ways are of Boundless Abundance – and there is nothing you have made scarce in reality or in possibility.

5:26 - Your Cosmic Womb is forever caressing, convolving, and flowing with common creation, or with undiscovered old and new creation.

5:27 - Under the Light of your Supreme Intelligence, O'Cosmic Being of beings, your children travel through endless worlds, universes, super-universes, and grand-dimensions, from discoveries unto discoveries, or from one life unto numberless other lives of eternal progression.

5:28 - O'Most Unfathomable One, your marvels and wonders, are at times, so unbelievable to both humans and ex-humans that angels and folks have called certain conditions of your presence "illusion." Nevertheless, real illusion does never exist beyond the shortcomings of human faculties – and all the so-called illusion is woven out of the fabric of your direct Presence, in and as substantive and inherent Reality.

5:29 - You are the Only All-Inclusive Reality and the Original Impetus of Power, Wisdom, and Love that will enable humans to the realization that they are the children of The Creator of goddesses and gods and that they are themselves destined to someday become conscious and mature goddesses and gods.

5:30 - Throughout the Cosmic, you are the Absolute Supreme Being and Ever-Present counselor, who forever teaches all beings how to attend one another with your Blessing and Love.

5:31 - In form, creations actions and significances, and for the good of All, O'Ever-present Cosmic Supreme Being, thy Will, Power, Wisdom, Freedom, Beauty, Joy, Labor, Light, and Love be forever done!

To the Glory of the Ever-present Cosmic Supreme Being, The Creator of All that is All!

⚘ The Sprout Café

Two years into living at the house with my roommates, Billy moved to the West Coast, and he and his girlfriend decided to end the lease. I was then faced with finding a new place for Son and me to move. Because of the felonies on my record and having no rental credit, I wasn't sure what place would accept me.

One day while speaking with Brooke, she mentioned that the apartment complex she lived at had an easy application process, and she'd be open to being a reference for me. I went forward and filled out an application to give it a shot. I applied to a one-bedroom, which Son and I would share. Thankfully to God, I got approved, and we moved in.

Son spent most of his time in the living room doing his work as he normally would. He was always fully focused on where he was in his consciousness, at the complete exclusion of what was going on around him in the room. Anytime I would ask him what was happening in his process, he would gladly pan into the room and explain to me the conversational exchanges that were taking place between him and other beings in the other realms. As schizophrenic as it sounds, if you were to hear the detailed and concise accounts of what his work on the other realms consisted of, it was fully coherent and beautiful, with a depth of meaning that was truly sacred.

As Son described it, The Creator had him teach the laws, knowledge, and wisdom of The Creator to various aspects of creation who had disqualified themselves in existence. He would describe the exact names of the beings he was speaking with and what the specifics of the conversation were about.

I continued to spend my time reading, studying, and learning from Son while furthering my ability to make healthy food. Eventually, I got a job as a prep chef at a new raw food restaurant in Roswell, Georgia called the Sprout Café. I only made around eight dollars an hour, but the experience was priceless.

Sprout Café would go on to be an extremely serendipitous place for me. This was the place where I met my first teacher of the healing arts, who introduced me to energy healing. The Sprout Café was also where I first came across the couple that fourteen years later, would become my close friends and mentors in the healing work I currently do, assisting Angels.

My dedication and determination to further myself was always without hesitation and sometimes against all odds. To make it from my apartment to the café required taking two buses, a train, a taxi, and a long walk. Although it wasn't practical, I didn't let that stop me — my mind was wholly committed to what I was learning. I now look back and realize the importance of having pure-hearted determination while on the path of furthering oneself. This was the very beginning of me embarking on a multi-decade journey of training and paying dues in the healing arts.

That journey began one day when I was given a ride to work at the Sprout Café by a friend named Gwen. Gwen was one of my past roommates at the place that the police raided a few years prior. Gwen saw this woman's small sign stating that she was doing Reiki sessions and decided to try it out. I watched the session from a slight distance, and I noticed her getting quite emotional, tears were running down her face. Knowing that Gwen wasn't a massive believer in this type of thing, I knew it must have been legit because I could see the effect it had on her.

Afterward, I was curious. I walked over to the woman, whose name was Jeanne Johnson, and asked her if I could schedule a treatment the next day. She said yes, and I thanked her for whatever it was that she'd done for my friend Gwen.

Throughout my workday, my mind kept getting pulled back to this experience with Gwen and this lady Jeanne earlier that day. The next day when I arrived at the café, I purposefully came an hour early to have enough time to do the session with Jeanne.

At this point, I was years firmly and devoutly on the path of my studies of *A Course,* and Cosmic consciousness from Son, but I'd never experienced any aspects of the healing arts. The thing called "energy healing" and "Reiki" were all new to me. I had never thought about *receiving* "healing," or, for that matter, doing therapy of any type (though there was much in *A Course* which was aimed at clearing the past and self-healing work through God). I was a bit skeptical of this "energy healing" thing, and at the time, on a personal level, I was pretty closed off to anyone being in my personal physical or emotional space.

The next day, during my session with Jeanne, I sat in her massage chair while she lightly rested both hands on the top of my head for an extended period, not moving them. I noticed a warmth emanating from her hands, but it was a subtle feeling. The next thing I knew, the gentle, peaceful, and slightly tingly sensation became a strong current of energy moving through me as if the volume had been turned up to a hundred.

Since this was my first experience of the sort, with no past reference for what to expect, I just thought that it was a natural part of it. Then, Jeanne said in a surprised tone, "Whoa, we just had a *master* come through the energy — that's something that rarely happens." I didn't know what she meant by that comment, so I didn't make anything of it. The experience was a peaceful one and I enjoyed it. We concluded the treatment, and I was left with a natural high type of feeling: ethereal and peaceful — enhanced and uplifted in a unique type of way.

As I went about my workday in the kitchen, I kept thinking that I'd like to learn more about what I'd just experienced. I was quite impressed by the whole thing. I didn't understand it, but I enjoyed the session and found it beneficial.

The next day when I arrived at the café, I asked her if she ever taught classes, and she said yes, occasionally. As someone who was only making eight dollars an hour and spending most of it on rent and public transportation, I was concerned I wouldn't have the financial ability to take the class. Thankfully, when I asked her how much it cost, she said that it wasn't about the money with me, and I should just come, that she'd be honored to teach me. I was enthusiastic to learn, and I was super grateful to her for the offer! I felt an invisible hand directing me forward through my studies, training, and teachers.

Even now, 20 years later, her generous offer is something I'm forever appreciative of. And it's something I pay forward to my students and clients whenever it is needed.

I continued working and learning at the restaurant and began to think that I could potentially earn a living being a raw foods chef. Day in, day out for months, I was soaking up my training and advancing in my ability to make gourmet-style, vegan, raw food commercially. Working at the Sprout Café, for next to nothing financially, was like an internship for me where I learned a vocational skill that allowed me to earn a living through my twenties while pursuing my training in the healing arts.

The environment at the café was very progressive and advanced — this was uncharacteristic for anything in Roswell, Georgia. The café served as a powerful hub for giving a stage to teachers and speakers who had valuable information. There was a teaching and presentation area in the café, where teachers would come and do demonstrations about all types of topics about healthy living and alternative healing.

One of the presenters who came through and did a demonstration was Peter Selby, accompanied by his wife, Anne Selby. Peter Selby demonstrated how they do extrasensory healing work guided by Angels. That being something revealed to him by the Angels, fifteen years into his career as a physical therapist. I was extremely drawn to their work. It had a purity about it. Sitting there thinking about Angels brought me back to the three times during my childhood and teens that I'd experienced them.

Peter and Anne's demonstration was happening while I was on my work shift. With a deep pull to their presentation, I reluctantly asked my boss if I could clock out for a bit and sit in on the presentation. She obliged. I did my best to follow what Peter was talking about, but a lot of it was completely over my head.

After the demonstration was complete, I wanted to meet them both. I was hoping to gain insight into my experience at 18 when the entity entered my field, and the Angel that helped me. However, after the demonstration, I had to go back to work, and a flock of people surrounded Peter. Anne was nearby, gathering all their things to wrap up the presentation, so I approached her. I was nervous, and my words weren't coming out of my mouth very clearly. In a very condensed way, I attempted to describe the experience from the past and told her that I had been around very dark people. she listened to me with a patient and open heart.

Then I asked her what the easiest way was to connect with the Angels for their help. She looked me in the eyes, like an Angel herself, and pure-heartedly said, "From within your heart, just call upon them." What occurred next was the most indescribable and unexpected feeling that began moving through me as she spoke the last words of the sentence. It was massive, scary, beautiful, sacred, and ungrounding, all at the same time — a feeling that I *absolutely* had never experienced before!

As I stood there, feeling as if I was going into some type of upheaval energetically, it was quite an ecstatic out-of-body feeling. She could tell that I was having an intense moment. As I was there attempting to gather myself, Anne told me to take slow deep breaths and when I get home to take an Epsom salt bath.

When I got back to my apartment that night, I took the Epsom salt bath. After about three days this ethereal feeling pouring through me finally settled down. Still, to this day, other than the experience mentioned in Chapter 13 (which inspired the title of this book), I have never experienced anything like the response I had to the conversation with Anne Selby that night.

Little did I know that in the distant future, this enchanting couple would become two of my most influential and present-day teachers, mentors, and beloved friends. Fourteen years later, the hands of destiny brought us together, and I had the honor to reconnect with them. This would lead to the most important work of my life and the pinnacle of my training.

❁ Healing Arts Training

Around a month later, Jeanne was teaching one of her first classes. She invited me to come to participate and learn. By this time, I was increasingly interested in her practice, and I made sure to make it. Over the next three months, through Jeanne's guidance, I went through all the levels of training to level three, which is the "mastership," teacher training level.

Upon my completion, and even as my training advanced and ability developed, I never felt right about calling myself a "master." The term or title seems like something you should only earn with proper experience. Like, once you've made it to the ten-year mark of continued training and application in the craft. I held the same sentiment years later regarding my hypnotherapist training and career. I also share the same view for the work I now do with the Angels. I feel this premature title of "master" in the reiki branch of the healing arts world is a bit misleading and unhealthy for the minds of the students and the expectations of clients.

I continued to read and study the training materials I received. I began to practice on myself and as many other people as I could. I couldn't help but notice that the flow of energy emanating from my hands seemed limited. When I did sessions with others, the results were subpar to barely noticeable — it seemed like something was missing. I continued to seek, learn, and develop as much as possible.

My training would lead me through many different modalities. They all seemed loosely related in their essence. I would take the bus to the local metaphysical/spiritual bookstore and sit there for hours at a time, reading every book I was drawn to. I didn't have enough money to purchase the books so I'd just go and soak up as much reading as I could while I was there.

One of the schools I was strongly guided to was called Tera Mai. It took me around two years before I could proceed forward with training in Tera Mai. Once I eventually proceeded in my training in Tera Mai, it massively upgraded my capacity to help others during sessions, especially on an emotional level.

⊛ Skeletons

At this point, I was almost 25 years old. Around this time, I was coming to terms with my past and cleaning out my final skeletons. The main skeleton was from when I had been unfaithful to Brooke in the beginning of our relationship. I hadn't yet confessed to Brooke about my past infidelities.

Since our break-up, we had both moved on with our lives. Although she had a new boyfriend, we remained family friends. We lived in the same apartment complex, and we'd still see each other now and then.

I kept feeling the time had come for me to confess what I had done to her. It was time to heal that wound between us. I called and let her know I needed to speak with her. When I sat down with her, I told her about the three times that I had been unfaithful in the first two years of the relationship. Watching her cry was the worst feeling. Especially considering how loyal and real she was towards me as a girlfriend. At that moment, I made a vow never to be unfaithful to another woman who had given me her heart.

It was something that I never will repeat. To this day, I'm still apologetic about it. When she asked me how I could be unfaithful if I loved her, I reminded her that my struggle with drugs had my judgment upside down at times – and I was selfish. To add to that, I didn't even love myself, which makes it difficult to fully love another fully.

In our past together, especially in the first few years, I didn't know what love truly was in its totality. Back then, life was about being high, making fast money, and furthering my social status in the drug game. Due to everything I'd gone through emotionally, I was closed off and didn't wholeheartedly trust women. It speaks absolute volumes to the type of woman and unconditionally-loving partner Brooke was that we made it five years together.

As time went on, she continued to be by my side, like an Angel escorting me safely through my hell. I eventually opened my heart toward her fully. In the final three years of our relationship, I was completely faithful to her. I had been closer to her emotionally than with any other woman in my life. She was the person who taught me what being a caring and loving human was about. She was the firsthand, living example of what unconditional human love is. To this day, I see her as one of my greatest teachers. Brooke taught me about loyalty, *real* human love, vulnerability, honesty, and integrity, which I still carry with me to this day.

Before I healed and grew to know God's love, I was limited in my capacity to love anything or anyone else. Brooke was, and is, my best friend and someone I trusted and respected, and I still do. We were real partners — boyfriend and girlfriend — and the five years we were together were the best five years of any relationship I have ever experienced.

Seeing her there in tears while expressing my infidelities taught me a valuable lesson. This is a lesson I carry in my heart today: Keep it real with people – especially women who share their heart and soul with you!

⊛ Riding the Light

I continued to work at the Sprout Café as a day job. My studies continued with Son, *A Course*, and the healing arts. At home I spent my time in the kitchen or reading in my bedroom.

Son spent most of his days in the living room doing his work on the other side. Son worked around the clock at times. On an energetic level, it was intense to be around him. Most uninitiated people would think he was off his rocker — but I knew the purity of his message, teachings, and the nature of his work.

One of the things he wrote was titled "Womanhood is Humanhood and Beyond." He was a major advocate for the women's movement in existence. When it came to this earth, Son would often mention that it is a place that was originally designed by The Creator to be led by women. He would always say that if the women of this earth were consciously in The Creator's Light, then all the food and crops would grow on their own effortlessly, at a rate that would produce more food than anyone could ever eat.

He also taught that The Creator had designed specific partners for each other, and he would always warn against having sex with just any woman. I was taught that before engaging in physical intimacy, you should check in with The Creator first, to avoid moving forward with anyone whom The Creator doesn't permit you to be with. We are energetically designed to be with specific partners who are aligned in The Creator's design for us.

Son sometimes mentioned a court system on the grander scales of existence, which he had assisted in creating. This was called the "Tribunal of the Whole." This court seated a type of judiciary committee held by what he called the original forefathers, or creator-gods of existences. This court was for holding beings in existence accountable for defaulting from Cosmic Law: spirits and groupings of spirits who had committed crimes in existence, which were consciously opposing The Creator's Will. He explained that there were major organizations of this world that were part of a larger group of systems in existence called 'the movement of all evils," and that their primary game was to be a movement that was to replace The Creator's unified plan for existence with their own plans, rooted in a selfish agenda of greed and gain.

Son shared much of his work with me, including the nature of how he met The Creator. He explained that the process unfolded within him, specifically during two years of his meditation practice: 1976-77. This process allowed him to attune to, and be carried by, the Light through all the levels of manifest creation, all the way unto the unmanifest Presence of The Creator of All. Being extremely curious, hungry, and diligent in my quest for understanding, this was one of the most important things I was hoping to know. When I asked him about the process, he began to explain it to me, and as he did, at a point, it looked as if the flame of a candle enveloped his body – visually it was totally next level to witness.

After explaining all of this to me, I naturally asked him if he would share the steps of the meditation process this experience revealed within him. He gladly obliged and began to write out the step-by-step process, which took about a day. Once he was done, he gave it to me. I was beyond honored. He then said that I could teach this in the future to students to assist them in reunion and communication with The Creator.

I have another published book titled *The Creator of All - The Cosmic IAM* that contains this meditation system and some of Son's other works, which give insight into The Creator of All and Cosmic consciousness.

⊛ Counting My Blessings in Disguise

One day while I was making food at the apartment, I received a call from a friend, who told me that he had just seen on the news that Billy and his friends had been involved in a federal drug bust in Southern California involving a LARGE amount of pure MDMA (ecstasy). On the news, it said that it was the largest federal drug bust of ecstasy of that purity that they had ever seized. A federal informant had set them up.

The realization immediately struck me, and I knew with every fiber of my being, that if I hadn't gotten busted, which caused me to change my life, I for sure would've been there with them in Southern California. I would've been looking at a decade of federal prison time. What had once seemed to be one of the most tragic betrayals and misfortunes of my life, ended up being two massive blessings in disguise. My arrest was a catalyst for my spiritual growth, and it kept me from getting into FAR more trouble in the future.

Billy went on to receive a steep federal prison sentence. To me, no number of profits, or fun, is worth losing years or decades of your life, and youth for. Although a troubled kid, Billy was an intelligent person who came from a very well-off family. In all reality, he didn't *have* to be selling drugs for financial reasons.

At this point, Billy wasn't the only one I'd seen lose significant years of their life. So many intelligent young men go to state or federal prison because of drug sales — when they could have done any number of other things with their lives.

❀ Closure

With around three months left on my apartment lease, things were ending at the Sprout Café, and they, unfortunately, had to close. Simultaneously, I'd begun to feel like I'd outgrown Atlanta, and it was time to leave. I had advanced through my training and studies, and Atlanta contained little opportunity for people on my path.

I was also feeling drawn to go and heal with my mother in Los Angeles, California. I wanted to try to help her in whatever way I could while there was still time and an opportunity to. I wasn't going to be able to help her financially the way I had thought in the past. Knowing that I had acquired a greater understanding of nutrition, supplements, fasting, food, spirituality, and the healing arts, I thought that I could surely help her somehow. It had been twenty years of being away from her and there were things that I wanted to heal between us.

At the time, I was barely making ends meet and didn't have much money coming in. I was also on intensive probation, though I had completed three of the originally scheduled five years. Another major factor was that I was caretaking for Son.

I knew if I were to make it to the West Coast, I would need a couple of things to align. One of the main things I needed to figure out was how to get my probation changed from supervised to unsupervised. I was clueless as to how I could pull that off.

The next time I reported to my probation officer, I decided to come right out and ask if there was any way I could relocate to California. I explained why I wanted to move, and to my surprise, he said yes — under a few stipulations. One of those stipulations was that I would have to pay off my fines and the remaining two years of my monthly supervised probation fees. The other stipulation was that I pay off the remaining fees in cash. I was so excited to hear his response that I completely overlooked his fishy request about it needing to be in cash. Not being the most grounded person, on top of being so excited to be off the hook, I didn't stop to think twice about it. I was on my way forward, off probation, and not looking backward! This exchange between my probation officer and myself would come back to bite me in a big way years later – in one of the most unexpected and unfortunate ways!

I came up with the money to pay off my probation fines through doing personal catering and then selling my kitchen tools. I also informed my grandmother and my mother that I would be coming to California.

Once I obtained all the money to pay off the remaining twenty-four months of probation fees and fines, I met with my probation officer and gave him the cash. He proceeded to sign me off supervised probation. I signed all the paperwork, and he told me to stay out of trouble and that there was nothing else for me to do.

I began to contact all of Son's friends and close associates to explain to them that I needed to go to California, and I could no longer take care of him. Son didn't want to leave the apartment — and in a way, neither did I. That had been such a simple and beautiful stage of my life, but I knew I needed to go try to help my mother.

Son continued to live in the Atlanta area. Throughout the next ten years, I only saw him one other time after this and only spoke to him on the phone a few times. During one of those conversations, I asked him about "plant medicines," and he explained the reasoning behind not using substances when you could learn and communicate directly with The Creator of All.

Josiah Osuagwu, the Cosmic Son, continued living in the Atlanta area, doing his work for 13 more years, eventually leaving this realm in 2018.

Son's teachings and inspirations continue to live on in my heart and fuel my conscious commitment to, my direct relationship with, and my understandings about The Creator of All. To this day, he is one of the most influential mentors in my life. His work and teachings deserve the highest of honors.

I gave away my furniture, packed my bags of clothes, and then flew to California from the Tennessee airport. I flew from Tennessee rather than Atlanta to save money on the ticket. Brooke ended up giving me a ride there to the airport. The goodbyes were cathartic, and many tears were shed. It felt like the closing of a beyond profound chapter in my life — a chapter that began nine years earlier, the moment I stepped off that Greyhound bus in Downtown Atlanta, arriving from a small beach town in North Carolina.

Grandma Diane (2008)

CHAPTER 6

❖ HEALING THE PAST ❖

❂ California: Part 2

Upon arriving in California, I first went to my grandmother's house in San Juan Capistrano. I wanted to take time and gather myself there before stepping into the situation that would be my mother's environment. When I arrived, my cheery, loving grandmother, as always happy to see me, met me with a warm welcome. It was good to see her and spend time with her. Her presence was always nourishing for my soul.

Coming from my situation in Georgia, I had no money saved, nor did I have gainful employment lined up. As I often did throughout that stage of my life, I was trustingly flying by the seat of my pants. I had no plan and simply let life present itself. I was somehow able to do so without any fear or concern.

The financial side of life was my only dysfunction, but I was unphased by it. My priority was my application and study of *A Course* – regardless of if it didn't help my financial situation. Moving to California, a place very progressive when it comes to healthy eating, I hoped my well-developed skill in preparing vegan raw food would translate into making a decent living.

Regardless of any of the challenges that I may be met with, I was there to honor my original intentions — to help my mom and heal our relationship.

When I arrived at my mother's house, it was not the warmest of welcomes. She was in the middle of a multi-day bender, high on crack cocaine. In that, she seemed distant and disconnected. She was in and out of the house constantly. The situation was one where you could feel how her conflict had broken the spirits of her husband and her son, my Stepbrother Larry.

Larry was born about 12 years after I was taken from my mom as a child. Larry is a beautiful-hearted, kind young man, born with Asperger's syndrome. He was raised in the most intense of situations – one from which I was spared. As a gifted artist, Larry used his art as an escape into an inner world where he developed into a genius political cartoonist.

The living conditions at my mom's house were horrible. It was a dirty, unkempt apartment in Venice. There were roaches galore. When I slept, I would put tissue paper in my ears to make sure that none of them crawled into my ears.

At this point, I had been studying *A Course* very intently for years. Of the many important lessons that I'd learned from my studies, the most important one was about to be tested in the most direct way: the ability to see beyond the nightmare appearance of what my mother had become, to witness unto her innermost Light and sacred essence.

From the normal, human perspective, everything about the situation I was stepping into with my mother reflected tragedy. Instead of being completely crushed emotionally, I maintained my center and kept my mind focused on the sacred. In this, I was able to behold her Light beyond the darkness. In this, I never ignored the conditions at hand that may need improvement. There was no "spiritual bypassing" (the term many like to use nowadays). I continued to attempt to help her physical situation become a better version of itself – without getting blinded by it.

Because my mom was still running the streets and rarely home, I didn't see her much. When she was home, she was usually passed out, catching up on the sleep she had lost during her tornadoes. I was hoping that our being reunited after twenty years of being apart would inspire her to make positive changes. But it was the exact opposite. My presence instigated her deepest demons of suppressed guilt. Her attitude toward me was distant, resistant, and uninviting.

Upon seeing the continual pain and disregard for her well-being, I did everything I could to convince her to put down the hard drugs. She even used crack cocaine right in front of me on one occasion. This was a blatant call for love. It felt like her way of overtly saying, "Yes, this is how bad it is, and this is why I couldn't raise you." She told me the horrific things she had done in the name of her addictions. It made my heart sink to hear it.

As deeply rooted as my focus was on the sacred divine within her, watching her smoke crack in front of me was heart-breaking. I attempted to get her to use marijuana instead and take other natural herbs such as Milk Thistle, which would help cleanse her liver and her body, but all my efforts were to no avail.

That she was still alive was a small miracle. When my mother was younger, she had heart surgery to repair the damage caused by her drug use. Part of the surgery required that she get the valves replaced so that once the artificial valves they put in had worn out, she would be able to remain alive. It was around twenty years past the time that she was medically required to get the artificial valves replaced, and she never did. It was even more surprising that she was still living as a hardened drug user, going multiple days in a row using crack cocaine and other forms of drugs, at will.

I feel that the root cause of her heart complications and self-destructive behavior was due to long-running, unresolved emotional pains that she carried within her from her relationship — or lack thereof — with her father.

After about a month and a half at my mom's apartment in Venice, I concluded I needed to find a different place to live. A relationship wasn't building between us. She made it clear that she didn't want me to stay there on multiple occasions. She often complained about the smell of garlic coming from me, which was a natural byproduct of my way of eating. However, I can understand her complaint. On top of the garlic smell coming from my garlic-rich diet, I also wasn't showering every day because the bathrooms at their place were warzone-looking caves for her drug use.

⊛ Building on Quicksand

I spent most my time outside of their place. The conditions in their house were nothing desirable. Not having a car, or even a license yet, everywhere I went to was on foot. I enjoyed being out exploring Venice Beach and Santa Monica. And just as I had expected, the raw vegan healthy eating community was flourishing. I met and networked with as many people as I could.

On my daily journeys through Santa Monica, I began to look for a viable commercial kitchen where I could begin any form of raw food operation. I eventually found a place on Main Street that had previously been host to another raw food chef. When I discovered this location, I approached the owner, introduced myself and my talents, and asked if I could do a nightly raw food menu there. The owner was open to the idea and told me to create a business plan that he would look over, and we could speak more about the possibility from there.

I immediately began to work on the business plan while also brainstorming how to accrue the financial support for funding the operation. Upon expressing my progress to my grandmother, she said she would be open to helping me if I made a solid, detailed business plan.

Although through my spiritual practice, my head was in the sky, when I wanted something enough, I could buckle down and be grounded. I spent the next two months fine-tuning my business plan. Once I had everything together, I presented it to the venue owner and my grandmother. They were both impressed by the details and decided to greenlight it. I named my food operation Bites of Light, and I was in forward motion.

For my food operation to move forward, it would require a business loan of $10,000. My grandmother agreed to give me the loan, but it was unclear when the funds would be available. Patiently I waited, while my day-to-day reality was challenging. West L.A. was a super expensive area to be in. Without having a consistent form of income yet, I was living off small rations and handouts coming from my grandmother.

For two months during this time, I was homeless – staying on friends' couches or on small boats in the marina. Finding a new place to live was also difficult. After weeks of looking, I finally met someone who had a condo in Marina del Rey near the Venice-Marina del Rey border, not too far from the beach. I rented out the roof area of his place. In that my room was on the roof, it didn't have a ceiling and was exposed to the elements. It was like I was living outside, but up in the air, in a nice part of town. I quickly jumped at the opportunity and was grateful to have found anything at all, especially considering my minimal finances, poor credit, an eviction on my record, and felonies. The opportunity was the best I could do at the time.

While awaiting my startup money, I continued going to vegan raw food functions, meetings, potlucks, and gatherings as I could to network with the community and promote the soon-to-be operation. This gave me an opportunity to look for people who could work for me when the time came.

One day, I was walking through Santa Monica, and an Eastern Indian man approached me. He had a strong Indian accent and seemed to be a yogi of some sort. He proceeded to tell me that he had psychic abilities from his yogic training in India. He told me that, in a past life, I was a revered saint and teacher who had students following my meditation practice.

Without telling him I was starting a business, he then proceeded to tell me the exact date that I'd be receiving funds for a business I was starting. My skepticism of him left upon hearing this. How would he have known I was about to start a business if he wasn't legitimately dialed into the ethers. He offered this information kindly, without asking for any fee. I listened to what he had to say, took a mental note, thanked him, and simply moved on with my day.

Weeks later, I got a call from my grandmother. She told me the specific date she would be able to deposit the funding for the business, which interestingly, was the exact date that the Indian man had predicted it would be — I was astonished by his accuracy!

The news gave much more credence to his other mentions about my previous life as a revered teacher of meditation. As I reflected on what he had said, it dawned on me how easy it was for me to pick up meditation once I was introduced to it. I also remembered the time I'd read the Bhagavad Gita, and the language seemed like second nature for me to understand.

Aside from that, I was grateful to receive the news about the funding, and I was glad for the opportunity to move forward with my food operation.

When I finally began my food business, I had a head full of steam — I felt like Superman! I had a determination and focus that seemed to be unbreakable. I was able to completely block out all the other challenges to ensure I was making progress.

Because I was putting this all together with limited funds, little money was allocated toward hiring help. My budget required me to wear virtually every hat of the operation. I did all the food shopping and ordered the ingredients. I also prepared all the food. I was the prep-cook and head chef, making all the menu items. When the food was prepped, and orders came in, I also plated every dish for each customer. On top of all that, I was also the busboy and the dishwasher.

Somehow, I was pulling all of this off without any form of personal transportation. There was no Uber or Lyft back then, so I got around West L.A. on foot, bicycle, or public transportation.

Doors opened for me, but they were doors that required unearthly strength and effort to hold open. However, along the way, I did receive amazing breaks. For instance, I had a friend named Amy Gayheart, who was a tremendously-gifted graphic artist from Atlanta, who offered to do the graphic design for my menu in exchange for meals. And the job she did for me was absolutely epic!

I was breaking my back in every possible way to make the food operation run smoothly day in and day out. My challenges were more than I could allow myself to take notice of. My mindset was of pure determination, and I barreled through any difficulty that faced me in a do-or-die manner, with my blinders on.

One of my struggles was my living situation. It was super cold sleeping on the rooftop of the condo at night. Living in Marina del Rey, I'd wake up with a coating of marine layer condensation all over me every morning. It always felt as if I'd been sleeping in light rain all night.

To add to it, my roommate had preconceived notions of ways that I would be contributing to the household and assisting him. When I couldn't meet his expectations, he became oddly passive-aggressive, which didn't make things any easier.

⊕ Seeing the Sacred

A few months into beginning my business, my mother ended up in the hospital for what I believe was an overdose mixed with general poor physical health. Although I could see her Light, I was carrying turmoil in my heart knowing that I couldn't get through to her. By then, I'd surrendered my hopes of establishing a healthy relationship with her the way that I had hoped to.

When I visited her at the hospital, seeing her Light was fully present within my heart and mind. There was a deep serenity in this. As I sat with her, at one point, I could see a luminescent glow about and around her — it was beautiful. That moment resonated as one of the most humbling and sacred experiences of my life. It was an immensely healing experience. With every engagement with another, we are the liberator or the imprisoner in how we choose to perceive them.

As I stood there gazing upon God's Light in her eyes, I realized the meaning of the Angel's message from 10 years prior, when I had asked about my purpose. Whether or not a brother/sister can remember their own Light, witnessing unto and recognizing their Light for them awakens a deep unconscious sleeping part of their mind that knows their divinity. This is something that happens on a soul level. To "save my mother" was not an act of financially, physically, or even emotionally saving her. Instead, it was an act of seeing her truly; an act of seeing her as the the perfection of her innermost Light, rather than seeing her through the eyes of sympathy, judgment, and/or condemnation.

❂ Unstable and Unsustainable

At the ten-month mark of being in Los Angeles, I'd been running my food operation, Bites of Light, on Main Street in Santa Monica for around seven months. I was making excellent food that was being very well received, but I was working myself to the bone with minimal resources and with no measurable reward. I was doing so while facing every challenge possible in the process.

Around this point, Brooke decided that she wanted to visit me. Upon arrival, she noticed that my living conditions, work conditions, and family situation were in a collapsible state. She began trying to convince me to come back to Atlanta and get away from my situation. It wasn't easy because I had invested so much time and energy into my operation, but eventually I listened to her. It was helpful to have a new set of eyes from someone I trusted, who could see what was happening from an outside perspective. I had been operating off sheer will with my blinders on.

In a week's time, I concluded my time in Los Angeles. I sadly closed the food operation in Santa Monica. Then I left my rooftop room in Marina del Rey. Before leaving, I took the remaining days to spend as much time with my mother as possible. Brooke was able to meet her as well. Meeting my mom was something Brooke had always wanted to do for years. Being the angel that she is, Brooke accepted her with open arms and a loving heart. Brooke's conclusion was the same that I came to as a young boy in North Carolina: my mother was sick and battling her own demons. That was the last time I saw my mother in the flesh.

With my tail between my legs, shaking my head a bit in disbelief, I left Southern California and headed back to Atlanta, Georgia.

CHAPTER 7

❋ PICKING UP THE PIECES ❋

❁ Renovation

When I arrived back in Atlanta, I felt deeply disappointed at a certain level. I wasn't exactly sure where I would be living. I couldn't stay with Brooke because she had a new boyfriend at the time. Once again, I had made another big move in my life without any forethought or plan. As usual, I surrendered to the guiding force of the universe, while part of me was also in a scramble trying to figure out where to stay.

Not only did I need to figure out where to live, but I also needed to figure out where to work and earn money. On top of that, I had to face the fact that my entire business and family loan were flushed down the toilet. Although I was able to salvage my food preparation equipment, I couldn't recoup enough money to pay back my grandmother what she had invested.

Thankfully, I had a group of friends, Ian being one of them, who'd gotten a house in Midtown Atlanta. They were kind enough to bring me in and give me a place to stay until I could get back on my feet.

I was carrying emotional density within me from having to walk away from my food operation. It was defeating having to flush all that time, energy, and money down the drain. I was also frustrated that my attempt to establish a healthy relationship with my mother had failed.

To add to my gauntlet were the felonies, past house evictions, underdeveloped credit, and a very niche skill/vocational craft. My expertise in vegan raw food preparation was an uphill battle considering Atlanta is a city of Southern comfort food.

I was financially depleted and didn't know what to do. The pressures of the world had me partly checked out. Through it all I remained inwardly focused on my spiritual disciplines. This theme would be a consistent pattern continuing through many stages: my heart and soul being at peace while my material life was in red-alert shambles, in dire need of stabilization.

Although I was grateful to be in a safe place around familiar people, the situation was of partial wreckage. It was a real effort to keep my emotional state balanced. I had little money coming in, and I still had to ask for handouts and assistance from my grandmother to simply eat or take care of the smallest aspects of life – which was unsettling to me.

I did my best to hit the ground running once I got back to Atlanta. But it felt more like quicksand initially. I began to network with people I knew in the healthy-eating community from the past. Still, everything was slow-moving. Whether or not it was a test of my spiritual endurance, the realities of what I had gone through in California, mixed with my present challenges, took extreme mental and emotional strength to overcome.

I had no money, and I wasn't eating correctly at all. I continued attempting to maintain my strict raw food diet, but due to minimal finances, I was eating far less than my physical body and brain required to be healthy. My weight was about 135 pounds (as a 6-foot-tall man). My financial situation mixed with my hardheaded determination to maintain dogmatic eating standards of a vegan raw food diet, was a bad combination

I eventually got an opportunity to do guest nights preparing raw food specials for a restaurant my friend Cory managed. It helped, but it was nothing that could pay the bills. There was a stretch of about six months when work was slim, and I made zero financial progress.

Being back in Atlanta, it was good to reconnect with family friends. Cory in specific, being one of the few people who was a brother on the spiritual path who aligned with my interest in the realm of esoteric knowledge and wisdom. It was good to be around kindred spirits and people I knew had my back.

After a little while of living with my friends at Midtown, their lease ended. I wasn't sure how to proceed. My head wasn't all there, and I still didn't have the financial means to get my own apartment. Part of me was in give-up mode. While I sit and write this, it's headshaking thinking about how incapable I seemed at the time.

My friend Ian ended up finding me a place on Craigslist. It was a perfect situation with a couple from Washington State. They were both into healthy living and yoga, and one of them was a Thai massage therapist. It really couldn't have worked out any better.

Luckily, tides turned quickly. Shortly thereafter, my friend Ian also got me a job waiting tables at a vegan restaurant called Café Sunflower. I then picked up a second job at a small health food store on Peachtree Street in Buckhead. My financial situation stabilized a little bit, and I was able to pay all my bills and eat correctly.

❀ Tera Mai

Gaining stability allowed me to proceed with my training in the healing arts. The healing arts school I'd been guided to was called Tera Mai. I found a local instructor that lived forty minutes away, outside of the reach of the public transit system. Not having a car, I had to get rides from friends, and typically, the person who would be there to help me, once again, was Brooke.

I continued my studies of *A Course*, healing arts, metaphysics, and at this point Jungian psychology. My training in Tera Mai was set up in levels that got incrementally more expensive. I wasn't sure exactly how I would afford to progress through the training, but I knew I would make it happen!

Immediately upon completing my first few classes, I observed an increase in my capabilities. I was very enthused about the training I was undertaking, and I began to practice on others with great results.

To complete the third class took me quite a bit longer, primarily because the cost of the training was $1200. Since I was only making a modest amount of money working at the restaurant and the health food store, most was going toward rent, bills, and general living expenses.

I wasn't going to allow anything to deter me. If there was one redeeming helpful quality that I gained from my biological mom, it was undying determination! With me, there was always an extreme dose of "Where there's a will, there's a way." And I took that to a whole other level when it became, "Where there is *God's* Will, *there is nothing stopping me!*" Any time I got my mind deeply fixed on obtaining something I really wanted, I would go for it with max force. Though the third class required more money than I knew how to earn, at this point, I refused to revert to fast money.

The way I obtained the money was entirely out of the left field. Strangely enough, it happened during my walk to work. The health food store was within walking distance from my apartment complex. Between the apartment complex and my place of work was a McDonald's. Most days, I would shortcut through the McDonald's parking lot, which had an inclined, chewed-up driveway with potholes in it. One day while walking to work, it was raining, and I crossed through the McDonald's parking lot and walked up the inclined entrance, I accidentally stepped in one of the potholes in the driveway and rolled my ankle, spraining it very severely — it was almost broken. I fell to the ground, holding my ankle in immense pain. While lying there clutching my ankle in pain I also almost got run over by a car entering the parking lot.

I picked myself up, limped into McDonald's, and filed a formal grievance complaint with the manager. I then hobbled my way into work, and my boss told me I should go to the emergency room and contact a lawyer. I did both, and months later, I received a settlement for $1500 from McDonald's, and they paid my medical bills from the hospital. So, I used $1200 of the $1500 settlement to pay for my teacher training class in Tera Mai.

Once I completed the third level of my training, I continued studying and furthering my understanding. I reread my manuals repeatedly and was ardent in my practice.

Eventually, my training grew through different methods. The way I saw and understood the human being grew to a much broader perspective. I began to understand the cause connected to how and where dysfunctions and imbalances come from. In this, I also began to understand the limitations of most of the healing methods I'd been learning. They were operating on the symptomatic energy level, leaving the root cause still there, most often unaddressed.

I learned that the physical body reflects the health of the subtle levels of self: soul, mind, and emotion. Usually, once an issue shows up as manifest in the physical body, it has already oozed its way forward, unchecked, from the other layers of a person's consciousness. For the physical manifestation of an issue to be healed fully, the root cause must be addressed. Even if a healing arts practitioner helps a client achieve relief of a symptom, it's usually only temporary if the root cause on the mental/emotional level isn't addressed.

✺ Kelsey

By 27 years old, I'd been celibate for around 6 years. I began finding myself drawn to the idea of being in a partnership again.

During one of my shifts while waiting tables at Café Sunflower, I saw a beautiful girl eating by herself. She had the most stunning blue eyes. Luckily for me she happened to be sitting in my section. Toward the end of her meal, I decided to compliment her on her eyes and asked her what her name was. She smiled and said, "I'm Kelsey." Her reply was inviting to I decided to give her my telephone number. Upon doing so I told her to give me a call sometime if she'd like.

Another month and a half passed before I heard from Kelsey. Finally, one day, as I was checking my voicemail messages, I had a message from her. I returned the call and she told me she'd been out of town at her uncle's ranch for a little over a month, and she'd just recently returned to town. I naturally asked her if she would like to get together, and she said yes, so we arranged a time to meet about a week later.

She came to my place, and we watched a movie and got to know each other. When I first met Kelsey, she was 19 years old, and I was 27. We were both Cancerians and automatically had a great connection. She was the only girlfriend I ever had who would dress herself in clothes that matched mine when we went places together.

While I was with Kelsey, she was very grounding for me. She helped me get my mind more back in the world and financial obligations. She brought out a much more responsible side of me. While I was with her, I finally got my driver's permit and eventually got my official driver's license, too.

Kelsey was coming from an abusive relationship with a previous boyfriend, who was constantly on drugs and physically abusive towards her. Her physical and emotional trauma would show up as overreactions to the smallest disagreements. Sometimes if we were in a disagreement, she would shield herself and shell up as if I was going to physically assault her — something I would never do to any woman.

Kelsey had been part of the massive '90s boom in prescriptions of the pharmaceutical drug Adderall. Adderall was a pure amphetamine; not much different than the street drugs I had illegally sold as a teen. As a child, she beamed with high energy, genius, and creativity, but those qualities were suppressed by the Adderall, which tends to turn people into robots of emotionless intellect. It also has a similar addictiveness to street crystal methamphetamine or cocaine. On top of the Adderall, she was also prescribed valium. She expressed a desire to not take either one but went through the immense challenge of breaking the developed dependency to them. At times it was heartbreaking watching her jostled between detoxing off both substances. The only thing that helped her was marijuana. I grew to develop massive respect for her efforts to overcome the use of those substances.

When I met her, she was living with her parents and had expressed wanting to move out. We decided to get an apartment with one of my old friends, named Allie. It was a nice apartment in Sandy Springs, which Kelsey decorated immaculately.

After we moved in together, I stopped working at the health food store and the vegan restaurant. I found my way into well-paying catering opportunities, preparing gourmet, vegan raw food for local health enthusiasts. My clients were financially well-off and had taken an interest in my cooking when we met through raw food gatherings and potlucks.

One of the people I grew close to was a man named Veggie Joe. Joseph was a kind and intelligent Lebanese Rastafarian who was around 60 years old. He was once a big-time accountant for commercial chicken farms in the Southeast. He ended up meeting a woman who was a vegan, who converted him to veganism. He eventually became involved in the vegan food movement and as well dealing cannabis. He had authored books on veganism, and he was also very well versed in commercial, vegan food operations.

Joe showed interest in the two of us starting a prepared, packaged, vegan raw food operation, supplying products to the health food stores in the greater Atlanta areas. He was open to funding and operating the business, while I would steer the preparation side of the business. We were in the process of putting all the plans together for two months before an unforeseen snag of epic proportions.

❀ The Warrant

I got my permit to drive at around the two-month mark of my relationship with Kelsey. One day, we decided to get food from a raw food café located inside Life Grocery in Marietta. At the time, I had just finished a three-day juice fast.

When we were driving back from Life Grocery, we got in an argument. I didn't want to be arguing with her while driving. I decided to pull over at a Burger King parking lot on Northside Drive. I'd never spent time in those areas, so little did I know it was close to a bad part of town. It was a place where people park and use drugs that they had just obtained from drug dealers up the street.

Kelsey and I sat in the car in the middle of an argument about something trivial. The managers of the Burger King saw that we had parked and weren't getting out of the car to come inside. Thus, they thought we were drug users, and they called the police on us.

When the police pulled up, I was in the driver's seat. The police officer walked up and asked me for my driver's license, which I gladly gave to him. He asked me why I seemed so upset. I explained to him of our argument and that I had decided to pull over. He then took my license permit back to his cruiser, ran my name, and returned to the car. Upon returning he informed me that I had a warrant out for my arrest for a probation violation in DeKalb County — I was in stone-cold utter disbelief!

Kelsey, who had never been in a situation like this before, began crying. The officer asked if he could search the car, to which we consented. He found the prescription pills in her purse and asked us about them, and she explained they were prescribed to her by her doctor.

I asked what the warrant was about and told him that I had completed my probation years ago. The officer said he didn't have any details other than that there was a warrant for a probation violation in DeKalb County. Again, Dekalb County being where my probation officer had put me on unsupervised, non-reporting probation and signed off on me moving to California. I was on my way to jail, standing there dumbfounded, with no earthly clue why there would be a warrant for my arrest.

At this point, I still hadn't eaten anything in three days. I had just gone and bought what was my first meal after fasting and hadn't eaten any of it. Kelsey, in tears, begged the officer to allow me to eat before they took me to jail because I hadn't eaten in days. The officer was kind enough to let me out of the handcuffs to eat, but I only had time to take a few bites before they transported me to Fulton County Jail.

Upon making it to the jail, things didn't get any better for me. Another past probation violation in Fulton County, from ten years previous, which I never showed up for, somehow popped up! It never surfaced during my past arrests or judicial proceedings in 1998–1999, but now here it was, rearing its ugly head.

It was a double whammy! Sitting in the holding cell, I was in total disarray. This news of my second extra probation violation was deeply concerning. For years, it had been haunting me in the back of my mind. There was a period when I had recurring nightmares about being in a courtroom because of judicial obligations that I'd overlooked. I never understood why it never came up as a warrant previously. Now — after completely changing my life – far removed from the drug world — this was all surfacing!

To make matters worse, I had to deal with all of this in the harsh, cold, concrete environment of Fulton County Jail after just coming off a multi-day fast. I had eaten next to nothing in days, and my blood sugar had sunk through the floor. I was vehemently opposed to eating any of the jail food. I also wasn't open to drinking their facility's tap water. I was in a difficult situation. Prayer and meditation were the only reason I didn't have a full-blown psychological breakdown!

To add insult to injury, this was all happening right as I was a week away from obtaining funding from Joseph for the raw food operation we'd been planning. The expected venture would have allowed me to grow massively and begin making significant, legal money for the first time in a long time. It was a nightmare unfolding in front of me at the most inopportune time.

Kelsey contacted Brooke, who then contacted my grandmother. My grandmother gave them the money to pay my lawyer, Michael Mann. Michael began to investigate the situation and find out why I had a warrant for a probation violation in DeKalb County in the first place. However, he said there was no reason to utilize his time and energy to address the probation violation warrant when Fulton County needed to be dealt with first.

With the first installment of $1500, my lawyer cleared up the hold from Fulton County and got the past probation off my record within five days. During those five days, I sat in jail awaiting the news of my potential punishment, and it was agonizing. That situation was something I wouldn't wish upon anyone. I could've been sitting in Fulton County Jail for God knows how long, dealing with a violated probation and resentencing.

I was under an avalanche of concern and total confusion. I wasn't worried about the inmates or violence. At that point, I had been in county jail four times and boot camp twice, and I'd never had an altercation with anyone. For that matter, I'd never been in a fight in my whole life. Knowing how to move and be respectful, I always avoided violence.

Once I was moved to the general population, I relied on eating the fruits they handed out at breakfast and lunch and would trade all my meat-based foods for other inmates' fruits.

After about four long days, I got the news that Fulton County had dropped the hold, and Michael Mann was able to clear my past probation — I was deeply relieved! This allowed me to go to DeKalb County Jail to face the next probation violation warrant. However, to take care of the situation in DeKalb County, my lawyer required $5,000, which I simply couldn't come up with.

By this time, Billy, my past roommate, and friend in federal prison, had discovered I was in jail after calling our house phone and talking to Kelsey. Luckily for me, Billy happened to have an aunt who was a lawyer in DeKalb County, who was open to helping me. Since I was a family friend, and because it was a simple case, she took the case on pro bono. This was crucial because I had no way to produce the $5000.

Once I got to Dekalb County Jail, the first blow to the soul was when I learned that it takes them three months to set a probation revocation hearing. It was a frustrating three months and by far worse than any time I'd ever been detained in the past, primarily because I knew I'd done nothing wrong – and there was no way to speed up the process.

Over the next few months, I spoke with Kelsey on the payphones as much as possible. Both she and Brooke would come to visit me together. Kelsey was a young, 21-year-old girl raised in affluence, and she didn't know how to deal with that type of situation. Having Brooke accompany her was extremely helpful for both Kelsey and me. With Brooke, who was familiar with the situation, it was comforting to know she was there to support me.

I spent the next three months doing what I had previously done in the county jail — reading and furthering my studies in spirituality, metaphysics, psychology, and the healing arts. I read and read... and then continued to read even more.

The situation was extremely straining on Kelsey. I could see it on her face whenever she would come to visit. It was nothing she wanted to be dealing with in any way. We had only been living together for three months when this all happened. While I was away, she was shouldering the financial load for living expenses and rent the entire time.

When the time approached for my court date, my lawyer was able to find out exactly what had happened. She informed me that there had been a group of corrupt probation officers in the DeKalb County probation system, which had been committing fraud by taking money from people on probation and keeping it for themselves.

As I reflected on my last few interactions with him, all I could do was shake my head upon remembering my probation officer telling me I could get my intensive probation reduced to unsupervised, but to do so, I would have to pay the remainder of my monthly fees with *cash*.

I figured the warrant had been there since I was in California. I was both relieved and angered all at the same time. Beyond it all, one thing I knew with complete confidence was that my experience with the judicial system was finally ending, thankfully, finally!

During my day in court, the situation was explained aloud, and I was given a ruling of immediate release. I was processed out of the DeKalb County Terror Dome by the next day. Upon my release, I was met by Kelsey and a healthy meal.

The whole thing had worn on Kelsey. My relationship with her was strained and never recovered from that point on. Even while in jail, I could tell she was already over it. We were coming to the end of the lease at the apartment. Within three months of my release, we decided to break up and move out in different directions.

While I had been in county jail, another local raw food chef had moved in on my opportunity to begin a raw food operation with Joseph. I was quite upset when I learned the news, but I wasn't sure if I should be upset at myself, Joseph, or the probation system of DeKalb County.

When I got out of jail, I got a job waiting tables at a friend's pizza place in the West End area of Atlanta. It was my only means to earn money, and although I was grateful to have a gig, I was heartbroken that the raw food business had passed me by.

Months later, through my persistence, Joseph and I reconvened talks on creating a second prepared, raw food delivery operation alongside the one he'd already started with the other chef. Our talks progressed until we came to an agreement. However, it went on to be a contentious and competitive working environment between myself and the other chef.

Kelsey and I moved out of the apartment. She moved back to her parents' house in the affluent confines of Cobb County, and I moved to Midtown with a friend of mine named Charles. Charles was a close family friend of mine; someone who was a talented artist and a kindhearted, conscious-minded individual.

✹ Soul Exhaustion

When I moved out of my place with Kelsey and started my food delivery business, I experienced massive adrenal fatigue. Financial uncertainty had mounted massively, and it impacted my nervous system and energy. I was still determined to progress successfully in my new food venture, but plain and simple, I was exhausted from all that I had been through.

The food operation I was running with Joseph was like my past operation in Santa Monica — I was doing it all on my own. I prepared all the food, went shopping for all the groceries, packaged all the prepared foods, and delivered them to the health food stores. And I was doing all my cleaning. There seemed to be a common pattern with me in the health food industry: I always wore all the hats at once.

For side money, I was still waiting tables at Café Sunflower. I would work there between the times I was preparing my own food for the business. There was never a moment I wasn't working. Determination was the only thing pushing me through the constant adrenal exhaustion. I was in survival mode, running myself thin, trying to juggle too much on my own.

My exhaustion caused me to make mistakes often and negatively affected my ability to properly pay attention to detail. Some of these mistakes were very costly — one almost cost me my life. One night after just getting out of a movie, I totaled my first car, a Hyundai Accent, I had just recently gotten for the food operation. As I approached a traffic light at an intersection leaving Little Five Points, a friend called my phone. As I looked down at it, I blew through a red light and hit another driver going thirty miles an hour. Thankfully, the injuries were minor, but I could've killed us both. It was a massive wake-up call, and from then on, I knew I needed to get more sleep *and* avoid my cell phone while driving.

⊛ My Mother's Passing

In the fall of 2006, I received a phone call from my grandmother with the news that my mother had just died. She'd been arrested, and when she was released, she went on a three-day crack cocaine bender. Once she finally came down from the high, she fell asleep. At one point through the night, she woke up and said a few things to her then-husband, and then drifted back to sleep. Shortly thereafter she had a heart attack and passed away.

When I received the news, I was relieved for her. I knew that her passing was for her best. I said my silent goodbyes, with blessings to her soul. I reflected on one of the last times I saw her in California years earlier, lying in the hospital bed. I deeply cherished that moment of seeing the beauty of her Light. I was at peace regarding her.

Tears were shed for the times we couldn't have together. I reflected on my time with her through my first five years. It took me back to beautiful moments of her playing the guitar and singing to me. I remembered times of her holding me in her arms and telling me she loved me. I thought about the insanity that was my first five years, pounding the pavement with my mom through the streets of Venice Beach. I thanked her for the qualities of strength and undying determination she imbued within me. As well, how she taught me to accept people of any condition, social background, color, culture, and race and to not judge people in broken dark places in life. She was a heart-torn woman with unresolved fury. She was a rebel, in the sincerest sense of the word. But she loved me with all her heart and soul, and I will always love her.

Crack cocaine and heroin are indeed an utter tragedy. My heart goes out to the young men and women who've ever been addicted to such a substance. My heart also goes out to their children. As I have grown up to become a professional in the healing arts, I always hold an extremely focused tone and heart-filled dedication when someone addicted to these substances comes through my doors seeking help.

✸ Portland

After a year of living with Charles on State Street, our lease ended. At this point, I had to come to terms with the raw food delivery business not profiting the way it needed to be. I shifted my gears to doing private catering and delivering prepared meals to locals in the Atlanta area. It was yet another blow to my momentum to walk away from another business I'd once been so enthused about. I was now further in debt as well.

After moving out of the house with Charles, I lived with different friends, bouncing between Brooke's house and my friend Cory's house. They were both kind and open-hearted toward me. However, it was a little strange living at Brooke's house, platonically sleeping in the same bed with her, while she had a boyfriend.

Homeless, I went into a bit of a scramble mode about what to do and where to live. I was quite unclear about the next steps forward. I had recently discovered mind-focusing techniques that helped influence one's progress and growth. Shortly after implementing them, a new opportunity showed up.

One day I received a call from Ian. He was contacting me from Portland, where he moved and began working at a successful vegan restaurant called Blossoming Lotus. This place happened to need a head chef, and they were interested in expanding the raw food section of their menu.

Ian set up a phone meeting between the owner and me, and the conversation went very well. Everything quickly led to a green light, and I prepared to relocate to Portland and begin my job as the head chef.

Over the next few weeks, I once again said my goodbyes to my friends in Atlanta, packed all my stuff into my small Hyundai Accent, and drove across the country from Atlanta to Portland. It was my first cross-country drive. Upon arriving in Portland, I was given a cash advance to get on my feet in the new city. I stayed with Ian for a while until he and I got a place together. I integrated into the city quickly and loved Portland.

As I began working for Blossoming Lotus, things seemed good for the first month. But I soon ran across unexpected expectations. Having had a head full of steam going into the opportunity, I'd missed a crucial detail during my initial discussions with the owner. Much of their menu was cooked food, and since the owner wanted me to be the head chef over the entire operation, I was also being asked to oversee the cooked food. The problem with that was that I had absolutely no training in cooking food – I only had training and experience in making *uncooked* raw food.

The miscommunication created a rift among the owner, the prep cooks, and me. Overlooking this crucial detail was the demise of the opportunity. While the job seemed to be exactly what I imagined, there was a devil in the details that I was overlooking. For years, not being thorough and detail-oriented was my Achilles heel.

My opportunity in Portland ended within three months of getting there. I quickly realized that my time and desire to be in Portland was as well. I loved the city, but ultimately, I was just passing through for a visit.

For purposes of the story, my friend Ian went on to get married and have two daughters. He created a successful health beverage company called Good Wolf, based out of Portland, Oregon. Ian was a brother that was always helpful. He's someone I'm proud to say I've watched with pride, grow up from the darkest of paths with me, and become a great father, personal success, and light on this earth.

CHAPTER 8

✹ THE WORLD'S UNDERTOW ✹

⊛ California: Part 3

After my chef opportunity in Portland ended, I quickly exhausted my financial resources. I relied on a small amount of money I made from selling my recipes to the restaurant owner before I left. The money I had was barely enough to get me out of Portland.

I was unclear as to the direction forward. As I reflected on what to do, I kept getting the sense I was being guided away from work in the food industry. When I prayed and meditated to gain clarity on the direction forward, I continued to get the message that a career change was upcoming. I just had no clue what exactly that change would be.

I continued to live in the present, trusting God and maintaining inherent belief in myself. I knew if my decision-making always came from a heart of healthy intention, then I would remain in harmony with the universe. As much as my use of forethought was missing and how ungrounded my mind was, I still held true to my trust in Destiny and always felt my guidance from The Creator would lead me in the correct direction.

Before I left Atlanta for Portland, I had begun a long-distance relationship with a Latina woman named Marcella. She was living in Long Beach, California. Marcella was a woman I had met online through a vegan raw food website. The relationship grew while I was in Portland, with her coming to visit me while I was there.

When things were ending in Portland, I decided that the best course of action would be to move back to California. I didn't know what to do or where I would stay when I got there. I didn't have any friends there other than Marcella, my friend Kyle who lived in Ventura County. I also had my grandmother, who lived in San Juan Capistrano.

At the time, my grandmother's husband of twenty years had recently passed away, just before my mother. My grandmother was living alone for the first time in her whole 81 years of life. As I figured out where I would stay when I got to California, my first option was to stay with Marcella in Long Beach until I got on my feet.

I drove straight from Portland to Long Beach, stopping only to get gas. It was an incredibly long drive, but it was necessary, seeing how I didn't have enough money for a hotel. I couldn't nap in my car because my small Hyundai Accent was packed with all my stuff, and I couldn't recline the seat. I made it to Marcella's house in the wee hours of the morning.

I had a deep soul connection with Marcella. But again, I wasn't looking at the day-to-day details of the situation. At that time, she lived in a small apartment while attending nursing school. She was constantly buried in her studies and seemed stressed out by it.

She was the type of person who had an extreme academic focus. School had always been her escape from early-life emotional trauma. School was a safe place from her family and past abusive boyfriends — it was a protective shield of sorts. Beyond that, nursing school required an enormous workload, so this allowed little time and energy for our relationship.

While I was there, I would make food for us and spend my time researching opportunities in the area. Although I sensed that my involvement in the health food industry was coming to a close, at the time it was still my only option, so I did my best to network with people in the community and figure out what my options were.

After about two months of us living together, Marcella hit her ceiling and deemed that me living there, and the relationship, were too much while having to deal with school. She decided that she wanted to put the relationship on pause and suggested we revisit it in the future. Although I understood, at the time I viewed it as weakness. Someone who could become overwhelmed that easily and glitch out was someone in which I couldn't place my emotional trust. My response was that I wasn't interested in revisiting the relationship in the future.

Typically, when something I'm invested in ends, I move onward with my life and don't circle back around. Looking back on it now, with us, that was an unfortunate stance to take because our potential was great, and we were aligned on the deepest levels. She's a woman I could've spent my life with.

◉ Agonizing Period of Transition

As my time with Marcella ended, I decided to stay with my friend Kyle in an area north of Los Angeles called Ventura. He opened his home to me and allowed me to stay with him for a little while until I got on my feet. I was grateful to him for doing so. Being in Ventura County didn't help with my next steps forward though. I eventually decided I would be much better off at my grandmother's house in Orange County because there was a larger community of health-minded individuals, which would potentially offer greater opportunities.

Through the time I was staying at Marcella's, Kyle's, and my grandmother's place, it was a period of uncertainty, and the transition seemed to last a lifetime. I continued to explore every opportunity with which I was aligned.

As this holding pattern continued, I found myself in a frustrated state, eager to make progress, yet unclear what or how to do so. I felt like a car in neutral that had the gas pedal pressed. All attempts at moving forward in the food industry turned up with nothing. This strange type of dissociated state came over me, where I seemed checked out. Almost defeated.

As kindly as possible, my grandmother tried to do everything she could to help. Though, her concerns often added to the pressure and conflict I was feeling. She was an extremely pragmatic, grounded, financially responsible woman. She'd been around very capable, extraordinarily successful, wealthy men throughout her life. She was Ms. Inglewood in the 1960s, and at one point in her life, she had the president of Mexico courting her as a romantic partner. I could sense her respect for men was oriented around a man's ability to produce worldly and financial success In her work career, she was one of the first executive-level women in the 5-star hotel industry when she was in her late 30s and 40s.

My grandmother didn't have the highest view of people of a spiritual nature who weren't successful or connected to the pragmatic world of finances. She looked down upon the spiritually-minded types, who were incapable on a worldly level. She would always sight one of her ex-husbands who drifted away from the world in pursuit of studying eastern Indian Hindu mysticism, which led her to have to support them both.

While I know she certainly loved me unconditionally, I could sense her disappointment in me. I noticed passive comments from her, which added to my unrest. The scenario led to an unspoken tension between us, which was the last thing I wanted.

As time crept forward, with me stuck at my grandmother's house, my frustrations rose, and so did my impatience.

I wasn't finding any legit opportunities, and zero significant opportunities were finding their way to me either. My desire was strong for any legitimate opportunity, which reflected my values. Regardless of my desire and searching, I continued coming up empty-handed and unclear. At this point of 2008, the money area was slim to none, and I had barely gotten by for the better part of nine years. I really grew to understand and appreciate how monks, yogis, and sadhus live with little to no money, mostly from donations and offerings. I still had to borrow from my grandmother to survive in the simplest of ways, even for simply buying groceries. I was mostly subsiding from almonds, bananas, and dates.

I eventually got a short-lived job at Marie Callender's in San Juan Capistrano. That wasn't for me, and I dreaded it. Back in Atlanta, I had told myself that I was moving on from being a server at restaurants, and I'd never do it again. Yet frustratingly, and from a place of desperation, there I was – and it wasn't even the type of restaurant from which I would even personally eat. I only lasted for about a month before my oppositional side marched me out the door.

Living and doing things my way, which was against the grain, was most natural to me. However, doing things my way, by far, wasn't the easiest, or even the wisest, from a financial perspective. At this point, I didn't want to conform and take the safe path. Amid the mounting pressures, I remained rigid in my position and refused to give up. I refused to change the direction of my path simply out of survival fear, financial need, or hardship. Did I have enough personality skills to do great in almost any sales-related job? Yes! Did I have the intelligence and determination to learn academically and be a working professional? By all means! Regardless of this, and regardless of how unclear the road ahead was at times, the reality was the nature of my destiny had its own direction and inertia. I recognized that I'd been given the opportunity to learn under great teachers and mentors in the past. Somehow, though unclear of the exacts, and with my faith wavering, it was all building toward something that would answer my hopes and eventually be self-sustaining.

I was being tested, and the test seemed mightier than ever before. Through hindsight, I now recognize that, at the time, regardless of how long and difficult this transitional stage went on, I was simply being ushered into a new stage of life. It was like everything in nature that takes its natural pace and course. Sometimes things require that little bit of extra patience for the road to open. At that point, the challenges make more sense, and your progress is even sweeter.

We are all encoded with what The Creator has designed for us. We're all prescribed a purpose, and the knowing, doing, and accomplishment of that is our soul's birthright – this is Destiny. Destiny is Law in existence. Everyone's organic part is of equal importance to the Whole. No matter the road to arriving at this, stay the course.

⚙ Pressure: Burst Pipes or Create Diamonds

My challenges, debt, and financial pressures were mounting. While in the previous nine years of my life in Atlanta, lack of money was more bearable. But for some reason, this stage of financial pressure was breaking down my patience.

Time continued forward, and the story remained the same. I was hitting a tipping point. I was unclear about what direction to go. I was becoming more face-to-face with my earthly challenges. My worries and frustrations around finances almost became my undoing. Being a man of self-respect and still asking for handouts from my grandmother to eat was humiliating.

I needed money, but I had always been opposed to receiving government assistance such as food stamps. That's not because I feel I'm too good for it, but because I thought it was an ingredient for potential complacency and codependence. I knew I could eventually pay my grandmother back, and I didn't want to get used to government assistance.

Not only was I borrowing money from my Grandmother, but I also began to borrow her disappointed perception of me. Unfortunately, I began to judge myself as incapable on a worldly level due to my spiritual mindedness. With haste and frustration, I became resistant to contemplative reflection and my spiritual studies and practices. I stopped praying and turned away from my relationship to God. In the name of being grounded and what I thought was, more "responsible," I shifted my sole focus onto the material-financial world.

Over the next coming years, this phase and change in me would bring forward a much lesser version of myself. A version of myself which wasn't indicative of all my spiritual studies and training through my twenties. It was a time filled with a handful of bad decisions and being in survival mode. The two things that remained the same, though, were: my awareness of our immortality as Spirit, and my desire to be truly helpful.

In hindsight I realize that all I really needed was balance and more patience. Being on the path of the sacred divine doesn't require renouncing the world. You can be fully spiritually awake and financially wealthy. The key is that you never allow the world and money to become your leading motivation. Our spiritual faculties should be given the opportunity to honorably guide our worldly life forward.

I eventually began to realize that money isn't the "root of all evil." It's the misuse of money, and/or the abuse of others for obtaining it, that is compromising. I gradually learned that the more success you have, and thus the more financial reward you receive, the more you can help others. So, bring value to the world and keep climbing and keep shining, and keep helping others up with what you've got.

✹ The Road Opens

After the tenth month of an extremely long wait for my next opportunity, I eventually discovered a woman who was a vegan raw food chef named Jenny Ross. Jenny owned a restaurant operation in Laguna Beach and was in the process of beginning a restaurant in Costa Mesa.

I contacted Jenny to arrange a job interview. When I met with her, I told her about my extensive experience with making food. She graciously offered me a position on their team. The pay was not much, but that didn't matter to me. I was super excited to be able to take a step forward and do something in alignment with my values. My job description was "prep chef," so I would work in the central kitchen and wait tables once the restaurant opened.

By this time my grandmother had begun promoting me to the local organizations and community groups she was a part of. She spoke to others about the healing arts methods I'd been trained in and that I was a gourmet raw food chef. One of the people she spoke to was a woman named Aileen. Aileen owned a retirement home in Orange County, and she was open to alternative healing treatments. She contacted me and eventually became a long-time client of mine.

Regardless of my grandmother's concerns and often sideways comments, she has always been my biggest fan and supporter. She is one of the people who showed the most belief in me, and I will always dearly appreciate that. There were times of difficulty when I began to lose belief in myself, but she was always there to push me forward and encourage me.

◉ Proposition 215

One of the biggest mistakes I made in this period was exploring the California medical marijuana movement. At this point, I'd been away from all mind-altering substances, including marijuana, for years. Although I had a general respect for cannabis, and knew it had its place, it wasn't conducive to disciplined spiritual practice and development.

The idea of this useful plant — which had been veiled with so much criminal stigma in my past — now being acceptable was something I found alluring and interesting. I decided I wanted to investigate. I received my medical marijuana license and began to use this extraordinarily potent, high-grade marijuana. With my highly addictive personality, occasional usage became frequent use, frequent use became stay high.

This marijuana was by far more powerful than anything I'd ever experienced in Atlanta. I had never had any herb that was this potent and disorienting. Being half out of my head would go on to play a hand in very questionable decision-making, which ended up teaching me more avoidable lessons.

For example, on one occasion, I had a friend named Ryan from Atlanta who was visiting the Orange County area. Ryan was a young man who, in the past, was one of my partners in crime. He was a recovered drug dealer who had reformed himself through traditional Christianity. At the time, he was out in California with his church group and wanted to connect with me. He happened to still be on probation from when he was arrested years previously.

When I went to meet him, I had just gotten off work at the raw food kitchen. The plan was to pick up Ryan and another friend, Sara, and take them to eat at the restaurant where I worked. Before heading out to pick them up, I went home and showered, and decided to puff some trees in my car at my grandmother's house.

Upon pulling out of my grandmother's driveway, I still had my herb on me. I picked up my friend Sara first and then Ryan, who was staying at a hotel in Lake Forest. I was in the process of leaving the hotel with the three of us in the car when I noticed there was a police officer parked on the other side of the street. Where the hotel was located, the exit was onto a street with a double yellow line. As I pulled out of the hotel parking lot, I needed to go left, and I crossed over the double yellow line to do so. Quickly after, the Lake Forest police pulled me over.

The police officer who pulled me over said she could smell the marijuana I had on me and immediately began to question me. I told her I had a license for the marijuana. She went back and forth with me about why I didn't have it in the trunk. In all the previous times I'd dealt with the police, this was the first time that I talked back and wasn't very compliant, which didn't help the situation at all.

The officer asked me to get out of the car and gave me a field sobriety test. At the time, I felt like I had passed, but she had a different view of the situation. The police then ran my record and discovered that I had an extensive criminal background. I was placed into custody and taken to jail for a marijuana DUI. I had to spend the night at Orange County Jail in Santa Ana.

The police allowed my friends to take my car. The next day Sara picked me up when I was released. I did not see or speak to Ryan for a long time afterward.

Although I respect the plant in its various useful applications, I was recreationally misusing it. I was consistently staying so high it was clouding my mind. My run-in with the law was a clear warning sign. This nonchalant attitude toward marijuana eventually led me to open doors that should've never been opened.

I eventually went to court for the marijuana DUI. With the representation of a public defender, I beat the charge. I had it reduced to reckless driving for crossing over a double yellow line. I stopped driving under the influence of marijuana after that, though its habitual overuse would continue for another few years.

CHAPTER 9

❊ SATURN'S RETURN ❊

It's said that between the ages of 27 and 32, the Universe presents a window of heightened tests and temptations. These tests represent the lessons you were supposed to learn through your teens and twenties. The process is referred to as "Saturn's return." Saturn's return acts as a rite of passage of sorts to determine if you're ready to move on to the next phases of your soul evolution. If you pass these tests, you move forward. If you don't, then you remain in a similar environment to your past experiences and lessons to relearn them. Revisiting and passing these karmic tests cement the steps for growing forward into new versions of oneself.

The first three-plus years of these tests – from 27 to 30 – I passed with flying colors. Though the final year of my Saturn's return, 31 years old, would prove to be a cosmic carrot dangle of temptation, filled with people making big, fast money and opportunities in the illicit designer drug world. Tests that tempestuously pulled and played upon my financial desperation and challenges at the time.

I had spent my twenties dedicated, disciplined, and humble, walking firmly on the path of my soul's growth and awakening. I had removed myself from the elements and influences of my teens. My life had changed, and I had shifted my values. I thought I was in the clear and that my past had been left in the dust. However, here at the end of my

Saturn's return, the ripest of opportunities for bad decision-making, fully reflective of my past, were about to land in my lap.

Simultaneously, at this same point in time, the next steps for my career training in the healing arts was made clear and laid out in front of me.

❀ The Revealing

The time was 2008, and I was 31 years old. I was beginning to spend more time in my native land of Los Angeles rather than Orange County at my grandmother's house. My hours at the vegan restaurant in Costa Mesa were slowing down. I thought it would be a good idea to begin networking in the city so I could find my way into more opportunities for financial growth and stability.

I began meeting people in the Los Angeles health-conscious eating community – which happened to intersect and be fused with the Burning Man, Grateful Dead, medical cannabis, psychedelic, and electronic music industry.

Some of my new friends were living lives of extreme financial abundance like I hadn't seen since my teens. This vast new social circle of friends opened doors to potential financial opportunities that were of massive temptation, considering how I was chronically in debt and struggling financially.

At this same juncture, I reconnected with groups of my friends from the past in Atlanta, who had moved to Los Angeles. Friends from the past and now new friends from the present were all converging into a singular social circle. Through all of us hanging out, everyone ended up meeting and going on to develop close connections. The next thing I knew there was an absolute inferno of abundance. There were parties, huge gatherings, feasts of the most nutritious foods, trips to Vegas, and amounts of money that were enticing for me at the time. The people I was meeting in these communities were very open-minded and easy to get along with.

I was introduced to friends of friends and more people quite quickly. One of the people I met in the Los Angeles scene introduced me to his older brother, Richard. Richard, or Rich, was my age, and was someone with whom I shared similar values and interests with.

Richard was a highly intelligent, multi-talented person, a music producer, musician, day trader, and a seasoned raw food chef. He was exceptionally well-versed in advanced nutritional health practices, Chinese herbalism, psychedelics, mineral supplementation, yoga, and martial arts. He also had a foot in the door of the boutique marijuana world and had been selling modest amounts of medical marijuana in Los Angeles for years. Richard had a vast social circle of wealthy, socially-influential people.

Richard and I hit it off immediately and developed a solid rapport of mutual respect. As I spent more time in Los Angeles, my friendship with Rich grew quickly. There seemed to be a soul-understanding between us. Like myself, he didn't drink alcohol, and he was into health-conscious living. He had a general grasp and open-mindedness to spiritual matters, but he also knew how to carry himself in the streets. He had a grounded mind regarding money, business, and resources. He lived in Santa Monica, which was close to most everything else.

Beyond being a successful producer, Rich also owned multiple medical marijuana shops in the Los Angeles area. To add to this, he also owned commercial-size marijuana farms up north. He was an extremely resourceful person. He knew everyone in the psychedelic community. He had bicoastal connections and involvement in commercial business operations, which were at a whole other level.

Rich's social circle was vast. While hanging out and building our friendship, I met most of his friends, customers, and connections in the cannabis world. Most were farmers and cultivators from both Northern California and Southern California. I was suddenly integrated into a community of successful people in their industry. These people had access to hundreds upon hundreds of pounds of boutique marijuana – people with resources at the largest scale imaginable. I saw they were all safe, good-hearted people.

There was something about the abundance and the excitement of it all that was alluring to me. Before this, while stowing away at my grandmother's house for the last year, I'd been removed from any form of social interaction. I had only been around my grandmother for quite a while up to that point. After coming out of this hermit's stage, I found it stimulating and nourishing to be meeting so many new progressive people.

While spending more time in L.A., the doors finally opened where I discovered what the next steps to my slowly-unfolding vocational training in the healing arts were going to be. During one of my visits, I was getting food at a local restaurant and happened to pick up one of the LA spiritual newsletter magazines. I scanned through it to see what was going on in the community and learn about events and practitioners of the healing arts who were promoting themselves.

As I got to the back of this publication, I saw a full-page ad for a hypnotherapy college named Hypnosis Motivation Institute. The ad grabbed my attention in a way that would not let me go – it grabbed my attention on a Soul level. With everything in me, I knew that I needed to look further into this school and pursue it as my next step in education in the healing arts. I researched more about the school, such as their intro classes and where the school was located, and I began to assess the possibility of enrolling.

Hypnosis Motivation Institute

Shortly thereafter I went and took a tour of the school and enrolled. I felt the peace of Destiny in my soul about the training. I could feel with all my heart that it was exactly where I needed to be. The school was in Tarzana, California, which is the northern area of the Valley. The only drawback was the distance between the school and where I was living in San Juan Capistrano. With Los Angeles traffic, the drive between the two places was approximately two hours.

Luckily for me, my friends offered me a place to crash as I began my training at the college. Having places to sleep part-time was crucial, and it is something that, to this day, I am still extremely grateful for. At the same time, these environments in Los Angeles put me right smack dab in the middle of lifestyles and opportunities that in hindsight, was a wild environment for me to be in considering my checkered past.

My curriculum at the hypnotherapy college required me to be in regular class two times a week and weekly practicums and weekend workshops. I was right at home in my training at the school. The school, HMI, was super professional and highly reputable for being the first accredited college for hypnotherapy. It was the first official *school* environment I had been in for vocational training in the healing arts.

❀ Fool's Gold

At this stage of my process, I had a well-developed social circle, had a car, and had begun school. Though I still needed to figure out how to create supplemental income. I needed to pay for my food, travel, and bills while living between Los Angeles and South Orange County for school. I was making a small amount of earnings doing sessions in my then *avocational,* healing arts practice, but it was just crumbs – not even anything I could cover my food and gas expenses with.

I was around friends who were millionaires, and the environment was exceedingly abundant. They all knew I didn't have money, and they were always very sharing and helpful when I needed it. I was treated like royalty. All the luxuries and fruits of their lifestyle were shared with me freely. There were large group vacations, big parties being thrown, and as much of the most expensive health food as you could imagine.

It was all very seductive at the time. There was visible abundance and wealth all around me. Though I still couldn't afford my own place to live or even pay my bills. I would've been homeless if it weren't for my grandmother. My financial reality remained the same as it had been the last ten years — standing next to zero. I never at any one point in time had more than $2,000 to my name. My bank account was perpetually in overdraft.

My survival challenges had been present for so long that I started to expect it would always be that way. It was like a constant vacuum of inertia pulling me into further financial need, debt, and concern.

To add to my financial need, I was also witnessing my grandmother begin to lose her house. This was all happening a short while after the 2008 housing market crash. She had already remortgaged her home, and she spent every day worrying about losing her only remaining life investment. Considering all the help she had given me countless times, everything in me wanted to help her salvage her home.

Richard, noticing my struggles, gave me twenty pounds of marijuana to try and sell at the local medical marijuana dispensaries. From an ethics standpoint, I saw nothing wrong with selling farm-grown California marijuana. I deduced that there was nothing morally wrong or dangerous about the situation. I knew the medical marijuana was from honest sources, hippie farmers, and that my efforts would not be leading to profits that funded people whose values were inherently unaligned with mine. No one involved was affiliated with mafia groups or huge criminal enterprises connected to cocaine, heroin, methamphetamines, or illegal firearms.

After two vastly disappointing weeks, I discovered the industry was already extremely flooded with inventory. The shops had all the suppliers they needed to keep their shelves fully stocked. My every attempt proved to be a futile waste of time, energy, and gas money, driving from place to place, chasing the dangling carrot of Los Angeles medical marijuana profits.

Once this didn't work, other potential opportunities were presented to me, both by Richard as well as other friends. What I noticed was that with each new opportunity, the risk versus reward ante was upped majorly. I was fully trusted and accepted by everyone around me, so any resource I wanted to try my hand in was readily available to me. The tug-o-war between huge financial resources and my situation was a real struggle at this stage. Not having money and being in constant neediness for so long had become an old story. My willpower was wavering.

The opportunities offered to me were gargantuan – some of which were downright dangerous. But all of which would have given me the opportunity to make hundreds of thousands of dollars, get out of debt, and help salvage my grandmother's home.

One of the opportunities offered to me was to manage and co-own a massive mushroom growing operation. That was followed by an opportunity to broker thousands of pounds of boutique cannabis through various cities on the east coast. Another group of friends wanted me to be the liaison for moving thousands of pounds of Mexican cartel marijuana every week. I had another friend give me more than a pound of DMT on consignment to go sell. There were opportunities to get involved with sales of gargantuan amounts of all types of psychedelics for that matter. I had another person offering to help me start a large medical marijuana growing operation.

The interesting thing about these opportunities was that the Universe just wasn't having it. Either before or immediately after the starting line, things would end up in some form of massive sabotage.

As well, although I was desperate and in survival mode, with every opportunity, I was always one foot out and one foot in, and hesitant to go all-in. I knew the extensive amount of time it would require to be involved with the opportunities I'd been offered. It was a level of time and dedication I didn't have - and more importantly, it was a level of risk I wasn't willing to take.

I was in school and finally moving forward with my training in the healing arts and was on my way to becoming a professional for the first time in my life. I had to come to terms with the fact that I wasn't going to be able to help her, even though I had the means to do so.

❀ The Betrayal of Self

By this point, I had all but completely suspended my spiritual practices and the application of spiritual knowledge I had spent the previous 10 years developing. Marijuana had replaced meditation; worldly thinking had replaced spiritual focus; socializing had replaced contemplation; financial worries replaced my trust in God, and bullish self-determination had replaced surrender to inner guidance.

My mind had become out of coherence with Spirit. I no longer used deeper awareness to witness to and recognize the sacred Light within others. Instead, I was seeing people through the lens of opportunity: seeing others for the potential resources they offered for my survival and worldly well-being. This was blinding and dishonoring to everything I had grown to know as sacred. My heart remained loving and kind, and I still was committed to helping others, yet I was operating like a blind shell of myself, constantly high on potent marijuana and in survival mode.

Marijuana was always around me and given to me freely. But using it amplified my mental loop of thinking about my financial problems. Life kept happening, bills were ever-present, and I was in perpetual need.

Outside of when I was with my friends, I was eating little. My blood sugar was often so imbalanced my hands would be shaky. I was living on rations. Like through my twenties, I was primarily living on almond and banana smoothies. Regardless of being malnourished, I was running on survival adrenaline, and I had a *push through it* mentality. My body weighed around 130 pounds. Which at 6-foot height, that's not healthy.

Not only did I remain under the influence of high-grade boutique marijuana daily, at a point, but it also began getting combined with a mixture of loose-leaf, American Spirit tobacco, sage, and other forms of herbs. With my addictive genetics, it was one of the most foolish decisions possible for me to pick up a habit of tobacco use. In the past, I had a vicious addiction to nicotine. Tobacco and I were not the best of friends. This was a very foolish mistake, and it would end up requiring tremendous, inhuman effort over time, utilizing hypnotherapy and other tools, to pry the nicotine out of my system.

⚙ The Avalanche Begins

After the first year of spending time with my friends in Los Angeles, I began witnessing the most unfortunate series of events. With their growing profits came greater spending. Greater spending naturally led to people taking larger risks to support their lifestyle. Larger risks meant the size of potential disasters increased as well. When a project that had large money on the line somehow went wrong, it was devastating for everyone involved. A single fumble could mean everyone involved would lose their entire year's earnings. Failing projects and losses accumulated, and the next thing I knew, strange sides of people were emerging.

Around this time (at the worst time possible) the use of alcohol entered the mix. Its use was like pouring gasoline on a growing wildfire. It became a profoundly sabotaging element. With massive amounts of money, stress, huge losses, and alcohol use, integrity issues followed.

I was in disbelief at times at the things I was witnessing. The integrity issues were around misappropriation of money, and betrayals having to do with women. Things started going super sideways, quickly.

I'd never been a drinker at any point in my life, nor am I now, but in this period, I joined the charade and began consuming tequila here and there with them. This led to a few fun times, but more times than not it led to foolish mistakes and questionable decisions. Alcohol brings out the lower animal impulses. It induces heartless lust, which attracts astral entities and demons into people's auric field. These influences cause people to go after sexual partners they would never typically be attracted to – and as well, partners not in alignment with The Creator's Will for them.

Alcohol was just one of the ingredients involved in my friends' recipe for disaster. They began taking spontaneous trips to Las Vegas for alcohol-fueled *weeks* of gambling. I accompanied them on a few trips to Vegas. On one occasion I witnessed Rich sit down at a high-limit blackjack table and turn $10,000 into over $150,000. Although it was exhilarating to observe while it was happening, it was all seductively deceptive in the bigger picture. Winning money at a casino is nothing to throw yourself a parade over, but as it was happening, everyone was celebrating it.

I observed that winning at gambling, especially when mixed with liquor, lulls a person into a false sense of god-like confidence, which increases the impulse to gamble more. This usually always leads to losing more than you will ever win in the long run. Sure enough, in time, that was the case. Eventually, the money I observed my friends lose was in the hundreds of thousands. They seemed to be unphased by the losses. I couldn't tell if their nonchalant attitude in the face of massive losses was coming from confidence or irresponsibility.

Nonetheless, between the losses from business transactions going bad to gambling, it was all a bit over my head. Being someone who was in perpetual survival mode, watching people losing hundreds of thousands of dollars or more at a time, and simply dusting it off and moving on, unphased, was headshaking to me.

⊛ Held Hostage

As things progressed forward with Rich and his community, his slow avalanche continued. None of it was getting any better. Past failures and losing money while gambling and debts led to further misappropriation of money from different projects, creating a dangerous juggling act. The more he tried to climb out of certain holes, the deeper others got. Pressures began to snowball, and he was forced to bring added resources into his pipeline to help him take care of past debts from failed projects.

At times, I would reflect on the sequence of events since I had met Rich around 6 months ago. To me it was unfortunate what I was witnessing. There were enormous amounts of money lost; increasingly expensive lifestyles mixed with liquor and gambling; lack of integrity with women, and blind pride. But through it all somehow, Rich was still kind, sharing, and respectful toward me regardless.

Here I was, witnessing all of this, in an environment where I didn't belong – an environment that was about to lead to major danger by association for me!

Rich was a highly-resourceful person who was very generous to everyone around him. In business, he was trusting and optimistic – even irresponsibly trusting and optimistic. His business model was primarily based on consignment. When he consigned things to his customers and working partners, eventually, there were hiccups, accidents, or flat-out tragedies leading to substantial financial losses. Often these unfortunate events happened at the worst of times. From what I noticed when I was around, an avalanche was continuing to pick up momentum in its devastation.

The pressure mounting upon Rich became severe. He was a quiet-natured person and didn't like confrontation when things went bad. Although he had a very calm and passive disposition, the stress had to have been unbearable. The frustration that followed projects gone wrong eventually led him to retreat. At times, I wouldn't hear from him for weeks in a row. This was especially the case when people were upset over a business exchange gone bad. When suppliers didn't get their money by the expected time, or when projects led to a loss, he'd often avoid taking the call, which would only make things progressively worse.

Knowing I was a close friend of his, people would often come to me and ask me to help them track Rich down. Disgruntled people would even try to bribe me to help them find him. At one point, there were *many* people looking for him all at once, but I never sold him out.

On one of these occasions, Rich had obtained a large amount of boutique marijuana from a supplier that was from San Francisco. I would go on to learn that this person's money somehow got lost in the shuffle, and then communication was lost between the two. The supplier was a laid-back Northern California farmer, but little did Rich know, the guy had ties with gang members from Watts and Compton — a fact that I, unfortunately, came to discover firsthand.

After missing the agreed-upon date for payment multiple times, the supplier tried to contact Richard for two weeks straight to no avail. Once he finally contacted Rich, there was a new date set, which he also defaulted on. In response to this, the supplier gathered his friends and waited at the outer gates of Rich's home recording studio to try and catch him coming home or leaving. This went on for three days.

Through mutual friends, they tracked me down to a friend's house I was visiting. They approached me and asked me where Rich was. At the time, I had no clue where he was. I hadn't spoken with him in weeks. They explained the situation to me and sternly told me that I would have to come with them. They told me that I needed to locate him and tell him it was imperative that he show up and meet with them.

They made it clear that they were carrying guns. I was then escorted to their car. Once we made it to the car, I was hesitant to get in. I told them I was a convicted felon and couldn't be in the car with guns. The supplier said that he was a convicted felon as well, and he didn't want to be in this situation having to carry a gun either – especially over something so easily fixable. Sternly, he told me to get in the car. I complied and got into the backseat where his armed friend was.

They forced me to give them my ID, my car keys, my business cards with my home office addresses, containing my phone number on them. They ordered me to get a hold of Rich, however possible. Much to my concern, I couldn't reach him on his phone. They were very firm in expressing to me that they were willing to hold me hostage for as long as necessary until they got a response from Rich. I was nervous, but I kept my composure and did my best to track him down.

To reach him, I had to contact his then-girlfriend and explain the severity of the situation. I asked her to contact him and explained where he needed to meet us. She called him immediately and explained the situation. Here I was, held hostage for something I knew nothing about and was in no way involved in. All the supplier wanted was a sit-down meeting with Rich to discuss where his money was and how it would be repaid.

Thank God Rich showed up that night. They had their meeting, while I sat there in disappointment. They agreed on exact dates for when the money would be delivered, and they wrote down all my information, including my office addresses on my business cards, then gave me all my personal belongings back. They made it clear that if Rich didn't come up with the supplier's money, I would be getting a visit at work.

The scenario was on the serious side of things. I didn't want violence to come upon either one of us. Rich paid off his debt with them within the following month, and everything was fixed.

That was the final straw. To have my wellbeing, and even my life, threatened because of a friendship was sobering.

Afterward, I separated myself from Rich, though I still maintain a brotherly love for him. I hold a great appreciation for the times Rich, and everyone else, helped me: times when I didn't have enough money to simply eat, get gas for my car, pay a parking ticket, or get my car out of the impound. We had fun times, and I was able to develop a solid friendship with Rich and his community of pirates and artists.

I significantly distanced myself from most everyone in those social circles. And I did so out of self-respect and dedication to my true path. There were a handful of people from that time, the ones not involved with illicit business, that I went on to develop solid friendships with. There were also people I met in that period, who went on to become clients of mine in my healing arts practice.

Through all of this, I was somehow able to pass Saturn's return temptations and trials by fire and proceed forward to the next phases of my soul's evolutionary path. I reinforced my previous lessons *once again* around financial opportunism, healthy social environments, and practicing wiser boundaries.

⚙ The Avalanche Ends

Around three months after being held hostage, Rich's door was kicked in by the Ventura County police. They were executing a search and arrest warrant. They ransacked his recording studio and home looking for psychedelics because of multiple controlled sales cases that had taken place with a woman who had turned state's evidence against him. The police were looking for several drugs, yet they didn't find any. The only thing that they did find were pounds of medical marijuana that he was licensed to possess legally. Nonetheless, he was taken into custody and arrested for the controlled sales cases.

Things had been going badly for him for quite a while. The situation with the police was just the icing on the cake. A multitude of projects had already fallen apart, most which led to massive losses and debt. On top of the mounting pressures, he'd become an alcoholic in the process. The avalanche had been continual.

Rich, ultimately, was a good brother. He was someone who when I first met him, wasn't a drinker: a young man of a healthy and holistic mind, body, and spirit. He was extremely gifted and artistically talented as a musician and producer. But in an unfortunate swing of events, in a short amount of time, he had gotten swallowed whole by the game. People had taken advantage of him. He owed money in all directions. His property and cars were being repossessed. And people who previously trusted him had begun to lose confidence in him.

Life lessons can be unrelenting, sobering, and unfortunate at times. Every person is responsible for making their own decisions, with integrity. Speaking from personal experience, when, or if, a massive financial gain finds you, take it in stride and let the experience filter through the Light and beauty of your heart of hearts. Operate with integrity and maturity – and ideally use your abundance for creating things that bring true value to other people's lives and the earth.

For the story's sake, Rich went on to get probation, attempted to successfully rebuild his life, was met with more adversity, produced a successful record, and eventually met a woman with whom he began his life. They got married, had two children, and started a family. He eventually got clean and sober from alcohol.

CHAPTER 10

✸ DESTINY ✸

While attending HMI, I took it all very seriously. I naturally excelled, and the material all seemed like second nature to me. Having eleven years of training in the healing arts under my belt before I began school was immensely helpful.

HMI was like its own version of Hogwarts for the healing arts. I loved everything about the school — the trainers, the training, and the academic environment. The class size was perfect for learning, interaction, and practice. I met great people while I was there.

The things I learned at HMI gave me a well-rounded skill set that allowed me to help people on the mental, emotional, and behavioral level. It was a complementary addition to the spiritual knowledge gained from my past mentors and teachers.

While I was going through the curriculum, the students were assigned to a mentor and were granted complimentary sessions with them. The treatments were profoundly helpful personally, while also helping me to further my understanding of how the craft of hypnotherapy works. Throughout college, I would go on to receive around nine or ten sessions.

I went to school three or more days a week and applied myself to the best of my ability. Due to living so far away, and how the curriculum hours were arranged, I ended up falling behind on the hours I needed from weekend workshops and practicums.

My living situation posed significant challenges to my school life. Although I was grateful to have landing pads in LA, sleeping on couches and floors comes with its own challenges. By the third day of not sleeping in a bed, I felt a bit off, especially during the sweltering summer days. My friends who I stayed with in Burbank didn't have an air conditioner and lived smack dab in the armpit of the canyon — blazing hot, sweaty, and uncomfortable.

The financial pressures of not having money, mixed with not eating enough and marijuana use, had me a bit all over the place in my head. My sleeping arrangements added to my disjointedness.

After being in LA for part of the week for school, I would retreat to the cozy confines of my grandmother's place in Orange County, unwind, take a shower, and sleep in a comfortable bed. It was so peaceful there — a dramatic difference from the high-paced nature of Los Angeles.

At around the seven-month mark of school, my grandma and I were met with a new layer of adversity. She had an unfortunate accident one night where she fell and broke her hip. The accident led to a hip replacement surgery. Consequently, I had to spend more time in San Juan Capistrano to assist her and help her with day-to-day tasks. This caused me to fall behind on my curriculum hours at school. School and caretaking were a lot to balance, especially considering the two-hour drive between her house and school at HMI.

⊛ Serendipity

Around two months before my graduation time at HMI, I was still very behind on certain types of curriculum hours, and I was in jeopardy of not graduating on time.

Around March, the student counselor, Tanya Nord, pulled me aside and, with concern, told me the number of hours I was behind. She said that I needed to make up the hours somehow. Considering it was the stage of the training where our internship involved direct client sessions, she proposed I make up my hours through sessions.

At this point, with graduation only three months away, the only way I was going to pull off graduating in time was by being thrown to the lions and doing live sessions with real clients. I was excited for the opportunity but also nervous at the same time. This would be a true baptism by fire. I had confidence in what I had learned up to that point, yet there was a part of me that was frankly terrified of seeing clients so quickly. It was a major growth moment for me as I was forced out of my shell and comfort zones.

Though challenging, I knew these in-person sessions would give me the experience and confidence I needed once I graduated. Obtaining my hours this way became immensely helpful. Seeing so many clients in my internship primed me to become a professional as soon as I graduated – not to mention it allowed me to graduate on time.

As the months rolled forward, I worked with client after client. I was a bit rocky in my first few sessions, but everything got smoother and I stuck to my training. I ended up doing a little over 110 sessions in my internship. By the time I was complete, my confidence was blazing.

Many of the clients I worked with remained my paying clients after I graduated. The beauty of this was that those same clients began to refer their friends and family to me. On top of that, of those referrals, they as well referred their friends and family to me. To ice the cake, most of these clients were in Orange County, the area I would eventually find my perfect office and office partners.

I ended up graduating on time with a full-time practice in place. I was seeing between sixteen and twenty-five clients a week. Although I didn't know it at the time, an average of twenty sessions a week is a substantial amount for a hypnotherapist, much less a hypnotherapist just graduating. This momentum continued throughout my first year as a professional and set a great precedent for what to expect in subsequent years. Over 8,000 sessions of experience later, I credit my internship and the first year of my practice for laying the foundation for the long-term progress and consistency in my professional practice.

Sometimes people enter our lives and play a role or have an influence over our lives that is far bigger than they could ever know or understand at the time. Although she was just doing her job as the student counselor, the creative solution Tanya came up with for me paved the way for what became an extremely successful career. I am forever grateful to Tanya Nord, and anytime I can tell her, I do so. To this day, I view her as a major instrument of God in my life – an assistant to my destiny if you will.

⊛ Mental Bank

While at HMI, one of my classes was on a subconscious-mind tool called the "Mental Bank." The Mental Bank was one of the main creations that the founder of the school, John Kappas, had developed through his long and storied career as a clinical hypnotherapist.

The Mental Bank was designed to reinforce and strengthen clients' progress outside of sessions. It's a small journal that accompanies a book called *Success Is Not an Accident: The Mental Bank Concept* by John Kappas. The Mental Bank, when done every night before going to sleep, gradually, yet effectively, lifts the subconscious ceiling of limitation we set on our success and deserving of reward. Our success is contingent upon our subconscious beliefs and feelings of deserving.

The theory behind this nightly accumulative approach is that it plays into the pace the subconscious *most* prefers to grow. Working with the subconscious mind in this manner allows a person to succeed in higher levels of success without the law of subconscious homeostasis sabotaging things.

On the day of the Mental Bank class, the words streaming from George Kappas's mouth while teaching were like music to my soul. At the time, as mentioned in previous chapters, I was barely scraping by – if that! I didn't have money for food, and I was making less than $600 a month. Financially, I had felt perpetually stuck at zero for a long time. Every word of the Mental Bank class that day hit home with me. The class was emotionally moving for me. I had discovered the missing piece; a major underpinning in the cause-and-effect nature of the mind to our outer world reality – and I felt hope! So much so that I even shed a tear or two.

⊛ Graduation

After accumulating all the credit hours that I needed in my internship, I graduated with honors in 2009. My grandmother came to my graduation ceremony. In all honesty, it was one of the proudest moments of my life.

Here I was, a professional. I had a vocational ability to help others, and just nine years previously, I was a three-strike felony offender for drug dealing, addicted to methamphetamines, facing a potentially lengthy prison sentence as a career criminal.

I know many of my readers have far more academic achievements than I'm expressing excitement for here, but at the time, this was big for me — especially considering my past! In my eyes, success isn't purely about what a person has achieved or created. Success is more about the things people achieve relative to their starting point and what they must overcome to do so.

I went on to build my practice both full-time in Orange County and part-time in Los Angeles. My first year was massively successful. And to attest to the quality of training I received from HMI, throughout my first year, I shared an office with three other hypnotherapists, all of us sharing one group calendar. I saw between twenty and thirty clients a week, while all the others *combined* saw around six to eight clients a week at most — all of them having been trained outside of HMI.

While at my office doing sessions with clients, I was more at peace than I'd ever been. I was a professional for the first time in my life. I wore business-casual work clothes Everywhere! I wanted to always represent myself professionally, wherever I may be, prepared to promote my practice.

Although I was horrible at saving it, I was earning good money legally for the first time in my life. I was doing what I loved while helping people. It had been a long road of struggling financially and not knowing the road ahead. Finally, I was moving forward!

Although with magnificent progress, the first year of my practice was no walk in the park. Immediately upon graduating, there was tremendous pressure on my shoulders with the type of clients and presenting issues which I was helping people with. Serious issues that were as raw and real as it gets. People with severe, lifelong problems.

Most of my clients required a referral clearance from their primary doctor, psychiatrist, or psychologist, to work with them. These clients had a history of suicidal ideation, extreme emotional conflict, trauma, and/or abuse. These were clients with issues deeply rooted in their subconscious from childhood, oftentimes causing addiction issues they were battling against as well.

Regardless of how heavy the issues were, I was there to be helpful to the best of my ability. With every client I gained invaluable experience. I'd never experienced a greater peace than when I was there in my office working with my clients. That remains the same to this day.

⊛ Building Momentum

As the first year of my hypnotherapy practice unfolded, I took the responsibility of growing in my craft very seriously. I put down the use of marijuana and was making great strides in my professional practice. That first year I facilitated around nine hundred treatments. Ninety percent of my clients came from word-of-mouth referrals. With every session, my confidence grew. I learned exponentially about my craft in that first year of sessions – far more than I had learned in school.

The first three months of growing professionally and earning more money, I had to recondition unhealthy habits. Primarily the habit of not planning my meals and not eating regularly. I'd gone so long famished and in poverty, my forethought around caloric intake was almost nonexistent. Instead of pre-planning my food for the workday, so I could nourish myself in between clients, I would just barrel through the day on adrenaline rather than nutrients.

Eventually this changed and flipped into a different problem: spending way too much money on eating out at health-conscious restaurants.

In those beginning months of my private practice, I got into a bad three-car accident, totaling my Hyundai Accent. The accident left me in a situation where I had to borrow my grandmother's car.

On one occasion while using my grandma's car to see clients, a red-colored couch had fallen out of the back of a truck and was sitting there in the left lane of the freeway. As I began to hit the brakes in my grandmother's 1990's Ford Taurus, the brakes locked up, and the car fishtailed off the left side of the 5 freeway and flipped over. The police arrived and helped me out of the car, and by the grace of God, I survived.

In a brief period, I'd been in two serious car accidents, both partially due to the poor performance of the cars I was driving.

I needed a quality car for the constant trips between Orange County and Los Angeles for work. Since I was making decent money for the first time, I decided to invest in a nice car. I partly looked at it as a benchmark reward to myself for all that I had gone through getting there.

⊛ Paying Dues

The first few years of my practice, I only charged around $75 a session. Since I was in the early stages of my career, I saw it as a stage of building experience and paying dues. I wanted to build as much experience as humanly possible and so I purposefully set my rates low so that people could more easily afford the sessions. This proved to be an excellent strategy that helped me to build massive experience points and sharpen my craft.

I was busy and was doing better financially than I ever had in my legal life. I got a little spoiled by my instantaneous success and figured that my continuous growth would just continue that way.

Although I was earning a decent living, my relationship with money was still impulsive and irresponsible. I was finally able to pay my own bills, but all the rest I'd spend on eating out at vegan restaurants without budgeting my lifestyle.

Finally, having money to eat out at healthy restaurants, at will, for the first time in forever was a much-needed boost in my morale – especially after going through so many years of scraping by, eating soaked almonds and bananas, and having to ask for handouts.

My spending habits as an adult were a bit reflective of my teens as a drug dealer. As I made more money, I ramped up my impulse to spend. I still wasn't making enough to save or pay off any debts. The inflated gas costs, and most everything else in Southern California, were consuming my earnings quickly. I assisted my grandmother and stayed at her house, but I had an overhead larger than I'd had the previous nine years.

At the time, it was 2010, two years since the financial crisis of 2008. As mentioned in the previous chapter, my grandmother, who had already reverse-mortgaged her home, was in jeopardy of losing it. Knowing how much my grandmother loved her home in San Juan Capistrano and how difficult moving at her age is, nothing would've made me happier than to be able to help her save her home. She had helped me so much over the last ten years (to the tune of more than $25,000). Regardless of wanting to save my grandma's home, I had to accept once again that I wasn't going to be able to pull it off. I would need to be further along in my career to help her solely through my professional earnings, and I just wasn't there yet.

It was a sad time for both of us. Within four years, she had lost her husband after a long stretch of helping him through blindness and dementia. Within three months of his passing, she lost her daughter, my mom, after trying to help her through a tortured life. After this, her brother also passed away. She then broke a hip, which required hip replacement surgery. Now, she had to come to terms with losing her home.

By the grace of God, her sister had a small condominium in Long Beach about forty minutes away, which she invited her to live in. Through all of it, my grandmother maintained a kind and loving disposition. She has always been a ray of love that brightens my life.

It's one of my goals to eventually begin a nonprofit organization that helps save elderly widow's homes from being lost.

My first year in my hypnotherapy office

⊛ An Archangel Named Azrael

After the first year and a half of my private practice, as my 33rd birthday approached, I began to experience the first dip in clientele. My practice went from seeing an average of twenty clients a week down to around eight or less. I wasn't sure how to react to the situation, but at the time, I was worried. I hadn't saved any of my earnings from my practice up to that point. I had new financial responsibilities, debts, overdraft fees, and not to mention taxes. I had begun my career with such momentum I figured that it would always just be that way – the last thing I was expecting was financial uncertainty again. It was a feeling of *oh no not again.*

Going through another phase of financial inconsistency quickly began to wear on me psychologically. The uncertainty caused me to question if I was even on the correct path. I even thought about changing my career path out of the healing arts altogether and instead seek something that had more consistency. Familiar concerns and worries around survival crept upon me.

It was summertime, and as is the norm in Los Angeles, friends were visiting from various parts of the country. One was a friend from my distant past in Atlanta. When I met with this friend, he was very enthusiastic about me providing him with a hundred pounds or more of cannabis every two weeks. Although I had made up my mind that I would stay away from all those types of resources and dealings, the option was tempting considering my neediness. Another dangling carrot... at another point of desperation!

With my practice sputtering and in need, this opportunity would have allowed me to make upwards of 20k a month. I knew all the people necessary to facilitate this type of request. I was quite conflicted and decided to take some time and give the opportunity a second thought before getting back to him. The proposal had me playing tug-o-war within for a little while. If the opportunity were to work, it would have produced the finances I needed to potentially salvage my grandmother's home while also giving me a cushion during any dips in my practice.

I thought it would be a wise idea to do a series of hypnotherapy sessions in the face of my challenges. The sessions would be with my hypnotherapist, whom I had successfully worked with at HMI. I was comfortable working with her, and she had helped me significantly in the past.

When I saw my hypnotherapist, I explained the dilemma I was in and the opportunity in front of me. I asked her what she felt I should do, and her response was, "If you have the chance to make $20,000 a month, do so safely." I found her response to be a real head-scratcher! Especially considering that she knew about my past trouble. To this day, I'm still a bit in disbelief when I think about her response.

Regardless of her encouragement, and all other factors, I was hesitant. But I didn't know what to do. I held off on giving my friend any definitive answer to his request.

I decided to schedule my next hypnotherapy session for the day of my 33rd birthday - which was right around the corner. My hypnotherapist was generous enough to give me the session as a gift for my birthday. We decided in advance to do the session with a therapeutic focus on what is called "inner child" work. The thinking was that the root of my pattern of financial inconsistencies resulted from early childhood programming I had learned from my mother, who couldn't keep food in our fridge or a roof over our head as I was growing up.

I arrived at HMI for my session at around noon. It was all a normal process, and it felt like any other time we had worked together in the past, aside from the fact it was my birthday.

As I sat down and leaned back in the recliner, she began to guide me into the state of hypnosis. Naturally, I became very relaxed, as is customary when going into this state. My eyes closed, and I was through the usual progressive relaxation process. After the progressive relaxation, she began the suggestive therapy. Everything seemed like hypnotherapy sessions with her in the past.

Around two minutes into the suggestive therapy, I began to feel a series of undulating waves starting in my feet and moving all the way up to the top of my head. Wave after wave after wave, they continued. I took close notice, as I had never experienced this feeling during a hypnotherapy session before. The waves continued for about a minute. As they did though, my hypnotherapist's voice faded out.

The next thing I knew, a Being appeared, taking up most of the screen of my vision. This Being had on a golden robe. It had wings furled in, down along the side of his body, with long, silver-whitish hair. He had eyes that looked like mini suns. It was an Angel.

"Hello, my name is Azrael," this golden-gowned Angel said. "I've come here today to tell you not to worry. We've been preparing you for many years to do very important work in the near future." A great peace came over me and my previously-worried mind was calmed.

I was then shown a sequence of visual imagery, like a slide show in chronological order, all my teachers/mentors and learning guides that had been brought into my life since my teens. The string of visions began with Son. Then I was shown an image of *A Course in Miracles* and me sitting and reading it. Then my first Reiki teacher Jeanne followed by Kathleen Milner from Tera Mai. The final image was of the hypnosis school. After the visual sequence ended, I was looking at Azrael again. I attempted to look directly into his sun-like eyes, and it felt as if he was keeping me from looking directly into them.

Tears were running down my cheeks as I laid there in those moments. I had never heard the name Azrael ever in my life. As I just sat there taking it all in, the next thing I knew, Azrael was gone, and I could hear my hypnotherapist's voice again. She was closing the session and counting me out of the state of hypnosis.

A clueless look came over her face as I explained what had happened. I felt unearthly – yet it was a feeling of love and emotion. Tears were running down my face. I was in shock, but in a beautiful way. Standing there feeling ethereal, we wrapped up the session, and I thanked her, hugged her, and went forward with my day.

As I reflected upon it all, I hadn't a clue what was meant by the *very important work* they had been preparing me for. I thought it may have something to do with a combination of the things I had learned over the last 12 years. At the time of this occurrence, I hadn't studied anything about Angels. Other than the experiences in my teens, I didn't know anything about them. The furthest I knew about specific Angels was that there was an Archangel named Michael.

After the session at the college, I had planned to go to a health food store after my session to get a smoothie. When I got there, I noticed a few books at the end of the juice bar. When I looked more closely at the cards, I saw that one of the sets was about Angels! I immediately began to look through the booklet to see if there was such an Angel named Azrael. When I opened the book, sure enough, there he was! I read that Azrael is an Archangel and that he is the Angel of transitions between planes, who helps usher the deceased from the physical to the spiritual dimensions back to God. I learned that he is the patron Angel of counselors, and he assists those who help console the families, friends, and loved ones of those who have passed away. I immediately began to tear up again.

Although my worldly situation had challenges awaiting, after that experience, I wasn't worried any longer. I interpreted the meeting with Azrael as a clear message to stop freaking out and to not jeopardize my future by doing something stupid. With a firm conclusion, I reached out to my friend who wanted hundreds of pounds of cannabis and told him that I was not going to help him. I was done with that world for good.

This experience with Azrael was one of the most profound things I had ever experienced. I kept a grounded head about it all, and I didn't overthink it. I only mentioned it to select friends.

After this I did my best to keep my nose to the grindstone. I remained focused and continued gradually building my practice. As the year went on, my practice picked up to around twenty clients a week. My clients were still mostly coming from word-of-mouth referrals. But to complement that, I also began utilizing various promotional and marketing methods that I hadn't yet used in the past.

❀ Zenith

The next year, I was going into my third year of private practice as a hypnotherapist, and things were solid. I'd accumulated a vast amount of experience in my field in my first 3 years. I had developed great confidence in my abilities.

On one of my days off, I was visiting a local metaphysical bookstore in Los Angeles. There, I noticed flyers for a demonstration by the couple who worked with Angels — Peter and Anne Selby, whom I had met in Atlanta ten years previously, at the Sprout Café. They were coming to town and there was nothing that was going to stop me from making it to see them.

At the demonstration, Peter and Anne greeted me with a warm welcome. They remembered me from the Sprout Café. We took a moment to chat before the demonstration. I knew I was in the presence of two masters of their craft, working with Angels.

I explained to them that I had become a clinical hypnotherapist and had built a practice in the Los Angeles area. They were excited to hear about this. Our conversation was brief, and they began their demonstration shortly after.

I went on to learn that their work with the Angels was a method originally revealed by an Angel to Peter, unexpectedly, on what was supposed to be a normal typical day at his then, physical therapy practice. From that day forward, Peter, eventually, with the help of his wife Anne joining, worked intimately with the Angels to further develop the work.

After the demonstration, as is customary, Peter and Anne fielded questions from attendees. They also allowed people to sign up for live, one-on-one sessions. After waiting my turn to sign up, the only time slot available was 8:00 a.m. the next morning.

The next morning when I arrived at their house in Brentwood, I was a little bit early, and they were just wrapping up their breakfast. Once we began the treatment, they stood side by side, Anne holding the clipboard and Peter preparing for the Angel-guided evaluation of my field. They asked me for permission to begin the session for purposes of being shown by the Angels what was "most relevant for my healing." Immediately, I could see a massive amount of what seemed to be Light illuminating the room. As I stood across from them, watching Peter being guided by the Angels, he began to express things to Anne that the Angels were showing. She would then write it all on the intake form. This diagnostic process transpired without me giving them any personal details about me, my past, or the issues I wanted help with.

One of the first things brought up was the adrenal fatigue issues I was experiencing at the time. The next thing they were shown was the buildup of financial anxiety/fear in my system from past challenges. One after the other, everything the Angels brought up from a soul, mind, and physical health perspective, was spot on.

Close to the end of the session, Peter looked up at me and said, "I'm to teach you this work in the future, you'll be doing this." That's when the light bulb turned on about the message from Azrael. At the time, they'd never taught a class. I kept quiet in humble gratitude for the entire session.

Toward the end of the session, Peter also said, "I also need to tell you: Only say things that you can do. Only give your word to people about things you know you are capable of doing."

I feel the Angels had shown him a tendency of mine to be overly optimistic and over-promising at times. I picked this up as a drug dealer in my teens. I tended to tell people what they wanted to hear. And although I had good intentions, that's out of integrity and deceptive. It was a characteristic that I allowed myself to become aware of, and then worked to change it.

Peter's mention also reminded me of a similar lesson I had learned from a past teacher, who said that if you are ever uncertain about your ability to back up your words with actions, remember to include the words "possibly," "maybe," or "perhaps." Being congruent in your words and actions ensures that your subconscious mind views you as someone it can trust. It was a crucial message for me to hear. Although simple, it was truly relevant.

Once the Angels revealed everything relevant in the evaluation, the next step was a clearing. Peter proceeded by asking me permission for each part to be addressed by the Angels. Step by step, the Angels, Peter, and Anne addressed every area of the clearing. Then we concluded. Witnessing their work first-hand was moving. I was super appreciative of the experience.

After this interaction with Peter and Anne, I was inspired about the possible opportunity to learn from them. I was fixed and focused on the next steps, though I had no clue when that would be. But I trusted. No definitive details were spoken about the training after Peter mentioned it to me, so I remained patient and allowed everything to align as it may.

As the following weeks proceeded, the healing treatment I'd done with them settled in more deeply. I began to feel better in my core energy levels, and I was less fatigued. I was amazed at how subtle yet consistent the effect of the session integrated. As time went on, things got stronger. The strengthening of the results was quite different from energy-healing sessions, in which the effects gradually dwindle after the session. It was also different from hypnotherapy, which required three or more repetitions of sessions and at-home reinforcements for maximum results.

Around six months later, my mentors came back through town to do in-person treatments. I was able to get another session with them.

Like the first treatment, without me expressing any details of my past, the Angels revealed layers of things that were lurking around as unresolved conflicts that needed to be addressed – most of which were experiences from my teens, where I was psychologically dueling with the Draculas. The final things brought up during my session were imprints and effects from 2008 to 2010, when I had meandered into the marijuana and psychedelic world, with Rich and everyone.

By the end of the treatment, Peter said, "Anthony, it is a testament to the strength of your spirit that you never ended up practicing the dark arts or becoming a black magician in this lifetime." Knowing the feeding ground that was my teens, to that, I agreed

I concluded the session and immediately felt so much lighter on a soul level. These were massive clearings of things that were serious lessons from my past. Things which had been hanging out unresolved in layers of my field.

Peter & Anne Selby

❂ The Pinnacle of My Training

In 2012, I received an email from Peter and Anne saying that they were putting together a 2-week training course and that I was invited. They explained the structure of the three-day introductory class. The email then mentioned that the introductory class would be followed by a ten-day advanced class immediately after.

The classes were being held in Sisters, Oregon, at a large, ranch-like home that one of their clients owned. I immediately began to make travel arrangements. I didn't have the entirety of funds for the classes or the money for travel there and back. Once again, my grandmother helped me cover the costs.

At this point, my grandmother had stepped up for me *so* many times in the most crucial of moments. I owe so much to her for helping me follow my dreams and destiny. Therefore, I've largely dedicated this book to her. For the people I've been able to help in my work, I owe most of the credit to my grandmother.

When it was time for the classes in Oregon, I boarded a plane from Long Beach to Portland and then rented a car up to Sisters. The only available car was a Ford Mustang. I had never driven an American muscle car before, so I was unsure what to make of it. It was already dark by the time I arrived in Portland. The drive to Sisters was about four hours north. The trip was through snowy conditions. The roads were icy, and they twisted through the mountains. At times during the drive, the snow was coming down so hard I could not see five feet in front of me. Often during the drive, I questioned if I would even make it there alive.

Once I arrived, they showed me to my room, which I was sharing with another student who was already asleep. The next morning, we began the first day of the introductory class. Over the next three days, my eight classmates and I were taught the basics of working with Angels for purposes of discovery and self-healing of the multidimensional human field of consciousness.

I thoroughly enjoyed every second of the class. Although the training material was advanced, I could wrap my mind around the curriculum and understand most of it relatively easily. My previous 12 years of training in metaphysics and the healing arts gave me a great head start going into this training. By the end of the introductory class, I was fully trained on how to do self-healing sessions. I had a working knowledge of invoking connection to God and Angels to locate disturbances and dysfunctions in my own astral/auric field of consciousness. It was truly out of this world fascinating to learn.

After the three-day intro class, we immediately began the ten-day advanced course the next day. We packed an enormous amount of information into ten days in the advanced course. The ten-day course elements took me the better part of three years to integrate and fully understand. Most of my integration of this knowledge came through sessions with clients after the training concluded.

Teaching this work was a new process for Peter and Anne, yet they did amazing. I was so impressed at how the two of them complimented each other so gracefully while teaching. They exuded the beauty and essence of the Angels in human form. The way their partnership was connected was the most beautiful display of love on a human level that I had ever witnessed by two people.

During the class, I soaked up the information and insight, but at the same time, I was observing a display of connection and loving partnership that I'd never seen before between two people. This was something that I deeply yearned to experience for myself. Although way too idealistically, I remember thinking how I'd love to have a partner to share both my work and personal life with. Unfortunately, my trying to force this romantic notion ended up creating a bit of a mess in my life within the following year.

When we got to the part of the class where Peter did individual clearing work, he asked us to express our intention for wanting to learn this work. When it got to me, my answer was simply, "To be able to help as many people as possible through the Angels' assistance."

Since then, my other hopes and intentions are to be able to help the Angels move this modality forward for its expansion and visibility, thusly attracting future students. As well, I want to honor my teacher's legacy: my dedication comes from the reverence and respect I have for the time, energy, and dedication they've given to the development of this work. My desire to help the Angels comes from the deep appreciation I hold in my heart for all the soul-saving help they've given me.

Once the classes were completed, I made it back to Southern California. I continued to study and review what I had learned. I advanced my understanding of the work by doing gifted sessions with as many people as possible. One of the first people I worked with was my close friend Benjamin. Upon working with him, the Angels were able to show an unresolved betrayal in his field of consciousness from when he was younger, which was anchoring an astral snake into his field. The Angels revealed the exact year of the betrayal and what areas of his person were most affected by these events with precise exactitude.

As I moved forward with the work, I learned a great deal through firsthand session work. I began noticing the Angels showing me things during the sessions that hadn't been covered in the classes and weren't anywhere in my learning materials. The Angels began referring to things related to my understanding of the subconscious mind from my past hypnotherapy training. In real-session time, the Angels were adding to the diagnostic range of the procedure. I continued to pay attention and consider what they were attempting to communicate in sessions.

I would like to qualify and more deeply explain my use of the word "Angel," as well as explain in more precise detail my personal, professional experience with Angels. Angels have, in large, been misrepresented, in a very limiting way, sequestered to the realm of theoretical idea, allegory, mythology, or hopeful notions, which keeps them very impersonal and "out there" away somewhere. That couldn't be further from the truth of their existence.

In my personal experience *and* professional work, I have seen them arrive as consolers, wise messengers, healers, and banishers of evil. They've always come in the most loving and caring manner that could be. I observe them helping people with the most emotionally personal issues. Most of which being lifelong issues that people have been carrying around within them unresolved, sometimes for decades.

They can assist with the most personal nuances of our lives, emotions, and thinking. But their help requires an invitation and asking for their help and being willing to do your part in laying down the thoughts, attitudes, decisions, and choices at the root of the issues.

CHAPTER 11

❋ IDEALISM & MORTALITY ❋

⊛ Blind Idealism

Throughout 2012, I expanded on my work with the Angels. A yearning to establish a genuine connection persisted within me. Although I had dated, it had been a long time since I'd been in a committed, romantic partnership.

I kept reflecting on the graceful eloquence of how Peter and Anne worked together and how connected they were. I deeply admired how they related to one another personally and professionally. Everything within my heart wanted to create a version of this type of union with a partner.

Traditionally, when it came to what I really wanted, I had been relentless. This idealistic determination mixed with irrational optimism would go on to create a major blind spot in the year approaching.

One evening, I was invited to a gathering in the Orange County health-conscious eating community. While there, I met a Colombian woman named Isabella. It was a brief meeting, but a powerful magnetism was noticeable between us. Afterward, I couldn't stop thinking about her, so I looked her up online and messaged her. We began talking a short time after.

Isabella informed me that she had recently ended a traumatic marriage. After her divorce, she went to a yoga retreat to heal and gather herself for a full year. In our early conversations she also mentioned wanting to possibly go to a naturopathic medical school in California in the future.

Isabella was a deeply spiritual, loving, and kindhearted woman. She was raised by loving parents, who raised her well. From an early age, she was introduced to spirituality and meditation. She loved God and was dedicated to living a conscious lifestyle. Trained in yoga and meditation, she ate healthily and was in shape. She was very open-minded to my work with the Angels. On paper, she seemed like the ideal woman of my dreams.

At the time, I was thirty-five years old, and I was well developed in my career. On the other hand, Isabella, also in her mid-thirties, was not where she wanted to be in life. She had just given three years to her previous marriage while working in a corporate job. She was in a place in life where she felt she needed to establish her autonomy and define who she wanted to become in the world. My idealism and passion blinded me to this. Although she mentioned her turmoil, initially, I didn't fully note her sensitivity around feeling underdeveloped. I was one-point-minded in my vision of her and I working together, like Peter and Anne.

Isabella never gave me the outright message that she was uninterested in being together. A large part of her showed a deep desire for our relationship to move forward. She would say things to me that profoundly moved my heart and reflected her desire for us to grow together. Yet also, she sometimes presented reservations in veiled ways through various clues.

Over the next few months, we spoke often and visited each other three times. Our chemistry was powerful, and we were attracted to each other on multiple levels. As our long-distance relationship grew, we made plans for her to move to Orange County in early 2013. We planned to get an apartment together in Costa Mesa near my office. At times, she had a "Let's see" attitude, whereas I was thinking, "Let's make this happen!" My thinking was an us against the world mentality, and that nothing could stop us. If any challenges arose, we'd transcend them.

Isabella and I found a place in Costa Mesa close to my office. It was an affordable one-bedroom with vaulted ceilings near the pool area. The neighborhood was peaceful and quiet. Once we moved in together in 2013, I broke personal records in my practice. I far surpassed my previous bests and did over nine-hundred sessions in 2013. However, regardless of what I proved with financial results, she couldn't seem to shake her financial worries and uncertainties.

I brought Isabella into my work with the Angels even though she was untrained and unprepared for live sessions. I figured it would be like an internship-type of opportunity for her. But that was a miscue on my part. I was in a blur of ambition and not thinking things through thoroughly.

We collectively decided upon a name for our work together and had big plans to expand the work into Spanish, which she spoke fluently. We even designed part of our website to facilitate both languages.

While Isabella showed extreme interest, dedication, and effort toward building the practice together, over time, it became clear that her role in our work together wasn't enough for her. I noticed her frustrations, and she became more vocal about not being content with what she'd accomplished up to this point in life.

From there, her personal motivations took precedence. She began to express her desire to go to naturopathic school more. Once I realized she was more concerned with her singular plans, I disconnected from the idea of us working together. It seemed unfortunate considering our potential. I was a bit myopic in that I couldn't understand how anything else could be more important.

Her resistance didn't stop at the area of work. Negative attitudes began to be expressed about romantic love and relationships, in general. She once told me, "What's the point in opening your heart and giving it to a man when it will eventually fall apart?" This statement made me realize that there was more healing which needed to take place within her before we were on the same page.

With that, I began to gravitate away from her as time went on. I slept on the couch often. I not only was letting go of the idea of us working together full-time, but I also had to disconnect from the hopes of our relationship becoming what I once hoped it to be.

At the eight-month mark, I ended the relationship. I was completing the busiest year of my private practice to date, working myself into exhaustion. I had been seeing on average more than three clients a day, seven days a week, every month. I was so busy I was often neglecting my health by skipping meals. I by no means wanted to have to be dealing with any form of relationship problems on top of this.

The entire process taught me a valuable lesson about not letting passion and blind ambition, or idealism, keep me from seeing the actuality of a situation. I became much slower and more thorough in my pace when entering a new relationship.

Beyond the hardships, we had beautiful moments together. I loved her dearly, which made the breakup even more difficult. During our first year, we got a Tonkinese kitten. We named the kitten Lua. Lua was beautiful. She was a polydactyl, or Hemingway cat, having six toes on each paw. She was a bundle of exuberance. Lua would go on walks with us like a dog, but without needing a leash, she'd just follow along. Lua became my best friend! Looking back at it, those walks through the apartment complex with the three of us were beautiful moments and will forever be close to my heart. As simple as it all was, I still look back on our time together in Costa Mesa as some of my most deeply cherished and sacred memories.

Lua

⚙ Dental Procedure Turned Deadly

When our first-year lease ended, Isabella and I were faced with the decision to either close shop, uproot and move, or sign another year's lease. At the time, I had excellent momentum in my professional practice, which I didn't want to disrupt by moving and relocating. Isabella wasn't prepared to move either. She had recently decided to enroll in naturopathic medical school in Los Angeles, which didn't allow the time or energy to immediately find a new place and move on the fly.

Our intimate partnership had ended, but we continued to live together as friends through the next year. Then, in February of 2014, tragedy struck in the most unforeseen way. I began noticing pain in two neighboring bottom teeth. I went to a local chain dentist's office. I foolishly expressed to the dentist that I wanted to try and save the two teeth if possible. The dentist proceeded to fix the situation and save the teeth.

Over the next two weeks, I noticed the original pain from the tooth growing and expanding. It began spreading down into my jaw and neck area. The pain continued to spread further into the lymphatic areas on the side of my neck. When I went back to the dentist and explained what I felt, he simply gave me antibiotics and told me everything would be fine. That was the furthest thing from the truth.

The situation had grown from a dental problem into a serious medical health problem. It was one of the most challenging things I've ever had to overcome. The infection spread through my blood and began to affect my thyroid. Upon a visit to a medical doctor, I was diagnosed with hypothyroidism. The infection then spread to the lymphatic area around the underarms and then toward my heart. There were times when I could feel heart pains, which was serious I could tell. I was feeling extremely ill and lethargic, and my brain was foggy. This was the first time in my life I had ever been chronically ill. There were times when I would go to sleep at night and question if I would wake up the next morning. I remember one night specifically where I reflected upon my entire life, thinking it may be my last opportunity to do so.

My ability to see clients declined massively, and my private practice suffered. Not being able to see the number of clients I wanted to, or *needed* to, was nothing short of devastating in my mind. Especially considering how monumental the previous year had been in my career. To the part of me that deeply desired continued growth and momentum, the situation was heartbreaking for me.

At first, I tried to show up for sessions the best that I could. Some days I did excellent work, though other days, I had absolutely No business being in my office attempting to help people.

Eventually, I had to put seeing clients on an extended pause. As a result, my finances plummeted – which made everything so much worse! I couldn't pay my bills and living expenses. I couldn't afford the costly supplements and treatments I needed to fix my situation. I didn't even have the resources to eat correctly. I began to go hungry and lose weight significantly – my body eventually began breaking down.

What made the entire situation so difficult was the large gaps of time between getting treatments due to limited finances and being without insurance. It was an utter nightmare. My health situation became critical. I didn't trust going back to the original dentist who had mishandled the situation, so I didn't know who to turn to. I began to seek advice from other dental clinics, but they all wanted to charge me more than I could afford for their services.

I eventually found a holistic dentist who could slow the continuous spread of infection through my body. Upon X-ray, he pulled the two teeth in question then cleaned out the area utilizing ozone therapy. To pay for his services, I signed up for a dental credit card. At the time, going into further debt was the least of my concerns.

Although the dental treatment helped, multiple areas of my body weren't working well because of the infection. There was nothing I could do to speed up the detoxification healing process. I leaned upon every resource I had.

Thankfully, I had lots of solid relationships with great practitioners in various branches of the healing arts. For my healing process, a group of doctors and practitioners from an alternative medical center called Center for New Medicine in Irvine, was the most crucial in my healing process. I had previously worked at the center as their resident hypnotherapist. Thank God they were compassionate about my situation. While being without money and insurance, they were still willing to help me.

The situation forced me to surrender, trust, and accept in ways like never before. Upon coming to terms with my mortality and loss of control over the situation, it became futile to sit and focus on it all. I began making the best of the situation. I spent most my time with Lua, reflecting on the steps for accomplishing future goals, once my health was better.

Not being able to work left me with time for self-reflection and self-healing work. In those ten months, I did a clean sweep of self-healing sessions with the Angels on every micro-issue I could find within myself from the past that needed to be addressed. I kept my mental, emotional, and spiritual state as clear as I could through my work with the Angels. But my physical process was exactly that – a process – a slow-moving process.

I learned about my friendships during this time. This period showed me people's true colors. A few friends came through like champions in this time of tragedy. Others, some of whom had the means to help me, turned their backs and pretended they didn't know what was going on when I reached out to them. I learned that true friendship is most definable when going through tragedy. It's easy to be a friend when everything is rosy. Kyle really came through in the clutch a few times whenever I didn't have money to pay my rent.

My friend Adam, who owned a functional foods supplement company called Elemental Wizdom, blessed me with multitudes of supplements to assist my healing process. He lent me his portable infrared sauna, to put up in my living room, and allowed me to come over and do ozone therapy at his house whenever I wanted to. As well, even Rich was kind enough to give me a large amount of CBD concentrate to assist my physical healing process.

◉ Good Journeys Isabella

After 2014, Isabella and I ended our lease at the apartment in Costa Mesa, and we finally moved apart. She moved to Los Angeles to be closer to her school. I was in a situation where I had zero resources or money saved due to not being able to work. I had no other place to go besides the one-bedroom condominium in Long Beach with my grandmother. Her sister, who owned the place, really didn't want anyone else living there, much less my cat. But I had no other options. I was in the healing process, and both my health and finances were broken. Even figuring out how to get my stuff moved into storage was a challenge.

Isabella went on to finish years of rigorous education to become a naturopathic doctor and eventually start her practice. The last I heard from her, she was living back in Texas with her parents, building her private practice as she originally desired. Good journeys to her. I appreciate our time of partnership for everything it was worth.

◉ Broken

Throughout 2015, while living with my grandmother, I continued to remedy my health situation the best I could. I continued receiving intravenous ozone therapy from my colleagues at the Center for New Medicine under the generous allowance of Dr. Leigh Erin Connelly. During one of my visits, I had my bloodwork done. Upon receiving my results, I was informed by a nutrition specialist that my body was missing vital amounts of cholesterol to rebuild cells. She said that my body was so malnourished that it was breaking itself down. Naturally, she instructed me to eat more – regardless of if the food was vegetarian or not – ideally healthy fats and protein. This was a challenge because I couldn't work and therefore didn't have the finances to buy more food. If I had the money to eat correctly, then I wouldn't have been having to receive that advice in the first place. At the time, I was a bag of bones: weighing 125 pounds – while standing six foot tall. My body's normal healthy weight is 175 pounds.

Through my bloodwork results, they informed me of a bad bacterial infection, and excessive amounts of heavy metals in my blood. They suggested that I continue doing cleanses, ozone treatments, and staying away from sugar and carbohydrate-heavy foods.

To begin getting the proper amounts of food and nutrients, I needed money – money that I didn't have. My grandmother, once again, helped me as much as she could, and I began using credit cards for the first time in my life. I was diligent in my efforts around detoxification throughout 2015. I was taking the correct supplements and eating correctly. Eventually, my health improved a bit. I gradually began to feel my vitality returning to me.

My health was partially restored, but my finances were still suffering. I had fallen into various debts. I kept strong, and I did my best to forge ahead. Luckily, my bills were low at the time. Regardless of the hurdles in my life, I was extremely grateful to have regained part of my health, which was the most important thing. "If you don't have your health, you don't have anything!" There has never been a truer statement!

⊛ From the Ashes

2015 ended, and after living with my grandmother for about a year, we both had to vacate her sister's condominium. My grandmother was getting older and needed closer attention. My Uncle Steve and his wife decided that it would be best if my grandmother moved to North Carolina to be within arm's length of their care. They found senior housing for her near where they lived in North Carolina and moved her cross country. Although I knew it was best, I was sad to be apart from her, knowing she wasn't in visiting distance.

I was primarily living off of credit cards at the time. I knew I would need to come up with thousands of dollars to move into a new place. I decided to try and move back to the apartment complex where Isabella and I had previously lived in Costa Mesa. Since the staff there knew me well, I figured getting accepted would be straightforward. Regardless, it was unfortunate that I was once again tiptoeing on being homeless.

Unfortunately, when I applied for the place, they told me that my credit didn't meet their requirements. In addition, my bank records showed inconsistencies in my monthly earnings since I had missed 80% of my potential work over the last two years. To get into an apartment, I needed the first month's rent, the deposit, as well as an extra month's rent. This totaled a little over $5000. I had to get a cash advance on one of the credit cards I was using to do so. The move-in fees swallowed every dollar of the amount I could get from the cash advance.

I ended up getting accepted into the complex in Costa Mesa and moved back in February of 2016. My health was still on a bit of a hobble, work sputtering forward slowly. One of my concerns was that I wasn't at 100% health yet and was about to be making a massive jump in monthly financial responsibilities.

Once I regained 80% of my physical health, I was feeling good enough to see clients. My next hurdle was that my professional momentum had been slowed to a halt for so long it was difficult to get things moving forward at all – much less moving forward full-steam ahead. It had been almost two years of being stagnant and not building my practice.

My client base slowly picked up – and then slowly slowed down again. I yo-yoed quite a bit through the first half of 2016. I was barely scraping by and struggled to pay for rent. I would go days without eating. To offset my costs, I leased my one-bedroom apartment on Airbnb for extra money. While people stayed in my apartment, I would sleep at my office on my massage table.

CHAPTER 12

❋ THE CALL FROM HOME ❋

❋ The Call from Home

In July 2016, I had the opportunity to do an Angel healing treatment with my mentors. As always, the treatment was poignant and profoundly helpful. It couldn't have come at a better moment. When I received the session, I was still not in the best of physical health, and my mind was constantly wrestling with uncertainties around survival and resources.

After the session with them, my work improved. I also began to see greater glimmers of light in how my physical body felt. Thankfully, things were about to take an unexpected turn for the best – in the deepest most profound way.

Around the second week of September of 2016, I was about to step into an experience that would deeply change me forever. It was the most beautifully sacred and awe-inspiring experience of my life, the experience that inspired the name of this book: *The Call from Home*.

For the last 7 years, I'd been removed from my daily devotional inner work and personal spiritual practices. There wasn't anything of my own *doing* per se which brought about this experience. This was something unforeseen.

During my time in Costa Mesa, one of my favorite things to do was walk with my cat Lua through the forested apartment complex. One early evening, as we were walking, my mind was mulling over concerns about survival, work, and paying my bills. The next thing I knew, I had a clear, calming, and powerful voice speak to me, telepathically, within my mind. It felt like it came from both within my heart and from all around me simultaneously. This voice said in clear, simple words: "Tony, that is enough... it is time to come home now." I was taken aback. The message was followed by the most intense, unexplainable feeling of love you could ever imagine! It was a feeling of love that felt ancient beyond time. It moved all through me.

The only way I can describe it in a human context is that it was the feeling of if you were to combine the love of millions of the most loving mothers and fathers together into one – but even more so. This feeling of love just continued. It was a love that felt like something supernatural in its essence. I was simply in awe. The experience was humbling. As I continued to walk with this feeling of love coursing through my entire being, my eyes began tearing up.

This was, by far, the most beautiful, as well as the most intense, feeling, of any type, I had ever felt in my entire life. It was a feeling of love beyond anything I had ever known or experienced. Virtually indescribable. This is the love that The Creator holds for us all, as Its beloved child. This love is our *true* home – the home which is beyond time – the home that we will always *truly* share together.

With this unexplainably rapturous feeling pouring through me, I did my best to hold my tears back and contain myself. I walked back to my apartment with Lua. As I got there, I sat down and attempted to gather myself. I took time to take it all in. I tried to logically understand what was happening – but that did it no justice. The experience was completely breathtaking in its beauty. The whole of the experience was an emotional one, because the feeling of love was so nurturing and moving.

After a little while of sitting there in the living room of my apartment, I began to hear an Angel addressing me. It wasn't audible, though: it was a telepathic/mental type of communication. Things were being expressed about matters in my life that they wanted to bring attention to for helping me correct. It was interesting because as I sat there, the feelings moving throughout me was a mix of ancient, heavenly, and ethereal, yet the things the Angel were expressing to me were very down-to-earth day-to-day matters of my life.

Many of the inner prompts and inner communication I was receiving were about people to reach out and offer support and assistance to. Some people I was being guided to reach out to were for purposes of making amends with them: some for me to forgive, and some for me to apologize to. I proceeded to contact all these people and did as I was being guided. The guidance I received over those first few days resulted in necessary healing of the past.

The guidance around people to reach out to went on for a few days. One of the people I was instructed to reach out to was George, the person who attempted to influence me to sell my soul back in my teens, mentioned in chapter 4. I expressed to him that I remember what happened and that one day he will have to make amends with The Creator and apologize, and that God still loves him.

Throughout all my experiences with the Angels, same as this one, they always spoke without excessive words. Words spoken with love and wisdom, but very precise and to the absolute point. By this time, as previously stated, I had gone through a handful of experiences with the Angels, but all those were short in duration. What made this different was the exchange was happening in a fluid continuous daily, back-and-forth dialogue type of way, in which I was able to ask questions and receive the immediate answer.

As this unfolded over the following days, the Angels revealed new things to me. Although the process became gradually easier to integrate, it was all still intense for the next seven days. The feeling of God's love kept bringing me to tears of awe. There was no way I would be able to work in that state, as ethereally ungrounded as I was, so I took the week off from seeing clients.

Throughout the following days of inner communication, one of the things I asked the Angels about was my physical health. They continued to assure me that my health would be fine. At that time, I felt about 85% better for about two years, but I still noticed that my body was exhausted from the combination of thyroid and adrenal issues due to the infection.

I also inquired about various matters of existence. The Angels showed me the completion of a long-time conflict in existence. It was like the conclusion of what seemed like a war or battle of sorts. In this vision, what looked like demons, had submitted and were being ushered by Angels on both sides of them, back to The Creator. The demons' heads were bowed in surrender while being guided at an upwards angle, back unto the Light of The Creator of All. It all looked like a conclusion that had already occurred in existence. The whole visual process came with a feeling of deep peace. What I realized was that this scene I was being shown was a reality that this world is in the process of catching up with.

I continued through the week with this feeling of this incomprehensible love. It brought forward a peace from within me that forever changed me. I went from being someone in a headspace of worldly uncertainty, to being in my heart filled with peaceful trust. It was a rebirth. It felt as if this was the true beginning of my life.

Toward the end of this seven-day experience, after asking many questions, I began to inquire about intimate relationships. At the time, I had been single for more than two years since my relationship with Isabella. I was in healing mode and had been waiting very patiently before embarking on a new relationship. At the time, I had a few sincere interests in women I had been talking with. When I asked the Angels which girl they suggested, they gave an affirmative response to the one named Alexi.

Alexi was someone I had met one year previously, though our first meeting didn't go well. Communication had broken between us, but I still had a slight interest in her. At the time, the idea of us being together wasn't at the forefront of my mind, so it surprised me that the Angels' guidance was aimed towards her. She and I were so vastly different, at first, I was extremely hesitant to follow their advice. Alexi was an actor and a model who lived an extremely different life than I did. I didn't feel we shared similar values the way I did with the other women I could've pursued at the time.

As I was trying to reconcile the guidance the Angels gave me about Alexi, at one point, I was led back to when Son taught me that sometimes our personality preferences may not be aligned with The Creator's plan, and when that is the case, put your likes to the side and defer to The Creator's guidance on the matter. It's only common sense to do so. Nonetheless, I was having a tough time wrapping my head around this one. I questioned their suggestion about Alexi more than once. At one point, after my constant questioning, they firmly told me to "please stop asking" and again expressed that it was important to God that I move forward towards her. They went on to express that she was one of the "original queens of the earth." I took that to mean that in one of her distant past lives, she was one of the first people in civilization to occupy a position of royalty once those types of social hierarchies were established.

Knowing it was important, I put my reservations and preferences aside, and I stopped questioning the guidance of getting closer to Alexi. Shortly after, I contacted her and asked her if she would be open to meeting with me. She said yes, and we arranged a time for the following week.

On the final morning of this week-long experience, I sat in this cathartic reflection. I asked the Angels, "What do I do next?" Their simple reply was, "Share with others the message of the love that God has for us all."

As I proceeded forward back into life, I could feel the love and Presence of God upon my heart and mind. I was in love – that is The Creator. I picked back up on my personal spiritual work and began nurturing my relationship with The Creator, keeping my mind in receptive prayerful communication. My survival worries left me; I felt a trust and serenity like I had never known before.

My healing arts practice, especially the work with the Angels, grew tremendously. My receptiveness to the Angels in sessions, and my abilities as a practitioner, quantum leaped. After this experience, my physical body regained its health. After two long years, I was finally back to 100%. And with what I was about to go through, I needed every bit of it.

On my walk where I heard the call from home

CHAPTER 13

☀ TO DO ☀

Alexi had originally shown back up on my radar again because of a mutual friend. A girlfriend of hers named Mia, who'd been following my work with the Angels, was coming into town, and wanted to do a session. She was staying with Alexi and mentioned that she would want to have a session done as well. The plan was to do the session at Alexi's house, and from there, we were back on speaking terms.

I arranged for Alexi and me to meet before her friend came into town. When we met, she was very receptive to me, though I could tell she didn't quite know how to respond when I talked about my recent 7-day experience.

Once her friend came into town, I did the treatment with her. Then I worked with Alexi. Upon doing so I found a heartbreaking situation in her field of consciousness, which revealed unresolved pain from past relationships, and undone issues having to do with men. She had a profound response to the clearing work and reported immediately feeling emotionally lighter.

By Alexi's request, we went on to do more treatments over the following months. Interesting, yet sometimes alarming, things came to the surface during her sessions. As we went into the deeper layers, past conflicts and deviant survival mechanisms were revealed. All things which were constructed in her runaway teens while afraid, wild, and reckless – a story I was personally very well versed to help with due to my own past.

Beyond similar teenage experiences, the two of us weren't simply different – we were absolute opposites. I wasn't sure exactly how I would be able to bridge that gap. Everything in me wanted to have a solid connection with her, but it proved to be a perplexing alchemy.

Alexi was a woman who was overly concerned with the physical material world. She was inundated by the day-to-day minutiae of life, to the point that she was always volatile and on edge with stress. Upon hanging out, more serious red flags began to show. Survival fear and worry was the cornerstone of her reasoning. I grew concerned. I could sense an intense nervous anxiety within her about money that led to a nonstop busying of herself. It was an auto-response and something she'd become conditioned to.

Alexi didn't use any substances or alcohol. She had a super-human brain and was the type of person who could naturally stay awake for days in a row and still be productive. In the early stages of our relationship, I could see that she was high-strung and intense. Her brain was like a never-ending battery.

Alexi had come from a rough childhood, raised by parents who were not in a happy marriage. Upon her request, I won't disclose any further details about them and their treatment of her.

She had a long history of dirtbag boyfriends who'd all cheated on her – literally every one of them. Her trust for men was broken, which made it difficult for her to be open and emotionally intimate. Emotional intimacy would put her in a resistant flight mode.

She was very driven and had side jobs apart from her acting career. It almost felt like she was using her work world as an escape. Similar to how Marcella used academics as an escape. Prioritizing emotional connection and romance seemed to bring up more frustration for her than it did enjoyment. As she put it, primarily because it requires time that took away from work and earning money.

From our very first date, the thing that stood out to me was this hypercritical nitpicking about the littlest of things. That was something unfamiliar – I'd never been around anyone who criticized me like her.

Another issue was the explosive anger that would combust about the most nonsensical situations. She had her own grading system for her explosions, like how tornadoes and hurricanes are measured: F4, F10 etc.

On top of that, I had to address boundary issues between her and other men. Something that just wasn't cool with me. Not only is it not acceptable to me, but I see it as an act of disrespect when an intimate partner flirts with and allows her energy to be bait for the opposite sex. I made this all as clear as I could. It was all the ultimate test of my centeredness. My greatest test yet – by far!

As things continued between us, I braced myself for what was to come. There was a time in the beginning of the relationship where she looked me deeply in the eyes and with a serious tone of forewarning, she said, *"I am going to drive you crazy."* Then walked away.

As the Angels had originally expressed, I should've slowly taken more time to get closer to Alexi. As we progressed into the beginning stages of our relationship, we both moved very quickly in our own unique ways. I moved very quickly emotionally in opening my heart and mind to her, while Alexi moved too quickly when it came to wanting us to move into a new house together.

From a financial standpoint, I wasn't even quite ready to be in a full-on relationship with anyone yet – especially with a woman like Alexi, who was, as she put it: "extra extra." I was getting by client-to-client and trying to climb out of credit card debt. And here she was, a woman who had it all, who could've been with any wealthy man she'd like, and she chose to be with me instead. Initially, I gave her much respect for that.

Going into the first month of our relationship, her lease was running out at the house she'd lived for three years. She got it in her mind to begin looking for a bigger house that she, myself, and a roommate could all share, which would reduce all our rents. She barnstormed the idea with maximum effort and efficiency, and sure enough, she ended up finding a 6,000-square-foot home with five stories in the Hollywood Hills that had just recently opened. Just as she had planned, the house was in a price range that would allow our roommate, herself, and I to all pay less than what we had previously been paying.

I went to look at the house that Alexi had found for us, which was big and multi-storied and at the top of Lookout Mountain in Laurel Canyon. The house had a view overlooking the entire city, all the way to the ocean.

While the location was beautiful, the house itself was beaten down. The tenant who had lived there before us was an evangelical preacher turned heroin addict who lost his mind and painted the entire place pitch black. Nonetheless, Alexi had the vision and never-ending energy needed to fix it into a cool home.

Beginning a relationship by moving in with someone is undoubtedly the most intense way to get to know someone quickly. I don't recommend it. Taking a road trip with a new potential partner is a much wiser way to go.

Once we moved in together, I instantly saw that our priorities were quite different. When I wasn't working, I wanted to spend time together getting to know her. However, she was more fixated on the process of getting the house together and making more and more money. I give her credit for her never-ending work ethic — she could go for days without sleep while trying to get ahead financially.

She had developed a vampire-like sleep schedule, not going to sleep until the sun came up in the morning – and she didn't seem to care to change it. She lacked sleep and, as a result, was snappy, negative, and constantly complaining. Mixed with her explosive anger, things were tense. Although I was at peace in my heart, I felt uncomfortable in my environment. With Alexi I had to keep reminding myself of what I had learned in *A Course*, that there are truly only two human expressions: love, and the call for love. Her calls for love were coming out in more ways than I could keep up with.

After six months of living together, I couldn't tell if I was a boyfriend, father, brother, or live-in therapist. Initially, I thought that our relationship was for it to be a romantic, soul mate type of thing. But as time unfolded, it was more of a mission to help a sister who wandered into the realm of the lost souls.

The whole thing was like the scene from *What Dreams May Come* when the character Robin Williams plays is in the process of trying to bring his wife out of a house in hell that she had trapped herself in after suicide. Before entering the condemned house that she had trapped herself in, his guide warns him to be careful because he could lose his mind in there and forget who he was and why he came. Throughout the entirety of our relationship, there were times when I had to really root down into my Spirit and not let myself get pulled into Alexi's hell. That's even more challenging when you're sleeping with someone, and each other's auric energy is merged.

If the beginning of my time with Alexi was a test from my training in *A Course*, then I would've gotten a C minus or D. I found it challenging to remain focused on her inner Light, beyond her words and actions. I didn't know how to reconcile the situation: should I bring attention to and help her correct the issues, or should I see beyond it all and witness unto her ultimate inner truth? The answer was *both*.

There were times I had to draw firm boundaries with her. This period taught me that it is of self-love and self-respect that we maintain healthy boundaries with people when necessary.

❁ They Know Not What They Do

Over the next year we proceeded to build our relationship the best we could. Alexi was out of town most of the time throughout. I remained focused on my work with the Angels and building my private practice.

In 2018, in an emotionally vacant ghost town of a relationship, I made a discovery that was heartbreaking. I came to learn of a deception and betrayal that had been taking place for the better part of our entire relationship. After multiple conversations about my discovery, the nature of what was going on came more to light. It wasn't surprising, yet it was still happening under my nose without me knowing. Another first.

It took around three days before it all fully dawned on me. Feelings of pain, betrayal, and disrespect set in. I had been deceived. I felt disrespected. I was hurt. So much so that for a while, I couldn't even see clients for work.

Human heartache and feelings of resentment are natural responses to betrayal. I initially was bent out of shape, and I was taking it personally. After a few days I eventually found myself at the reminder within that humans act in unloving ways because they don't remember, and aren't consciously aware of, who or what they truly inherently are spiritually. There is a Light within everyone that most are currently asleep to. This Light is what we truly are. It is the binding substance that makes everyone one with you. Souls who are asleep to this are capable of all the atrocious acts that happen in this world.

The key to everything I had grown to know and hold sacred was found in being able to know this and regardless, continue to acknowledge and see beyond their sleep unto the sacred essence that they truly are as your brother/sister: the beloved child of God.

The next thing I had to remind myself of was that most people don't realize that their thoughts and emotions are vibrationally causative. When charged enough, they can have interdimensional consequences and effects. Through what is called magnetic resonance, our thoughts/emotions signal to and attract varying types of lower-dimensional parasitic entities into our field of consciousness. This has traditionally been referred to as *possession*. These entities influence people in various self-destructive ways – sometimes to the point where much of a person's behavior is the byproduct of manipulation from the entities that they're taxiing around.

So, oftentimes, you're not just dealing with the person, you're also dealing with all the lower dimensional astral hitchhikers they're carrying around in their field. Knowing this, it is wise to draw firm self-respective boundaries when necessary.

Once everything was out in the open, Alexi took accountability, showed remorse, and asked forgiveness. She asked if we could do sessions with the Angels to revisit some changes that she was ready to make. For the first time in all the time I had known her, she was expressing empathy. She changed some subtle things and showed sincerity toward wanting to salvage our friendship. Month after month, she continued to step up as a much kinder version of herself.

When I spoke with the Angels about everything that had happened between Alexi and me. I expressed my confusion as to why I would be guided into the situation with her in the first place, with this awaiting me. Upon listening intently in prayer, the message I received was, "We knew you were the only one that could get through to her." That response sufficed. I didn't mind after that, and I was honored to have the opportunity to help a sister.

As I sat and reflected upon it all, the whole experience deeply reinforced one of the greatest pieces of wisdom I've had the honor to learn by way of multiple teachers in my life: The highest expression of free will choice is when it is used for yielding to the knowing and doing of The Creator's Will for you. This is what I term *true will*. Once you know what your true will is, then do it in the face of any dislikes, adversity, evils, or danger. Even if it's a massive mountain to traverse, do so without fear. When acting on God's revealed direction, one should carry forward wholeheartedly.

In the beginning, now, and in the end, we are all family together in our Creator's Beingness. There's a no-man-left-behind policy in the Kingdom when it comes to family in Spirit – even if it takes a thousand lifetimes for a soul to find its way back.

Alexi and I were able to find a family friend in each other, and ultimately, both become greater versions by being brought together. I've watched her begin her journey back Home, with a greater center of peace and a conscious connection to The Creator. And there is nothing more beautiful than that.

CONCLUSION

In closing, I'll say writing this book has been quite a journey. It's been a long three-year process. In these three years, since moving on from my time with Alexi, I also completed a book about the teachings of Josiah Osuagwu, titled *The Creator of All The Cosmic IAM*, as well as a book about my experience with the Angels titled *As Revealed by Angels*. Through word-of-mouth referrals, my professional practice in working with the Angels has grown massively. In this time, I also finally fulfilled my long-time creative desire to begin a conscious clothing company named Gold Encompass Clothing.

As life has progressed up until now, it feels as if the dust has settled, and there is a clear vision of the road ahead. I remain dedicated to my craft, distraction-free, and focused.

I'd like to say that beyond everything, I am simply grateful to The Creator for giving us life and existence. I am grateful for both life as immortal Spirit and life here in the physical temporal. I often stand in awe at the sheer amazement of it all. I am grateful to have made it to this point alive, with my soul, and be all in one piece!

Here is a summary of the most crucial lessons from the major themes of my life contained in this book:

❀ Parents Who are Addicts

When it comes to being raised by parents who are addicts, the most important lesson I can share is: know that it's not your fault. The despair and trouble that others put themselves through are not because of you. As you move through life, don't blame yourself for their sickness — or anyone else's, for that matter. Do your best to be there for loved ones going through their challenges, but never allow yourself to get dragged into their darkness.

In addition, remember that no matter how badly you may want to save someone you love, *they've* got to choose to save themselves. There are usually multiple factors and unresolved conflicts that contribute to people becoming addicts. Their response to those conflicts was to use drugs to bury their pain. Love them. Love them beyond their darkness. But love yourself equally and enough that you practice healthy boundaries when needed.

One of the best ways to help others is to do so well in your own life. Display self-love, and sometimes that can give others the inspiration needed to change, heal, and begin loving themselves.

I'll add three last things. The first is:

Establish a close communicative connection with The Creator and ask for Its love to fill your heart. Let that be the substance of the foundation of your experience here.

Next, do your best to face your own emotions and work through them. Feel them and know that you don't have to escape from them or suppress them. As you learn to face and work through your emotions, you will find that they then can be resolved and released from your system. This will help you avoid your parents' mistakes and ensure that you develop emotional maturity.

Lastly, find and gravitate toward healthy mentors and teachers throughout all stages of your life.

⚜ Self-Condemnation

Depending on the scenario, guilt, such as in the form that leads to remorse, can be a useful and necessary response to one's mistakes. It can be a conduit for change. But when guilt becomes overdone, and becomes habitual self-condemnation, it becomes a tool for self-destruction. This is often the case with kids who come from abusive environments.

Allow yourself to be okay with making mistakes. The human experience is designed for learning and evolving through mistakes. We learn how to get it right by first not getting it right. When it comes to your shortcomings, failures, and mistakes, be gentle and forgiving toward yourself rather than self-condemning. If your mistakes involve others, have accountability, and apologize wholeheartedly, then immediately reflect on what you learned and how you can improve. From there, make the improvements.

You don't have to be perfect – but you can become a great person through improving by learning from your mistakes. Self-condemnation or self-criticism causes us to not take chances. When we don't take chances, we don't evolve or grow. In this, we solely fall back on our comfort zone strengths without developing our weaknesses. We all have natural strengths and weaknesses. Appreciate your strengths, but don't let self-criticism, fear, and avoidance cause you to lean on your strengths like crutches. Allow yourself to mess up, make mistakes, learn, and give a focused effort to improve upon your weaknesses and shortcomings. It is healthy to face mistakes and develop through them — and while doing so, be patient and kind toward yourself, rather than self-condemning.

⚜ Never Compromise Your Soul!

Even in this limiting world, we've been given an immense capacity to learn, create, and achieve! Your Spirit, expressed through a focused mind, strength of will, consistency, and The Creator's guidance in your heart, has the capacity to accomplish things truly unimaginable. Most anything your soul truly desires can be earned and created.

Never forsake your soul, and never sell your soul for worldly gain and temporal riches! When I say, "Don't sell your soul," the words are meant in both uses of the phrase: Don't compromise your integrity, ethics, and values to get ahead in the world. But also, don't be a b*tch and compromise your soul through self-betraying pacts with forces of evil for material gain.

Success, achievement, wealth: they don't require taking the easy road. And it doesn't require the suicide of your Light to obtain them. The Creator is ALL things. It has made you eternally in Its glory, and It will always give you all that you want or need, in a way that is the healthiest for your soul – and in a way that will never compromise you! You may need to be patient and ensure you show up with your best effort. If it can't be earned in an honest, wholesome way that reflects integrity, it isn't worth having.

Dark forces are liars who only take advantage of people, leaving them washed up and more desperate than they originally were. At that point, that soul's Light has departed. You are the beloved extension of The Creator that is All, and your Light is the Crown Jewel of The Creator's heart. Nothing of this temporal world could ever measure up to that. Always maintain your soul – no matter how desperate or confused you may get!

✹ The Eyes of Vision – Choose to See Truly

This world that most everyone is collectively familiar with, agreeing upon, and mentally sharing, is a blindfold to the knowing of our eternal truth. It is a world of appearances which reflect the limiting and reducing belief that everyone is a temporary being of flesh.

Here, what we choose to see others as, is what we are bound to experience as ourselves. When the mind believes it is a physical existence, and thus projects that perception onto others, it sleeps to its inherent reality and is experientially limited to that. When one allows their mind to realize and understand that its inherent nature is immortal and of Spirit, and extends that acknowledgement back to others, the experience within oneself is profoundly different – a difference that is beyond explanation; the key to all magic; that is the seat of true beauty.

When you allow your awareness of others to rest upon the acknowledgement of their sacred Light, you experience a resonance of oneness with them which will light up a love in your heart that is not of this world. To do so brings a glow to The Creator's heart. It is an act that reverberates the beauty of holiness through all of existence to the joy of the Angels and the heavens and our Maker.

The key to liberating your mind from this shadow world of illusion, is found in focusing your awareness of your brother and sister in a way that extends their Light back to them. While the part of their mind that is aware of it sleeps, your silent acknowledgment, and awareness of their truth will awaken that part of their mind which remembers their Light.

Perception/how we choose to see is karmic and creative in nature. What you believe and what you see others as – spirit or flesh – is what you'll think and experience yourself as. Choose to see others through the knowing eyes of their immortal truth and you'll be blessed with new eyes – eyes that see truly; eyes that behold witness to the experience of our Supreme Being and immortality; and eyes which when utilized expand your own Source Light to full power.

❀ Unified True-Will

Our existence is one of free will. Freedom is a primary characteristic of God's Love, manifest in the design of things. We have every right, ability, and option to go off and do it all by ourselves. But we also can ask for The Creator's help, point of view, and guidance on matters of our life.

Although free will decision-making and learning through making mistakes is a common and natural part of human life, many needless mistakes can be avoided by aligning one's choices with wisdom. This opens a road of tremendous grace. The exalted expression of human free will is choosing to merge it with The Creator's guidance and Will. In hindsight, I can locate so many of my unnecessary mistakes and lessons that could've been avoided by taking the time to ask and listen patiently within.

Humans rely on determining things through their high-minded intelligence, reason, subconscious programming, and/or the familiarity of choices from the past. This is, extremely limiting. In this world of time, space, and bodies it seems that we've been left all on our own to figure it out, independent of our Maker. However, that appearance couldn't be further from the truth. With a sincere, open-hearted request, the very Maker of All can reveal and guide the way forward for us. Although free will is a fundamental element of existence, enacted by and fully respected by God and our Guardian Angels, there's not a single decision on earth they won't help you with if you ask.

The idea of suspending one's free will for guidance from God can easily become something that triggers fear or loss of control because it gets misperceived as involving having to sacrifice your autonomy, plan, and what you want. The Creator doesn't operate from deprivation and sacrifice, nor wants to sway you from what makes you genuinely happy — your Maker just wants to bring you the absolute best version of what will make you the happiest, and most fulfilled. To feel or believe that the Author and Supreme Intelligence within All Existence, the Maker and Sustainer of all phenomena and things, doesn't have a higher viewpoint of knowing as to what would be perfect for you, is a real head-scratcher to me!

To align your will with The Creator's Will and viewpoint on matters:

Begin with a true want and desire to know.

From there, it requires calling forward The Creator's guidance and asking questions.

Follow this by relaxing the intellectual thinking mind and need to control.

Next, using whatever meditative practices you'd like, get into a place of stillness of mind, and sincerely listen for the answer from the Voice of God within your heart of hearts. I say "listen," but ultimately, The Creator will guide you in the way that is most perfect for you: it may be an answer that comes through visual imagery; it may be in the form of a message extended into your heart; it may be just a deep sense and knowing; it may be a series of synchronicities and earth angels bringing door-opening opportunities into your life, at the perfect time.

It may take some patience and time to quiet the mind conditioned by the world.

If your requests are sincere, you will be answered.

Be vigilant to hear, know, and do.

When you ask and are given guidance, surrender fully. When you surrender to and submit to The Creator's Will, for this or that matter, do it sincerely with all your heart, soul, and being.

I feel it's important to add that when asking for assistance in knowing God's Will, understand that sometimes the nature of divine guidance can come in equal proportion to our preparedness. It is only wise to develop as many strengths as possible so that the way you can be utilized is more dynamic. For instance, if that request is wanting to know your soul's purpose, that can sometimes be a journey that requires patience and a persevering commitment.

❀ Don't Deviate

When you are on a path that you know is true for you, don't allow your human challenges or day-to-day difficulties of the world, derail you from the necessary steps forward. In coordination and orchestra with the Cosmic Whole of Existence, we all have a unique function to carry out and fulfill.

When you find yourself on the path of doing your true will, don't allow bumps in the road or distractions to compromise your process. Your true will often unfolds in progressions of development. All growth is sequential. All the while throughout the process, there may be trials and tests. Sometimes these trials may make you want to react with fear or doubt. Simply said: Stay the course! Remain courageous! Trust your process! Troubleshoot as you may need to – but do not deviate, quit, or compromise your progress! Remain focused on your path and the doing of your soul's true will!

I have witnessed tremendous God-granted potential and purpose in people, ravaged and sent into disappointment due to unhealthy distractions and survival-fear deviation. When on the path of The Creator's Will, the further down that road you get, the more you should be aware to avoid letting past, unhealthy distractions or fears try to derail you. When you become more self-aware and resistant toward things that distract you, you develop an exceptional quality of perseverance and focus. Both qualities are paramount for achieving greater heights of progress in your reason for being here: Your soul's true will.

⊛ The Creator's Love – Family

Our True Undying Reality is Spirit-Mind - the immortal child of The Creator. The Creator loves us as Its only child. The knowing of your inherent essence and immortal reality, and the knowing of the love that The Creator holds for you, are both your inherent right. The Creator's love is something that nothing on this earth can replicate.

What blocks the knowing and feeling of that love is the self-reducing belief that we are temporal, physical bodies of flesh, bound to death, separate from each other, and separate from our Creator.

You, in your innermost truth, are not born of the earth. Although your physical body was made through sexual exchange between your biological mother and father, your body is not what you are. It is only the temporary earth-carrier of you — *you* that is Spirit-Mind. Regardless of what the world has taught you to believe about yourself, you are the sacred, beloved child of The Creator, and you/we are immortal Spirit-Mind. We are the indwelling essence that is animating the body, and that the physical body is within.

We are spawned from, and born out of, The Creator of All as Its child – and our existence is forever held and happening within the Mind-Body of The Creator. Opening your eyes to this knowing allows you to see through the knowledge of our Eternal Truth. Recognizing and seeing that truth within your brothers and sisters is at the root of our eternal relationship. True relationship, which can never pass. A relationship bound by the fabric of our oneness and true beingness. This opens your heart to receive the Love that is beyond this world —

the love that The Creator has for us all – the love which our family and collective Kingdom is made of.

❀ Be Helpful from Your Heart

In this world giving to others is sometimes used as a mask of virtue, or for selfish manipulative reasons. Sometimes giving to others, especially excessively, comes from people overcompensating for not feeling deserving of receiving from others. All the above are distortions of charity. Be charitable to others from your heart – *when and how you are guided to from within your heart of hearts.*

Regardless of if this world tries to teach you that everyone you don't know are strangers, the fact is that everyone is your family in Spirit. When you give, do so simply and do so wholeheartedly. One day, this will all be gone, and when your final moments on this earth find you, you won't be thinking about how much money you made or saved – you'll reflect on how you treated others.

Sometimes the smallest acts of sharing can have the greatest impact on another's life.

❀ Good Journeys

I could've exited from this earth many times. I could've spent twenty or more years in prison. I could've lost the Light of my immortal soul. I have been counted out and dismissed by family, friends, and colleagues – I've even been counted out by my own self. I was not just an underdog; I was an almost deceased dog – ready for burial.

Through sincere prayer, the graces of God, and a solid dose of unbreakable will, you can overcome yourself and your past – no matter how monstrous or dark it was. Much of my life's progress was against all odds. Even so, with God's grace, I have built a successful twelve-year, full-time practice in the healing arts. In that time, I have facilitated more than 7,000 clinical treatments.

If I can overcome who I was as an addict and drug dealer to grow into who I've become, then so can you overcome your own adversities.

I'm grateful to share this all with you! That's my story thus far. And that's all for now. Good journeys, smy friends.

May you grow to know and fulfill your Destiny as The Creator has encoded it within your soul.

May The Creator's love encompass your heart – may you always remember how important, how sacred, and how loved you are.

To you all, brothers, and sisters, be well and may complete peace be with you.

Contact:

Instagram @gold.encompass

& @anthonyatonement

Twitter @Gold_Encompass

Gold-encompass.com

Goldencompassclothing.com